DATA MINING
A HANDS-ON APPROACH FOR BUSINESS PROFESSIONALS

THE DATA WAREHOUSING INSTITUTE SERIES
FROM PRENTICE HALL PTR

Planning and Designing the Data Warehouse

Building, Using, and Managing the Data Warehouse

Data Mining: A Hands-On Approach for Business Professionals

DATA MINING
A HANDS-ON APPROACH FOR BUSINESS PROFESSIONALS

Robert Groth

To join a Prentice Hall PTR Internet mailing list, point to:
http://www.prenhall.com/mail_lists/

Prentice Hall PTR
Upper Saddle River, New Jersey 07458

Library of Congress Cataloging in Publication Data

Groth, Robert.
  Data Mining: a hands-on approach for business professionals/
  Robert Groth
      p.   cm.
  Includes bibliographical references and index.
  ISBN 0-13-756412-0
  1. Data mining. 2. Data warehousing. 3. DataMind. 4. KnowledgeSEEKER
  5. NeuralWorks Predict. 6. Data mining—Software.
  I. Title.
  HF5548.2.G748   1997
  658'.00285'63—dc21   97–24689
                                                                      CIP

Acquisitions editor: Paul Becker
Editorial assistant: Maureen Diana
Production supervision: Nicholas Radhuber
Cover design: Anthony Gemmellaro
Cover design director: Jerry Votta
Marketing manager: Dan Rush
Manufacturing manager: Alexis R. Heydt

 © 1998 Prentice Hall PTR
Prentice Hall, Inc.
A Simon & Schuster Company
Upper Saddle River, New Jersey 07458

Prentice Hall books are widely used by corporations and government agencies for training, marketing, and resale.

The publisher offers discounts on this book when ordered in bulk
quantities. For more information, contact : Phone: 800-382-3419; Fax: 201-236-7141; e-
mail: corpsales@prenhall.com; or write to:
Corporate Sales Department
Prentice Hall PTR
One Lake Street
Upper Saddle River, NJ 07458.

Printed in the United States of America
10 9 8 7 6 5 4 3 2

ISBN 0-13-756412-0

Prentice-Hall International (UK) Limited, *London*
Prentice-Hall of Australia Pty. Limited, *Sydney*
Prentice-Hall Canada Inc., *Toronto*
Prentice-Hall Hispanoamericana, S.A., *Mexico*
Prentice-Hall of India Private Limited, *New Delhi*
Prentice-Hall of Japan, Inc., *Tokyo*
Simon & Schuster Asia Pte. Ltd., *Singapore*
Editora Prentice-Hall do Brasil, Ltda., *Rio de Janeiro*

To my daughter,
Elena Marie

Contents

■ CONTENTS ■

Series Foreword

P*lanning and Designing the Data Warehouse* is the first volume in the Prentice Hall series on data warehousing. As Series Editor, I wanted to put down my thoughts on what we would like to accomplish with this series of books.

Data warehousing is still very much an emerging technology. Some refer to it as an approach, a movement or even a set of technologies. Whatever the result of this taxonomic exercise, it is obvious that there is a strong need for a clearer vision of what data warehousing as a discipline is and where it is going; more rigorous definitions of its various components; a common vocabulary for enhanced usage; a better understanding of the skills needed to properly undertake the different functions involved. Furthermore, how does data warehousing relate to other disciplines within information systems technology? Does it fit best within computer science, management information systems, information engineering or some other such denomination? What business role does it play within an organization? What successful implementation strategies can be identified? In short, there are a significant number of questions that must, and will be, answered as data warehousing matures and blossoms.

Through this series we also expect to address some of the key technical problems that data warehousing practitioners are facing. Whether it be the issues related to datawarehousing architecture, data warehouse database design, metadata repositories, data mining algorithms, or other specific topics, we will bring the top experts in the field to share with us their best knowledge and experience.

Like other such endeavors, there is a substantial number of management considerations involved in data warehousing. From critical success factors to financial considerations, from cost accounting mechanisms to staffing issues, this collection will deal with them.

Ultimately, our goal is to present as complete a reference source as possible for individuals and organizations involved in planning, designing, building, managing and using data warehouses.

It is not a simple goal, nor an easy challenge; but it is convergent with The Data Warehousing Institute's mission.

As President of The Data Warehousing Institute, I am in the fortunate position of being able to draw on the resources of the Institute to address the demands of being the editor for this Prentice Hall series on data warehousing. The Institute is committed to expanding the use of this technology and enhancing data warehousing professionalism. As such, it runs a growing set of educational and technical programs that have become groundbreaking in their quality and scope. In the process, the Institute has brought together within its "faculty" some of the top experts in the field and has identified the pioneering "case studies" where organizations have implemented successful data warehouses. In short, there is a very strong cross-fertilization between the Institute's activities and the issues we will be addressing in future volumes of this series.

We are convinced of the importance of data warehousing as an agent of change within the information systems industry; and we are pleased to be at the leading edge.

Ramon C. Barquin, Editor
President, The Data Warehousing Institute

Foreword

A few months ago, I received a call from our long distance provider. The friendly voice on the other side of the line wanted to let me know they had reason to believe my calling card had been stolen. I looked in my wallet and found it safely tucked away in its usual slot and so informed the caller. She then proceeded to ask me whether I had made a series of telephone calls within the last 24 hours.

"Did you call La Paz, Bolivia yesterday at 2:45 P.M. from Kennedy Airport, New York, for about 45 minutes?"

"Huh?" I answered.

"And at 4:45 P.M. did you call Lagos, Nigeria from the same place?

"What?" I replied, even more incredulous, "I was in Cincinnati all day yesterday. Nowhere near New York City!"

"These calls and three others were placed using your card and PIN number from a pay phone yesterday and we wanted to check with you, since they don't fit your usual calling patterns. We won't charge you for these calls, and we would like to cancel your current card and issue another one right away with a new PIN number."

Bottom line: my calling number and PIN had been stolen somewhere, some way. And the phone company had been able to detect it early as a result of the application of what you and I now call data mining. Great work! Great save!

Of all the applications of a data warehouse, data mining is probably the one with the highest potential payoff. Enterprisers dream of discovering the patterns in their data that deliver early detection of credit card fraud, reliable profiles of customer buying behavior, or clear indicators of the effectiveness of a specific drug. Data mining promises to do much of that.

However, data mining is not a cybernetic Philosopher's Stone which will turn your data into gold. Those of us who have been around long enough know full well that there is no such thing. In fact, while data mining shows great promise, there is much that has to happen before the current set of data mining tools is able to deliver on their promises. For starters, users must be much better educated on exactly what data mining is, what the software can and cannot do, and whether the data that they currently have is truly exploitable; in other words, is it highgrade ore and really worth the trouble.

This is why Robert Groth provides a great service in putting together *Data Mining: A Hands-On Approach for Business Professionals.* It serves a very useful purpose for the practitioner who needs to know enough about data mining to be able to put in perspective what the boss is asking for, what is really needed to solve the problem, and what the product vendors are promising their tools can do.

His approach is very much on the mark for this purpose. There is enough attention to basic theory and definitions to provide the necessary intellectual framework, but the bulk of the book is aimed at the practitioner and thus includes many case examples and reviews several important data mining products.

At its very root, data mining relies substantially on statistics. Hence, you cannot get away from needing at least a basic understanding of the discipline in order to determine what type of technique best addresses a specific problem domain. And supplementing the statistical tools with neural net technology and intelligent agents gives the users a bigger arsenal of weapons with which to attack their problems. Furthermore, all this must be put in the larger context of knowledge discovery, which includes data mining as one of its components.

Mind you, we need as much help today as we can get in what is the age old process of obtaining meaning from a collection of data points or observations. Daniel Boorstin, the former Librarian of Congress, is someone I am fond of quoting. He addresses the problem in "The Age of Negative Discovery," an essay in his anthology *Cleopatra's Nose.* Pointing out that "for most of Western history, interpretation has far outrun data," he proceeds to note that "the modern tendency is quite the contrary, as we see data outrun meaning." He attributes this to the advent of the "mechanized observers" or machines that generate such vast numbers of observations, or data points, and make it essential that we learn to navigate these oceans of data. The key insight has to do with the importance of negative discovery. That is, determining that which "is not" and discarding all other data, through analysis, that does not contribute to a better understanding of our reality. Isn't this to a large degree what data mining is all about? The process of finding meaning from observations: knowledge production, knowledge discovery, knowledge management, data warehousing, and very specifically, data mining, tie these things together.

FOREWORD

The Data Warehousing Institute Series from Prentice Hall PTR is now in its second year. We started out with the two overview volumes where experts in the different fields provided introductory chapters in their subject areas. With *Data Mining: A Hands-On Approach for Business Professionals*, we start the process of providing in-depth coverage of each one of the many sub-disciplines within data warehousing. As Series Editor, I am very pleased with the choice.

Ramon C. Barquin, Editor

Preface

The process of knowledge discovery is certainly not new. Someone first discovered how to start a fire, that the earth was round, and that passing out pretzels to customers at a restaurant promotes drinking. Even before computers were used to automate the knowledge discovery process, statisticians were using probability and regression techniques to model historical data. Certainly, people have attempted to perform "data mining" before the popular term was first coined. So why is data mining suddenly reaching the covers of magazines and into the imagination of corporate America?

Hopefully by explaining the current field of data mining and introducing popular tools easy enough for you to use, this book will help answer this question.

Data mining is hot. An article in *Bank Systems & Technology*, January 1996, stated, "Data mining is the most important application in Financial Services in 1996." A 1996 commercial by IBM®, played during the SuperBowl, shows fashion models discussing the use and advantages of data mining. This is remarkable attention to an "emerging" market. Consider the projections in market opportunity for data mining shown in the figure on the next page.

Data Mining Software Market Opportunity

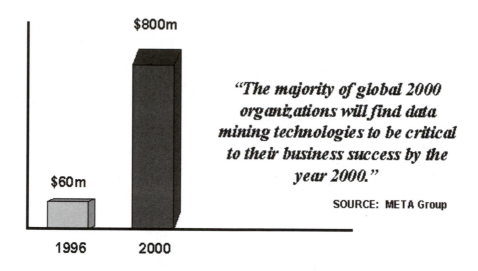

$800m

$60m

"The majority of global 2000 organizations will find data mining technologies to be critical to their business success by the year 2000."

SOURCE: META Group

1996   2000

Data mining, until recently, has been largely an academic field and required computer systems out of the reach of most business analysts. Something has happened to move knowledge discovery into the mainstream. Below are a few of the reasons why data mining has recently gained such popularity and, consequently, why this book was written:

- *The cost of personal computing power is decreasing to a point where data mining is now possible for business professionals.*

  A few years ago, only the IT departments of large corporations, like finance and insurance institutions, had the computers to perform data mining; today, you can perform data mining studies on a PC. Data mining is a computationally intensive process and it requires a fair amount of disk space as well. As the price of computing power and disk space continue to drop, the possibilities open to end users are mind numbing.

- *Recent innovations in methodologies used for data mining are making data mining more powerful and easier to understand.*

  Advances in computational power have enabled innovative, new algorithms for data mining to develop. New algorithms have increased the usefulness, power, and the usability of these tools. The mid-80s were a time when several techniques first appeared. Influential works by John Hopfield, on neural networks, and Breiman, Friedman, Olshen, and Stone, on decision trees, propelled data mining into the corporate world. By 1996, the number of new techniques applied to data mining were staggering, whether they be in the form of decision trees, neural networks, fractals, genetic algorithms, or the networked agent-based technology.

- *Software vendors are making data mining available to the end user.*

  A few companies are trying to bring data mining out of its traditional roots in acadamia and within the reach of the business professional. There will always be the need for experts in the field of statistics, but business analysts have largely had to rely on others to answer fundamental business questions. Analysts need a tool easy enough to use to point them in the right direction.

However you view this emerging market, a basic fact remains:

Data mining has become available to business analysts and end users.

That is an awesome statement! As a business professional, student, researcher, manager of information systems, or consultant, it should catch your attention enough to want to learn more about data mining.

The Purpose of this Book

This book is devoted to the business professional.

This book, *Data Mining: A Hands-on Approach for Business Professionals* resulted from the fundamental realization that data mining is heading into the mainstream, and that there are no books about data mining devoted to the business professional. This book provides an innovative, easy approach to learning data mining for business professionals, students, and consultants. The CD-ROM at the back of the book makes learning data mining a hands-on activity. You can try out several different software packages available for data mining.

The book discusses how knowledge discovery is used in different industries as well as discusses several of the data mining software products, which, although they may be appropriate for IT organizations and run on larger servers, also run on personal computers. The focus on products which run on personal computers is deliberate because they are the products that offer data mining to the widest audiences. Sample studies for specific industries, like retail, banking, insurance, and healthcare are provided.

This book takes a distinctly different approach to introducing data mining than the academic-focused books currently on the market. The emphasis of this book is on market focus and a hands-on teaching style.

Market Focus

Data mining is still largely an evolving field, with great variety in terminology and methodology. To gain a reasonable understanding of what data mining is all about, you must have a broad perspective on how it is being used within the market today and where to go to find information.

Information vendors and web sites are listed for you. Data mining tools currently on the market are also discussed to familiarize you with the market.

Chapters 7 through 8 provide examples of data mining in various industries, including:

- Banking and finance
- Retail and marketing
- Telecommunications
- Healthcare

This book broadens the scope of what is relevant to learning data mining. Not only should you learn the methodology and terminology needed to use data mining, you should also learn about specific examples of how to achieve fast results in the corporate environment.

Hands-On Teaching Style

This book also provides a hands-on approach to learning data mining. By devoting three hours of your time, you can use the enclosed CD-ROM to familiarize yourself with all the major processes.

Once we cover the concepts of data mining, we go directly to exercises to show how easy it is to turn data into information. *Data Mining: A Hands-on Approach for Business Professionals* includes a CD-ROM containing demonstrations of three end user data mining tools from Angoss® KnowledgeSEEKER™, NeuralWare's® NeuralWorks Predict™, and DataMind® Corporation's DataMind Professional Edition.

This book should increase your own marketability by showing how data mining is used in the database industry today. This book should provide you an answer to the following basic questions:

- What is data mining?

- How is data mining used in the market today?

- Why use data mining?

- Which vendors are in the data mining market?

- Where do you go to find information on data mining?

- How do you data mine?

Audience

Of the many books published to introduce data mining, this is the first devoted to the business professional. You do not have to have a statistics degree to use these tools.

This book gives a general overview of data mining and was written for a broad-based audience. The book will be useful to:

- ***Business Professionals***

    Anyone in business who deals with large amounts of data should be interested in data mining and this book in particular. A conscious effort is made to provide industry examples as well as make the use of data mining products understandable.

- *Database Administrators (DBAs)*

  Database administrators will be interested in this book from the standpoint of how end users can extract data from today's relational databases and data warehouses in order to mine data. This book discusses example data structures for different industries and what data fields are used in different types of data mining studies.

- *Marketing Analysts*

  Data mining is especially useful to a marketing organization, because it allows you to profile customers to a level not possible before. Some people refer to this as "one-to-one" marketing. Distributors of mass mailers today generally all use data mining tools. In several years, data mining will not be an advantage, but a requirement of marketing organizations.

- *Students*

  Students desiring a practical introduction to the basics of data mining and what is being done in the market can start with this book.

- *Systems Analysts and Consultants*

  Consultants can benefit from the discussions of the vendors involved in this market and by industry specific examples.

Scope of the Book

Data Mining: A Hands-on Approach for Business Professionals does not attempt to explain the algorithms used with data mining. If you want to learn more about the algorithms, I would suggest *Advances in Knowledge Discovery and Data mining,* by Usama M. Fayyad, Gregory Piatestsky-Shapiro, Padhraic Smyth, and Ramasamy Uthurusam. This book, at over 550 pages, is the most comprehensive work today on the academic approaches used in data mining.

This book is devoted to the business professional and targets an audience of PC users who do not necessarily have a statistics background and who want to try data mining themselves. Data mining for business professionals is just one market segment. Consider the segmentation of the data mining market in the figure on the next page.

Data Mining Market Segments

Business Professionals

IT Organizations

Managed Systems

While many data mining tools are available to business professionals, data mining tools are also sold into other market segments. For example, some data mining products are sold to *IT Organizations* and require sophisticated hardware and specially trained technicians to use them. They also usually require a system administrator and are often focused on vertical markets, like Falcon™ from HNC® software, which is used for fraud detection for banks and usually runs on mainframes.

Some data mining products are used as *managed systems*, and are sold with consultative services. For example, IBM sells outsourcing services where you can send data to them and they will return the result.

Data mining for business professionals does not imply "low-end", rather it requires tools that are accessible and understandable to business users who are not necessarily statisticians. Many vendors have PC versions of their products, but they also sell high-end servers. As long as these tools provide an integrated approach to data mining and make the reporting of the results straightforward, then they are selling closer to the business professional. The trend indicates that more vendors will be selling to this market within the next few years.

CD-ROM Installation Requirements

The minimum system requirements for installing the CD-ROM included in this book are discussed in Appendix B. Each of the three data mining software products included in the CD-ROM have their own requirements.

The installed software enables you to run the CD-ROM-based tutorial included in this book. Additional files have been added specifically for this book beyond those provided by Angoss Software, DataMind Corporation, and NeuralWare.

Organization of this Book

Data Mining: A Hands-on Approach for Business Professionals is divided into three parts:

Starting Out: The first three chapters introduce data mining, discuss the data mining process, and cover vendors involved in this market.

Chapter 1, Introduction to Data Mining, introduces basic concepts of data mining, discusses the models used for data mining, introduces terminology, and provides a brief history.

Chapter 2, The Data Mining Process, covers the process of data mining and introduces different types of studies as well as data cleaning issues.

Chapter 3, The Data Mining Marketplace, introduces vendors in the data mining market today.

A Rapid Tutorial: Chapters 4 through 6 introduce several of the leading data mining software products that are focused on business professionals.

Chapter 4, A Look at Angoss:KnowledgeSEEKER, covers the leading, commercial data mining software product based on a decision tree model that is focused on end users.

Chapter 5, A Look at DataMind, covers an innovative commercial data mining software product that enables business professionals to mine data and make predictions. The front end to the product is based on Microsoft Excel to make the product understandable to end users.

Chapter 6, A Look at NeuralWorks Predict, covers a leading commercial data mining software product based on neural networks and focused on business professionals.

Industry Focus: Chapters 7 through 8 focus on specific industry uses of data mining. Examples for each study performed are provided, with tips on how these can be performed on corporate database systems.

Chapter 7, Industry Applications of Data Mining, looks at types of data mining studies in banking and finance, retail, healthcare, and the telecommunications industries. Examples of companies performing data mining are provided.

Chapter 8, Enabling Data Mining through Data Warehouses, looks at how data warehouses provide a methodology for helping perform data mining studies. Four data warehouse industry examples are provided to discuss the type of data that would be integrated as well as introducing how some data mining studies could be performed using these data warehouses.

Acknowledgments

This book would not have been completed without the help of many individuals. Many thanks to my wife, Michele Groth, for her review of the book and to Leo Gelman, at Red Brick Systems®, who contributed greatly to the discussion on data warehousing in Chapter Eight.

Special thanks to Angoss Software, Belmont Research®, DataMind Corporation, HNC Software, MapInfo® Corporation, Neural Applications®, NeuralWare, Pilot Software®, and Silicon Graphics® for providing the use of images used in this book. Angoss Software, NeuralWare, and DataMind Corporation all contributed to the demo CD-ROM included at the back of the book.

Thanks to Penny Buckley and Fritz Vandenheuvel at Angoss; Patricia Campbell at HNC Software; Craig Zielazny and Casey Klimasaus at NeuralWare; Karen Gobler at Pilot Software; Lisa Jacobsen at MapInfo; A.J. Brown, Ram Srinivasan, Janet Fish, Karen Thomas, and Shaw Taylor at DataMind Corporation; Tracy Timpson, Mark Olsen, and Patricia Baumhart at Silicon Graphics; Jim Ong at Belmont Research; and Kurt Kimmerling at Neural Applications.

Chapter

1

Introduction to Data Mining

This chapter examines fundamental questions about data mining: what is data mining, why is it valuable, and how do you data mine? Methodology, terminology, and examples of the process of data mining are discussed.

The chapter is organized as follows:

1.1 WHAT IS DATA MINING?

Data mining is the process of automating information discovery. An analogy can be drawn to the process of finding a lost pet at two o'clock in the morning in an overgrown field: you could use a flashlight, but it sure

1

would be nice if you had motion sensors in the field to narrow down where you look.

Most analysts today use the equivalent of a flashlight to locate interesting information in their data. While tools exist to query, access, and manipulate data, the user is left to point the flashlight where they think they should go to find useful trends and patterns. Data mining automates the process of discovering useful trends and patterns.

Central to data mining is the process of *model building*. Creating a representative model based on an existing data set has proven useful for understanding trends, patterns, and correlations, as well as forming predictions based on historical outcomes.

While model building is a familiar concept to all data mining products, the methods of data mining can be categorized, grouped, cut, sliced, and discussed in many different ways. Clearly the market has not reached a consensus on how to characterize data mining. People were performing data mining before the term was popularized and have their own terminology and methods. For example, a statistical approach to data mining involves a process called *regression analysis*. Regression analysis methods have been used for years to model data and have only recently adopted data mining lingo.

In Colin Powell's book, *My American Journey*, he briefly discusses the use of regression analysis in the Viet Nam war:

> One of may assignments was to feed data to a division intelligence officer who was trying to predict when mortar attacks were most likely to occur. He worked behind a green door marked "No Entry" doing something called "regression analysis." My data got through the door, but not me. I was not cleared to enter. One day, the officer finally emerged. There were, he reported, periods when we could predict increased levels of mortar fire with considerable certainty. When was that? By the dark of the moon. Well, knock me over with a rice ball. Weeks of statistical analysis had taught this guy what any ARVN private could have told him in five seconds. It is more dangerous out there when it is dark.

Data mining certainly has progressed beyond where it was in the 1960s, but the most interesting point about this excerpt is that you would never have heard anyone refer to this exercise as data mining back then, but this is precisely what they were trying to do.

Query Tools and Data Mining

End users are often confused about the differences between query tools, which allow end users to ask questions of database management systems (DBMS), and data mining tools. Query tools do allow users to find out new and interesting facts from the data they have stored in a database. Perhaps the best way to differentiate these tools is to use an example.

With a query tool, a user can ask a question like: What is the number of widgets sold in the midwest versus the south? This type of question, or query, is aimed at comparing the sales volumes of widgets in the midwest and south. By asking this question, the user probably knows that sales volumes are affected by regional market dynamics. In other words, the end user is making an assumption.

A data mining study tackles the broader, underlying goal of a user asking a question like the one above. Instead of assuming the link between regional location and sales volumes, a data mining study might try to determine the most significant factors involved in high, medium, and low sales volumes. In this type of study, the most important influences of high, medium, and low sales volumes are not known. A user is asking a data mining tool to discover the most influential factors that affect sales volumes for them. A data mining tool does not require any assumptions; it tries to discover relationships and hidden patterns that may not always be obvious.

Many query vendors are now offering data mining components with their software. In the future, data mining will likely be an option to all query tools. Data mining discovers patterns that direct end users toward the right questions to ask with traditional queries.

Types of Data Mining

There are many different ways to classify data mining tools. For example, one recent paper suggests seven different types of data mining tools, depending on the algorithms each approach uses, arguing that different data mining algorithms are more appropriate for certain types of problems. Another paper discusses eight kinds of problems solved by data mining and differentiates data mining vendors by the problems that each vendor tackles. A reader looking for standards in the area of data mining will be sadly disappointed.

Even the meaning of the term "data mining" is open to debate. Data mining has also been referred to as *KDD*, or *knowledge discovery in databases*. The difference between data mining and KDD varies depending on the author you read or article you choose. Some argue that data mining is only the discovery component of the much loftier KDD process.

In this book, data mining is defined as a process of identifying hidden patterns and relationships within data. Data mining in this book is described in a functional manner with a specific goal: *This is a book about data mining for business professionals*. The use of the term KDD is avoided.

Business professionals look for data mining approaches that meet their needs. First of all, a business professional requires data mining to be *understandable*. Secondly, data mining must have good *performance* so that models can be built in a timely manner, and most importantly, data mining must be *accurate*.

This book defines three fundamental approaches to data mining, which encompass the thoughts of most business analysts when they define data mining:

- Classification Studies (Supervised Learning)
- Clustering Studies (Unsupervised Learning)
- Visualization Studies

1.1.1 Classification Studies (Supervised Learning)

This first example is an example of *classification* or *supervised learning*. This approach to data mining is very common in the business world.

An analyst for a telecommunications company wants to understand why some customers remain loyal while others leave. Ultimately, the analyst wants to predict which customers his company is most likely to lose to competitors. With this goal in mind, the analyst can construct a model derived from historical data of loyal customers versus customers who have left. A good model enables you to better understand your customers and to predict which customers will stay and which will leave.

The example of modeling customer loyalty, or churn rate, illustrates the process of defining a *study*. Studies formulate the scope of a data mining activity. A study will identify an overall goal and the data to be used. Having a goal in mind when data mining is not only useful, it helps define the data mining process. Goals do not have to be specifically defined in data mining.

By defining a business problem, you have already started the process of data mining and formulated a goal. You can easily state a goal in our example.

Goal

I want to understand what makes customers more likely to stay with or to leave my company.

A goal differs from the process of asking a specific question because you are not assuming any correlations. For example, you could have asked a question like: How many people whose line usage over six months is decreasing are no longer customers? This question assumes a link may exist between decreasing line usage and customers who are likely to leave. Query tools are able to ask specific questions; data mining tools prioritize the importance of information linked to a definable goal.

Subject of the Study

Studies require a *subject*. For example, Table 1-1 shows a historical data set of customers. The data set has a field, *Cust_Type*, that indicates whether a customer is loyal or has left to a competitor. We can use such a data set as the subject of our study.

Table 1-1 *Data set for customer churn*

Column Name	Type of Data	Value	Description
Cust_ID	Numeric	Unique values	Unique identifier for a customer.
Time_Cust	Numeric	Integer values	Days a customer has been with company.
Line_Use	Character	Very High, High, Medium, Low, Very Low	Minutes used by the customer in the last month.
Trend	Character	Increase, varied-increased, same, varied-decrease, decrease	An indicator of usage trends for a customer's last six months.
Status_Indicator	Character	Survey-High, Survey-Fair, Survey-Low, Unknown	Survey results on customer satisfaction.
Cust_Type	Character	Loyal, Lost	Is customer still with company (loyal) or no longer customer (lost)?

The table above shows data elements that identify a customer, describe the customer, and indicate whether the customer is loyal or has left the company.

Note that building the model of customer churn implicitly requires knowledge of which customers have remained loyal and which have not. This type of mining is called supervised learning, because the training examples are labeled with the actual class (loyal or lost).

The specific trait to be profiled from Table 1.1 is specified in column *Cust_Type*. This column specifies, row by row, whether a customer has historically been a loyal customer or has left for good (values: Loyal, Lost).

The column, *Cust_Type*, is defined as the *output* or *dependent variable* if it is used as the basis of the study, e.g., *the study profiles those who have historically been loyal customers and those who have left the company.*

You could also do a study on the characteristics of customers based on a satisfaction indicator. In the column

Status_Indicator, e.g., the study profiles individuals by their satisfaction indicator (Survey-High, Survey-Fair, Survey-Low, Unknown).

By defining the column, *Status_Indicator,* as the dependent variable, you have dramatically changed the goal of your study and the likely results.

1.1.2 Clustering Studies (Unsupervised Learning)

Clustering is a method of grouping rows of data that share similar trends and patterns.

Clustering studies have no dependent variable. You are not profiling a specific trait like in classification studies; hence, these studies are also referred to as *unsupervised* learning and/or *segmentation.*

Building the model of customer churn implicitly requires knowledge of which customers have remained loyal and which have not; the training examples are labeled with the actual outcome (loyal or lost). Clustering can also be based on historical patterns, but the outcome is not supplied with the training data.

A Clustering Example

Retailers want to know where similarities exist in their customer base so they can create and understand different groups to which they sell and market. They will use a database with rows of customer information and attempt to create customer segments.

Clustering techniques try to look for similarities and differences within a data set and group similar rows together into clusters or segments. For example, a data set may contain many affluent customers with no children and also may have customers with lower income and one parent in the family. During the discovery process, this difference can be used to separate the data into two natural groupings. If more such similarities and differences exist, the data set could be further subdivided.

The bitmap in Figure 1–1 shows a sample clustering study which takes customer data and tries to divide it into different segments.

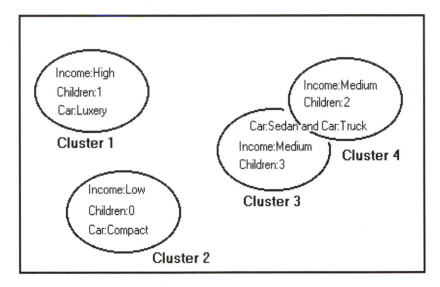

Figure 1–1 Customers are clustered into four segments

A chart like this one attempts to gain knowledge about the groups of data within a data set. Once clusters have been identified, an analyst can try to understand the similarities and differences in the clusters. In the example in Figure 1–1, four clusters are identified. Further investigation can show the reasons that these clusters appear different. For example, cluster 1 contains customers who drive luxury cars, cluster 2 contains customers who have compact cars, and clusters 3 and 4 four have customers who drive sedans and trucks. The data in clusters sometimes overlap, and, in the case of clusters 3 and 4, there were as many similarities as differences.

One question often asked when clustering data is:

Is there a way to optimally figure out how many groups, or clusters of data, exist in a data set?

Figure 1-1 magically came up with four clusters, but you might have gone with two or three. This is an area of continued research, but today, many approaches to clustering allow the user to decide the number of clusters to create within a data set whereas others try to come to a decision using one algorithm or another.

1.1.3 Visualization

Visualization is simply the graphical presentation of data. The process of representing data graphically is used today in most query tools. In fact, Microsoft Excel has graphing and mapping capabilities in its product. Still, visualization can mean much more than two-dimensional charts and maps.

Representing data graphically often brings out points that you would not normally see. Consider the map in Figure 1–2 from MapInfo Corporation.

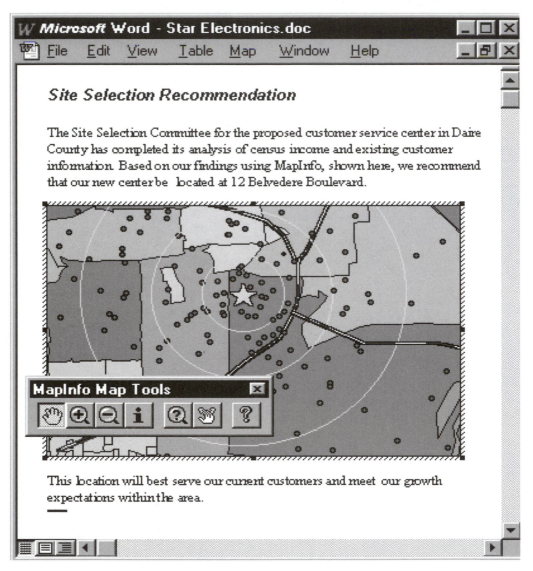

Figure 1–2 This map is used to help visualize good business sites

Figure 1-2 graphically shows locations of similar businesses to help choose the right location for new businesses.

Silicon Graphics, a provider of a spectrum of data mining tools, is a leader in visualization techniques for data mining, using their expertise in three-dimensional animation and rendering. Several data visualization examples using Silicon Graphics tools are shown in Chapter 3.

1.2 Why Use Data Mining?

The many articles in the mid-90s about data mining discuss it as an "emerging market", which is absolutely amazing considering how many companies use it. The best argument about data mining's usefulness is the number of companies that are data mining today and refusing to talk about it. The list of companies data mining looks like a Fortune 500 *Who's Who*.

Here are a few areas in which data mining is being used for strategic benefit. These companies were gathered by searching on the Internet, reviewing company literature, and by looking at investment reports for data mining companies.

Direct Marketing

The ability to predict who is most likely or most desirable to buy certain products can save companies immense amounts in marketing expenditures. Direct mail marketers employ various data mining techniques to reduce expenditures; reaching fewer, better qualified potential customers can be much more cost-effective than mailing to your entire mailing list. Users of such technology found by looking at software company literature include People's Bank, Sundance, Equifax, Reader's Digest, Group 1, Marriott, and the Washington Post.

Trend Analysis

Understanding trends in the marketplace is a strategic advantage, because it is useful in reducing costs and timeliness to market.

Financial institutions desire a quick way to recognize changes in customer deposit and withdrawal patterns. Retailers want to know what products people are likely to buy with others (market basket analysis). Pharmaceuticals ask why someone buys their product over another. Researchers want to understand patterns in natural processes. Wal-mart and the University of Rochester Cancer Center are two of the many institutions using data mining for trend analysis.

Fraud Detection

Data mining techniques can model which insurance claims, cellular phone calls, or credit card purchases are likely to be fraudulent. Most credit card issuers use data mining software to model credit fraud. Citibank, the IRS, MasterCard, Dun and Bradstreet, and Visa are a few of the companies who have been mentioned as users of such data mining technology. Banks are among the earliest adopters of data mining, including Chemical Bank, U.S. Bancorp, Bank of America, Wells Fargo Bank, and First USA Bank. One article estimated $800 to 2 billion lost each year to cellular phone fraud. Every major telecommunications company has an effort underway to model and understand cellular fraud.

Forecasting in Financial Markets

The use of data mining to model financial markets is used extensively. There are books on using neural networks for financial gain. Walkrich Investment Advisors, Daiwa Securities Company and Carl & Associates, among others, use data mining techniques to model the stock market.

1.3 HOW DO YOU MINE DATA?

In Section 1.1, the process of data mining was described as a process of *model building*. By building a model of a data set, data can be understood in ways that we may not have previously considered. Ultimately, models can be used to make predictions.

Here is a brief summarization of the data mining process. While not all vendors will describe the processes as the same, there are five main steps to data mining.

- Data manipulation
- Defining a study
- Reading the data and building a model
- Understanding the model
- Prediction

Below, each of these steps in the data mining process is described. Note that data mining is a circular process. One study sparks ideas that will lead to new studies which, in turn, may lead to more new studies.

1.3.1 Data Preparation

Some people would like to view data mining as a magical process that somehow takes raw data and distills it into a diamond that will save your business millions.

The reality is that data mining should always be considered as a *process* and data preparation is at the heart of this process. For example, if you want to find out who will respond to a direct marketing campaign, you need data about customers who have previously responded to mailers. If you have their name and address, you should realize that this type of data is unique to a customer and therefore not the best data to be mined.

Information like city and state provides descriptive information, but demographic information is more valuable: items like a customer's age, general income level, types of interests, and household type. This information can be purchased from many companies, but to mine it, the data must be merged.

There are several things to consider about data preparation in a data mining study.

- Data cleaning

  Data is not always "clean". For example, a column containing a list of soft drinks may have the values "Pepsi", "Pepsi Cola", and "Cola". The values refer to the same drink, but are not known to the computer as the same. This is a consistency problem.

  Another cleaning issue is stale data. Mailing lists have to be continually updated because people move and their addresses change. An old address that is no longer correct is often referred to as stale.

  Another data cleaning issue is typographical errors. Words are frequently misspelled or typed incorrectly.

- Missing values

Data often contains missing values. Some data mining approaches require rows of data to be complete in order to mine the data. Also, if too many values are missing in a data set, it becomes hard to gather any useful information from this data or to make predictions from it.

• Data derivation

Often the most interesting data may require derivation from existing columns. For example, if I have a column called *maximum$_94* and *maximum$_95* to describe the dollars spent in 1994 and 1995, an interesting derivation is *$_difference*, which is the change in the amount of money spent between 1994 and 1995.

• Merging data

The most commonplace data for business systems is stored is on a mainframe or in a relational database on a UNIX server or Windows NT workstation. Data in these systems are stored in the form of tables. For example, Figure 1–3 shows an entity level diagram of sales transactions for a retailer.

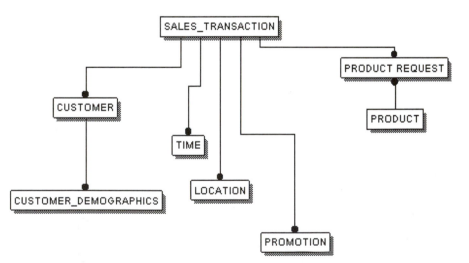

Figure 1–3 Tables for mailer response and customer information

In order to mine these tables, the data must be manipulated into a two-dimensional table. Merging data in a relational system can be achieved in a number of ways including merging these tables through a view, an SQL statement, or an export of the data into a flat file. Views are created by a database administrator to make a series of tables look like one. Query tools can merge tables by building a query that joins the tables into a resultant table.

1.3.2 Defining a Study

Defining a study differs for supervised versus unsupervised learning.

For supervised learning, defining a study involves articulating a goal, choosing a dependent variable or output that characterizes an aspect of that goal, and specifying the data fields that are used in the study. Good studies are tied to traits that can be described with your data.

The example used in Section 1.1 was a study measuring churn rate. The goal was to understand customers who are loyal versus those who are lost to competitors. The output was the data field, *Cust_Type* (Lost or Loyal). Finally, the data fields that are used in the study were defined as *Line_Use, Trend, Status_Indicator,* and *Time_Cust*. Each of these data fields has perceived value in describing customer loyalty.

For unsupervised learning, the overall goal is to group similar types of data or to identify exceptions in a data set. Grouping similar types of data, or segmentation, is used in many activities—most notably identifying market segments in direct marketing. Identifying exceptions is useful in discovering fraudulent or incorrect data.

There are a few important issues relevant to all studies. First of all, defining studies involves specifying a realm of data sets. You may use one data set for building a model, but you may wish to use another to validate that the model is correct, and yet another data set to make predictions on using that model.

Another issue in defining a study is specifying *sampling size*. It is not always necessary to mine an entire data set. You can often choose a subset of rows by random sampling. Determining the number of rows necessary to accurately represent the entire set poses several challenges, which will be discussed in more detail in the next chapter.

1.3.3 Reading Your Data and Building a Model

Once a study has been defined, a data mining product reads a data set and constructs a model. While all models vary, the underlying concept is the same. A model will summarize large amounts of data by accumulating indicators. Some of the indicators that various models will accumulate are:

Frequencies: Frequencies show how often a certain value occurs. For example, for 40% of the customers who left one company, the column *Status_Indicator* had a value Survey-Low.

Weight: Weights, or impacts, indicate how well some inputs indicate the occurrence of an output. For example, you would guess that the value Survey-Low in the column *Status_Indicator* has a high weight or impact for lost customers. The weighting indicates how relevant this "guess" is.

Conjunctions: Sometimes inputs have more weight together than apart. For example, it may not be true that males make loyal customers, but it may make sense that males who are pet owners and like to ski are loyal customers. The combination of inputs, males *and* pet owners *and* skiers, is an interesting conjunction.

Differentiation: As a marketer, you may want to know that scuba divers are likely to buy your product; but if scuba divers are much more likely to buy your competitor's product, then you are not likely to use this fact. Differentiation indicates how much more important an input criterion is to one outcome than another. It specifies the range between weights.

Noise

Models invariably will be imperfect if for no other reason than the data sets used to build them often contain anomalies of various forms. Errors or anomalies that appear in data mining are referred to as *noise*. In some papers on data mining, the terms "catastrophic noise" or "malicious training vectors" are used to discuss situations where anomalies cause models to fail. There has been much work

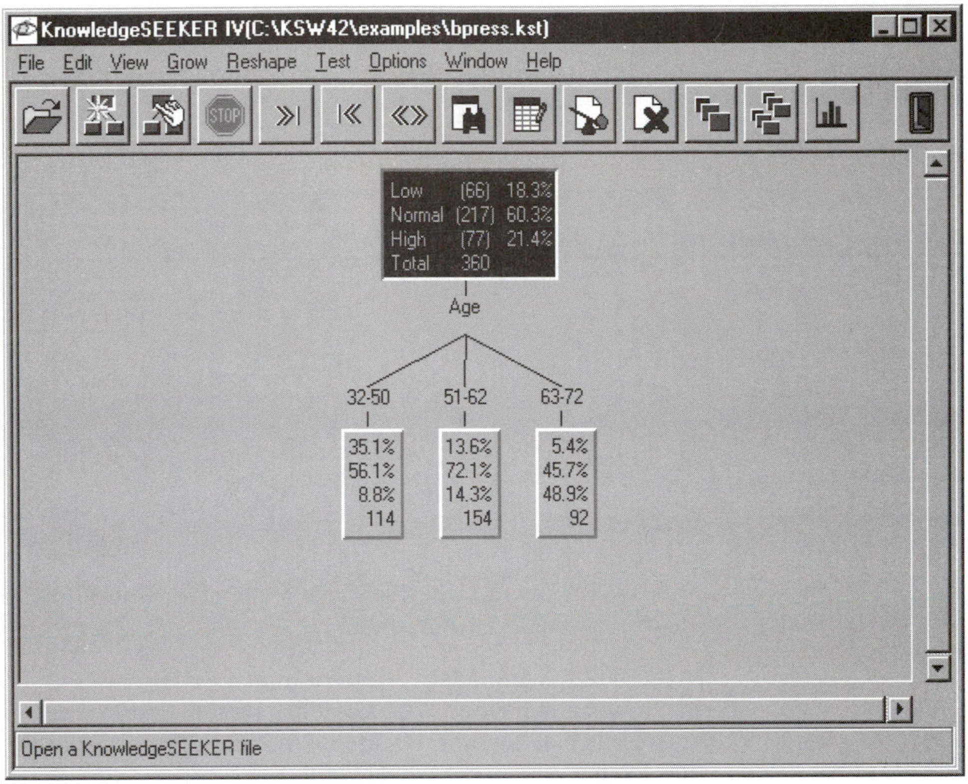

Figure 1–4 A graphical representation of a decision tree

in designing filters to soften the impact of noise in data sets and to improve the overall accuracy of a model. Different models will have thresholds that will allow you to dictate what amount of noise is acceptable for a model.

1.3.4 Understanding the Model

Model understanding takes different forms based on the type of model used to represent the data. Figure 1–4 shows an example of a decision tree model from Angoss (described in Chapter 4).

The screen presents a tree representation of a data set from a hypertension study. The tree shows a strong correlation between a patient's age and hypertension. The separation of data based on an attribute such as age is referred to as a *split*. There are many other splits that can be examined.

Definition of : Scenario #1						
Conjunction #	Input criteria	Required	Freq.%	Impact	Output criteria	
	Pmt_History 12		65.99	100	Account_Status Balanced	
	Occupation Principal		37.65	100	Account_Status Balanced	
	Pmt_History 11		16.6	100	Account_Status Balanced	
	Checking_Acct. No	Yes	100	36	Account_Status Overdraft	
	Pmt_History 1		44.83	93	Account_Status Overdraft	
	Pmt_History 0		9.2	93	Account_Status Overdraft	
&1	Marital_Status Single		49.32	219	Account_Status Payment Late	
&1	Home Rent		49.32	219	Account_Status Payment Late	
&1	Mo_Income 4|5		49.32	219	Account_Status Payment Late	
	Pmt_History 5		15.07	92	Account_Status Payment Late	
	Pmt_History 3		54.79	91	Account_Status Payment Late	
	Pmt_History 4		28.77	80	Account_Status Payment Late	
	Visa_Limit very low		5.48	60	Account_Status Payment Late	
	Savings_Acct. No		9.59	59	Account_Status Payment Late	
	Marital_Status Widowed		16.44	52	Account_Status Payment Late	
	Mo Expenses 1|5		80.82	49	Account_Status Payment Late	

dittx.DM — Control Center \ Model (1)

Figure 1-5 A model summary report from the Agent Network Model

Figure 1–5 shows a model summary report for DataMind, which is discussed in Chapter 5.

This model is completely different than a decision tree model, yet it is trying to accomplish a similar result. The main issue is how understandable the metrics are and how well the model is represented.

Another modeling approach shown in Chapter 6, from NeuralWare, uses neural networks. Neural network approaches have been criticized for being "black box", which means the models are not easily decipherable for understanding. This is not true for all neural networked approaches, but many neural network products today are used specifically for prediction and not for understanding.

Once a data set has been mined, the process of understanding the model created from the data set involves many different aspects. Below are several aspects of a model to consider.

Model summary: A model summary should show the weights, frequencies, and conjunctions that are important to describing the goal. A model summary, in any form, should be understandable and concise.

Data distribution: A model is only useful if it is based on a large enough representation sample. If a data set has 1 million males and 1 female, then it is not a valid study for females. Consider the data distributions in Figure 1–6.

Scenario #1 - Distribution of the criterion : Mo_Expenses (Continuous)

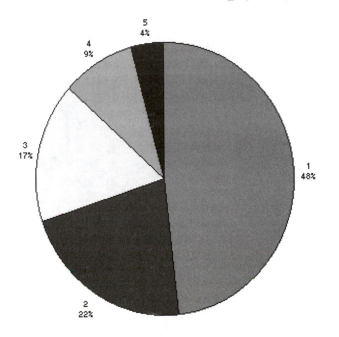

Figure 1–6 A proper data distribution

This is a valid data distribution. Consider the example of data distributions shown in Figure 1–7. Obviously Category 4 in this example encompasses most of the data. The real issue in Figure 1-7 is to ensure that the data is representative of the population from which the data is drawn. If categories 1, 2, 3, and 5 represented the number of occurrences of rare diseases versus Category 4, which was the number of occurrences of common colds, then the distribution may be okay. However, a better distribution is required if the categories 1, 2, 3, 4, and 5 represent equally distributed populations of patients.

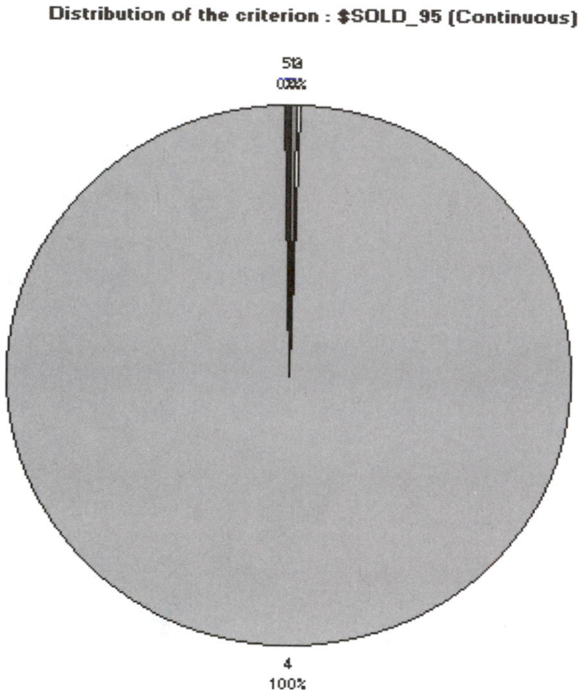

Distribution of the criterion : $SOLD_95 (Continuous)

513
00%%

4
100%

Figure 1–7 A skewed data distribution

Differentiation: Regardless of how good an input is at predicting an outcome, if it is equally predictive for another outcome, then it is not as useful. For example, most teenagers may frequent McDonald's, but they may also frequent Taco Bell. On the other hand, if an input predicts one outcome much better than another, it has a high degree of differentiation. For example, if people with red shoes and bow ties are ten times as likely to visit McDonald's than Taco Bell, then there is a high degree of differentiation for this condition.

Validation: Validating a data set involves making predictions using an existing model and comparing the results to known results. Choosing a separate data set from the one that was used to build the model is a better way to understand predictive capabilities. Figure 1–8 is an example of a validation graph from NeuralWare that compares real results and expected results. In a perfect model, the graph will look one and the same (disregarding observational noise).

Comparison

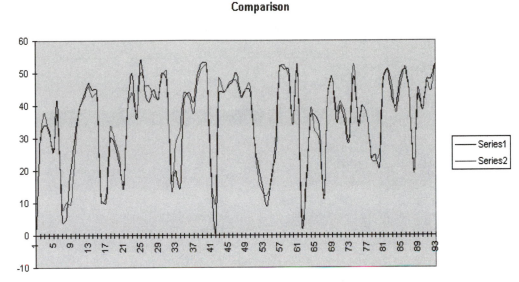

Figure 1–8 This cart compares real results and expected results

> *Profiling validation success and failure:* It is useful in model understanding to tell you why your model succeeds in correctly predicting and why it fails in correctly predicting as part of the validation process. This in not common to all techniques, but it is available.
>
> *Profiling cases:* It can also be helpful to point to rows of data that are most likely to predict an outcome. This ability helps you to understand real-world cases of when certain outcomes happen.

1.3.5 Prediction

Prediction is the process of choosing the best possible outcomes based on historical data. For example, this prediction screen from DataMind, shown in Figure 1–9, predicts that a customer is overdrawn. The second best outcome, or challenger prediction, had a score that was 42% less.

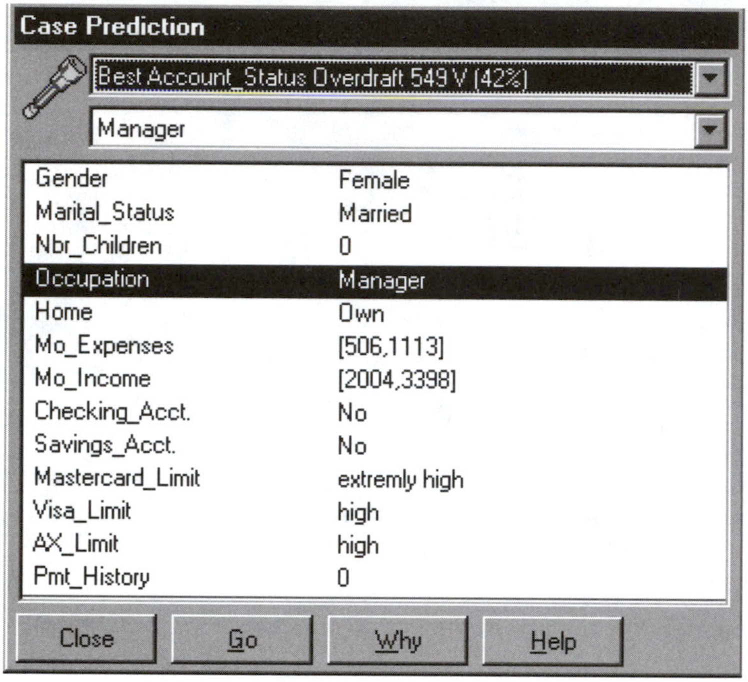

Case Prediction

Best Account_Status Overdraft 549 V (42%) ▼

Manager ▼

Gender	Female
Marital_Status	Married
Nbr_Children	0
Occupation	Manager
Home	Own
Mo_Expenses	[506,1113]
Mo_Income	[2004,3398]
Checking_Acct.	No
Savings_Acct.	No
Mastercard_Limit	extremly high
Visa_Limit	high
AX_Limit	high
Pmt_History	0

Close   Go   Why   Help

Figure 1–9 This window performs an interactive case prediction

Here are a few of the interesting predictive capabilities.

Understand why a prediction is made: Some models will provide the reasons why a prediction is made. Here is the screen you will see when you press the *why* button in Figure 1–9.

```
┌─────────────────────────────────────────────────┐
│ Prediction Influence                              │
├─────────────────────────────────────────────────┤
│  🔦  Account_Status Overdraft                     │
│                                                   │
│   Impact  Required   Criteria                     │
│  ┌──────────────────────────────────────────────┐│
│  │ 93                  Pmt_History 0             ││
│  │ 83                  Nbr_Children 0            ││
│  │ 53                  Mo_Income 1|5             ││
│  │ 53                  Savings_Acct. No          ││
│  │ 44                  Mo_Expenses 1|5           ││
│  │ 40                  Visa_Limit high           ││
│  │ 37                  Gender Female             ││
│  │ 36       Yes        Checking_Acct. No         ││
│  │ 31                  Marital_Status Married    ││
│  │ 28                  Home Own                  ││
│  │ 26                  AX_Limit high             ││
│  │ 20                  Occupation Manager        ││
│  └──────────────────────────────────────────────┘│
│                                                   │
│     ┌─────────┐        ┌─────────┐                │
│     │  Close  │        │  Help   │                │
│     └─────────┘        └─────────┘                │
└─────────────────────────────────────────────────┘
```

Figure 1–10 Why was a prediction made?

Margin of victory: If the best case prediction has a score of 100 and the challenger prediction has a score of 50, then the margin of victory is 50%. If the prediction has a score of 100 and the challenger prediction has a score of 99, the margin of victory would be 1%. Generally, the higher the margin of victory, the more likely the prediction is to be true.

Scenario playing: Some prediction models have the ability to change parameters to see how predictions change. Again, this helps in understanding why a prediction is made. Some models graphically model several scenarios of predictions at one time.

Understanding prediction affinities: Another interesting feature of model prediction is to set two variables constant and see what the other predictions would look like. For example, if a customer is affluent and owns a four-wheel drive vehicle, and all the other variables are varied, what does the set of different outcomes look like?

1.4 DATA MINING MODELS

At the heart of data mining is the process of building a *model* to represent a data set. The process of building a model to represent a data set is common to all data mining products; what is not common to all data mining products is the manner in which a model is built. Vendors often discuss the differences in models built using algorithms and approaches. To confuse this situation, there are hundreds of derivative approaches under the generic guise of names like neural networks, agent networks, decision trees, genetic algorithms, and belief networks. For example, NeuralWare offers a neural network product set that offers over 25 different neural network approaches. This section will discuss different modeling techniques. Several books are recommended for continued reading in this area as this in not the main focus of this book.

1.4.1 Decision Trees

Creating a tree-like structure to describe a data set has been used for quite some time in computer science, but it has not been a preferred process of knowledge discovery. The book *Classification and Regression Trees*, written in 1984 by Breiman, J. Friedman, R. Olshen, and C. Stone, was an important work in gaining credibility and acceptance for decision trees in the statistics community. The decision tree approach discussed in this work is commonly referred to as the CART algorithm.

J.R. Quinlan added popular new algorithms in a paper, "Induction of Decision Trees," published in the *Machine Learning Journal* in 1986, which introduced the ID3 algorithm. In 1993, Quinlan also published the book *Programs for Machine Learning*, introducing the extremely popular decision tree algorithm C4.5; the book includes source code for programmers.

In addition to ID3, C4.5, and CART, classification tree analysis has many different algorithms. A commonly used algorithm is CHAID (Chi-Square Automatic Interaction Detection) for categorical outputs.

Figure 1–11 shows the decision tree we showed earlier.

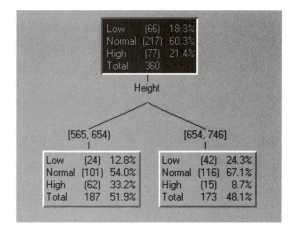

Figure 1–11 Viewing a decision tree model

The greatest benefit to decision tree approaches is their understandability; however, to successfully model data using the decision tree approach, several splits may be necessary. The tree subdivides the data according to height. It may be necessary to subdivide further on the basis of age and weight to learn, for example, that short, heavier people above a certain age have a greater incidence of high blood pressure.

How Decision Trees Work

Below is a simplified, stepwise discussion of building a decision tree. It should be noted that there are many approaches to decision trees used today. One approach is a statistical approach. CART is the best example of this approach. It uses statistical prediction and there are exactly two branches from each nonterminal node. Another approach is where the number of branches off a nonterminal node is equal to the number of categories. Examples of this approach are the CLS, ID3, and C4.5 algorithms. Another approach varies the number of nodes on a nonterminal node from two to the number of categories. This approach is exemplified by the AID, CHAID, and TREEDISC algorithms. Many vendors use a combination of these approaches. For example, Angoss KnowledgeSEEKER uses a combination of algorithms.

While all decision tree algorithms undergo a similar type of process, they employ different mathematical algorithms to determine how to group and rank the importance of different variables. For example, Quinlan, in *C4.5 Programs for Machine Learning,* discusses a gain ratio algorithm that "expresses the proportion of information generated by the split that is useful, i.e., that appears helpful for classification."

Step 1: Variables are chosen from a data source. From the variables presented in the data source, a dependent variable is chosen by the user. In the example in Figure 1–11, hypertension is chosen as the dependent variable, with outcomes low, normal, and high. An input variable for this study is height. This variable is shown in Figure 1–11, but there may be many such input variables.

Step 2: Each variable affecting an outcome is examined. An iterative process of grouping values together is performed on the values contained within each of these variables. For example, in Figure 1–11, the optimal grouping of values for height are examined. Through an interactive process of grouping and merging the numeric values for the variable height, the values are shown as divided into two categories: (565-654) and (654-746). The conclusion that these are the two groupings for the variable height is done by statistical tests like Chi-Square that attempt to maximize variations between the groups and minimize variations within the groups. The determination that two groups, not three or four, is the right number of groups is also dependent on the type of functional tests used for grouping the data.

Step 3: Once the groupings have been calculated for each variable, a variable is deemed the most predictive for the dependent variable and is used to create the leaf nodes of the tree. In our example, the variable height is selected as the leaf node of the tree because height was determined to be more predictive of hypertension than other variables. Frequency information is usually supplied to show the number of occurrences, by groups for the values of a dependent variable. In Figure 1–11, it is shown that shorter individuals are more likely to have higher blood pressure (32.2% of the people in the shorter height range had high blood pressure versus 8.7% of the taller individuals).

1.4.2 Genetic Algorithms

Genetic algorithms are a method of combinatorial optimization based on processes in biological evolution.

The basic idea is that over time, evolution has selected "fittest species." Applying this idea to data mining usually involves optimizing a model of the data using genetic methods to obtain "fittest" models. There is much active research in the area of genetic algorithms today, and, of all the modeling techniques, this appears to be the least understood. The roots of genetic algorithms start with Charles Darwin's work, the *Origin of Species*, in 1859. In 1957, G.E.P. Box wrote *"Evolutionary operation: a method of increasing industrial productivity"*, which was influential in linking genetic algorithms with business problems. Other influential works include a work by A.S. Fraser, *Simulation of genetic systems by automatic digital computers*, and one very influential work in this area has been by H.J. Bremermann, who in 1962 wrote *Optimization through evolution and recombination*. Genetic algorithms have often been used in conjunction with neural networks to model data.

How Genetic Algorithms Work

Genetic algorithms are good at clustering data together. For example, you want to divide, or cluster, a data set into three groups. A process to do this is discussed below.

Step 1: With a genetic algorithm, you can start with a random grouping of data. Think of each of three clusters to be created as a organism. The genetic algorithm will have what is called a *fitness function* that determines if a data set is a match for one of the three "organisms" or clusters. This fitness function could be anything that identifies some data sets as "better fits" than others. As data sets are read, they can be evaluated by the fitness function to see how well they relate to the other data elements in a cluster. In our example, a fitness function could be a function to determine the level of similarity between data sets within a group.

Step 2: Genetic algorithms have *operators* which allow for copying and altering of the descriptions of groups of data. These operators mimic the function found in nature where life reproduces, mates, and mutates. If a row of data in a data set is found to be a good fit by the fitness function, then it survives and is copied into a cluster. If a row of data is not a good fit, it can be crossed over to another set or, in other words, it can be mated with other clusters to create a better fit. A cluster will alter itself to create optimized fits as new data sets are read.

1.4.3 Neural Nets

The concept of an "artificial neuron" which mimics the process of a neuron in the human brain was captured in 1943 in a paper by McCulloch and Pitts discussing a Threshold Logic Unit (TLU). In 1959, Frank Rosenblatt introduced the concept of a Perceptron. Neural nets fell into disfavor following a book, *Perceptrons*, by Minsky & Papert in 1969, which showed that perceptrons could not solve a simple decision problem known as the XOR problem. Neural networks came into favor again when people realized that perceptrons with nonlinear thresholding units connected in multiple layers had considerably more power than a single perceptron. In 1982, John Hopfield published a paper showing how neural networks could be used for computational purposes. In 1984, Teuvo Kohonen introduced a new algorithm he called an *organizing feature map* that allowed for a process of using neural networks for unsupervised learning. This opened a new branch of neural network research where no "correct" answer is required to learn or train a network. Since 1984, a flurry of works have been improving on the process.

Neural networks are used extensively in the business world as predictive models. In particular, the financial market widely uses neural networks to model fraud in credit cards and monetary transactions.

How It Works

Figure 1–12 demonstrates a neural network. Each of the processing units takes many inputs and generates an output that is a nonlinear function of the weighted sum of the inputs. The weights assigned to each of the inputs are obtained during a training process (often back-propagation or conjugate gradient) in which outputs generated by the net are compared with target outputs. The answers you want the network to produce are compared with generated outputs and the deviation between them is used as feedback to adjust the weights.

The number of inputs, hidden nodes, outputs, and the weighting algorithms for the connections between nodes determine the complexity of a neural network. There are many approaches for finding the right number of hidden nodes and readjusting weights by a training process.

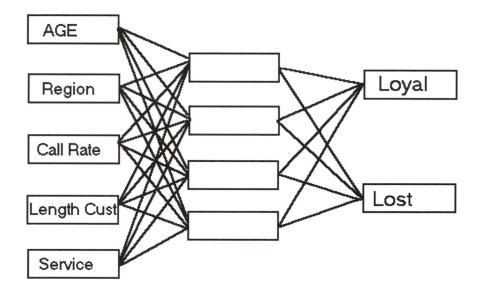

Figure 1–12 A neural network model

The hidden middle layer shown in Figure 1–12 can actually be multiple hidden layers. By far the most common neural network used is referred to as a *back propagation network*.

The set of outcomes, *y*, shown in Figure 1–12 is given by the set

$$y = \left[Loyal \; or \; Lost \right]$$

The outcome *y* returns a degree and is determined by a function, f(*x*), such that

$$y = f(x)$$

where *x* is the set of inputs. In this case *x* represents the values stored by the columns *Age*, *Region*, *Call_Rate*, *Length_Cust*, and *Service*. This input information could look like:

(*Age*=20; *Region*=South; *Call_Rate*=High; *Length_Cust*=10 years; *Service*=gold)

The outcome degree is determined by the weighted sum of input variables.

In Figure 1–12, there are four hidden nodes that connect the inputs and the outputs. The set of hidden nodes is h, and w is the weight where

$$y = w_1 h_1 + w_2 h_2 + w_3 h_3 + w_4 h_4$$

For more information on this method, a good reference is *Elements of Artificial Neural Networks* by Mehrotra et al.

1.4.4 Agent Network Technology

This method of model building treats all data elements, or categories of defined data elements, as agents that are connected to each other in a significant way.

This methodology is the process used by DataMind Corporation in their products. The Agent Network Technology was developed by Dr. Khai Min Pham, in France in early 1990. The early developments of this technology are discussed in *Intelligent Hybrid Systems*, by S. Goonatilake and S. Khebal, where the technology is described as a *polymorphic hybrid* approach, meaning it takes on the traits of different algorithms depending on how it is used. Figure 1–13 shows a model representation of the Agent Network Technology.

Agent Network Technology

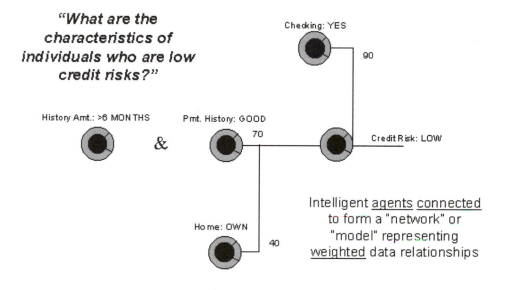

"What are the characteristics of individuals who are low credit risks?"

Checking: YES

90

History Amt.: >6 MONTHS   Pmt. History: GOOD

70

Credit Risk: LOW

Home: OWN

40

Intelligent <u>agents</u> <u>connected</u> to form a "network" or "model" representing <u>weighted</u> data relationships

Figure 1–13 An Agent Network Technology model

The Agent Network Technology distinguishes required conditions and contextual conditions. For example, owning your own home may affect your credit risk, but, in the example above, having a checking account is a required condition that must be met for you to have a low credit risk. Owning a home is a contextual link to having a low credit risk; having a checking account is a required link.

Central to the Agent Network Technology model is the concept of *impact*. Impact is a measure of influence of a given variable on another specified variable. Impact is measured on a linear scale that is closely related to posterior probabilities. The degree of association of a certain variable with another is a combination of impact and frequency (frequency is how often a value occurs for a specified outcome). For example, Figure 1–13 shows the input criterion *Home:OWN* is associated with the output *CreditRisk:LOW* has an impact on 40. To tell if this input criterion has a strong influence on *CreditRisk:LOW* requires a comparison of this score to other outcomes. If there are two other outcomes (*CreditRisk:MEDIUM* and *CreditRisk:HIGH*) and the impact for the criteria *Home:OWN* is 10 and 20 for these outcomes, then *Home:OWN* has a much stronger influence on *CreditRisk: LOW* than on the other outcomes.

Another important concept is that of a *conjunction*. A conjuction occurs when two variables together affect an outcome. For example, Figure 1–13 shows a low credit risk for people who have 6 months of credit history *and* good payment history.

How Agent Network Technology Works

Suppose you have the data shown in Table 1–2.

Table 1-2 *A frequency table of males and females with different account status*

Account Status	Male	Female	TOTAL
Balanced	176	71	247
Overdraft	58	29	87
Payment_Late	55	18	73
TOTAL	289	118	407

In order to calculate the impact of males on the status Balanced, a series of probabilities is calculated. These probabilities are referred to as conditional probabilities. For example:

P(gender = male) or P(A) is given as the probability that someone is male. For this example, it is 289/407.

P(status = balanced) or P(B) is given as the probability that someone is balanced. For this example it is 247/407.

The conditional probability P(A | B) is the probability that someone is male given that they are balanced, which in this example is 176/247.

P(A | $\overline{B}$) is the probability that someone is male given that they are not balanced, which for this example is 113/160.

A rough approximation of the impact calculated by the ANT technology is discussed in *Intelligent Hybrid Systems* and is given as:

$$Impact = \left(\frac{P(A|B)}{P(A|B) + (P(A|\bar{B}) \times (x - 1))} \right)$$

where x is the number of outcomes. In this case, there are three outcomes (Balanced, Overdraft, and Payment_Late).

1.4.5 Hybrid Models

There are many different modeling techniques using combinations of algorithms. Vendor tools that make use of more than one approach are referred to as *hybrid* systems. Being a hybrid system does not always imply that the tool uses a hybrid algorithm. Some hybrid systems just supply a bunch of genetic, neural, and decision tree algorithms and you are left to decide which one to use. Another "hybrid" approach that vendors offer is a suite of data mining algorithms. For example, Thinking Machines, with their Darwin product, makes use of several different mining algorithms. While the algorithms themselves are not hybrid, the product uses the algorithms in combination.

A hybrid algorithm, on the other hand, is one algorithm that makes use of several features. There is much activity in the area of creating hybrid algorithms.

1.4.6 Statistics

Statistics has long been used to create a model of data sets. The process of linear regression is a process using probability, data analysis, and statistical inference. Blaise Pascal and Pierre De Fermat introduced probability in a series of letters aimed at solving a gambling problem. Reverend Thomas Bayes (1744-1809) added what is known as the Bayes Theorem of Probability. Regression analysis was introduced around the turn of the century by geneticist Francis Galton, who discovered what is called *regression towards the mean*. He used probability and statistics to show that the height of children regressed toward a mean (taller fathers had shorter sons; shorter fathers had taller sons). The process of linear regression is an aggregate method of predicting the difference between predicted and actual data sets using the concept of regression towards the mean.

Some mathematicians may argue that all models used in data mining are really statistical methods in disguise. Statistics includes the realms of probability and statistical inference, which are routinely used to create models that represent data sets.

On Discriminant Analysis

Discriminant analysis is a study of finding a set of coefficients or weights that describe a Linear Classification Function (LCF) which maximally separates groups of variables. This LCF function can be given in the form

$$LCF = w_1 V_1 + w_2 V_2 + \dots + w_k V_k$$

where w is the weight,

V is the set of variables, and

k is the number of variables.

Discriminant analysis is popular for vendors attempting to find common groupings of variables. A threshold is used to classify an object into groups. If LCF is greater than or equal to the threshold, it is in one group; if LCF is less than the threshold, then it is in another group.

The weights are called *discriminant coefficients*. The data mining process of clustering attempts a similar process.

On Logistic Regression Modeling

A *regression equation* is an equation that estimates a dependent variable using a set of independent variables and a set of constants.

For example,

$$x = A y_1 + B y_2 + C y_3$$

is a regression equation where x is the dependent variable,

$y_1, y_2,$ and y_3 are the input variables, and

the constants are A, B, and C.

The equation above is referred to as a linear regression equation. Many techniques have been applied to regression equations, including a popular least-squares regression.

Linear regression models attempt many of the same things that data mining tools do, including making predictions for direct mail campaigns on whether a customer will respond or not.

Regression techniques can be used to perform prediction when techniques of conditional probability are introduced. The regression model used for predictive response is sometimes called the linear probability model (LPM). One type of regression model is the *logit model*, which is a model where all independent variables are categorical. A *logistic regression model* is similar to the logit model, but has continuous variables as well.

There are many types of regression models. For situations where no linear functions easily fit with data, there are nonlinear regressions and nonlinear multiple regression models. Coefficients of multiple and partial correlation can be defined using a variety of statistical methods.

1.5 DATA MINING TERMINOLOGY

Several concepts and objects are fundamental to data mining. The terminology defined here is purposely not all-inclusive. Some vendors go to great lengths to point out that there are many methodologies for data mining and name each approach. Vendors usually define each of these methodologies with their own terminology. There is a terminology war in data mining. Be aware that the industry has not reached a consensus in how words are used, but below is a list of concepts widely accepted today.

Classification (Supervised Learning)

The human mind naturally segments things into distinctive groups. For example, people can be lumped into the classifications of babies, children, teenagers, adults, and elderly. Classification provides a mapping from attributes to specified groupings. For example, the attribute age two years or younger can be mapped to the category babies. Once data is classified, the traits of these specific groups can be summarized. The very first data mining example, modeling customer churn rate at the beginning of this chapter, is a classification study where we were trying to group customers who were loyal and those who left and never returned.

William Shakespeare loved to classify people. Polonius's comments in Hamlet, Act I, Scene 3, are but one famous example:

> Neither a borrower nor a lender be: for loan oft loses both itself and friend; and borrowing dulls the edge of husbandry.

Clustering (Unsupervised Learning)

Clustering, or segmentation, is the process of dividing a data set into distinctive groups, e.g., in the case of fraudulent claims, the records may naturally separate into two classes. One of the categories may correspond to normal claims and the other may correspond to fraudulent claims. Of course, there may be some legitimate claims that are mislabeled as fraudulent, and vice versa.

For example, in direct marketing you may want to examine market segments. If you have nine customer segments, it may be interesting to cluster market segments 1 and 2 together in one group; 4, 7, and 9 in another group; and the rest in a third. Clustering helps determine what groups should be together.

Linear Regression

Linear regression is the statistical technique of finding how input data can affect a certain outcome, or dependent variable. Two very popular statistics packages, SAS and SPSS, are widely used to create models using linear regression techniques.

Modeling

Modeling is the process of creating a model to represent a data set. There are many different modeling techniques, as described in the last section. A model will not usually represent a data set with 100% accuracy. You can create a model that is 100% accurate on some approaches using one training set, but if you are using such a model for prediction, then you may have *overfit*, or *overtrained*, the model by making it too specific. For future cases, your model may be less accurate because, over time, general trends are more important than specific cases.

This brings us to an extremely important issue in data mining:

Will knowledge derived from one training set be applicable to other data not seen during the training process?

There is a fundamental trade-off between the complexity of the model (e.g., number of free parameters), the number of training examples, and how well the model will generalize to unseen data. If you have a training set that, when modeled, shows an influence on people with blue ties buying sailboats, the model created with this training set will not easily predict using another data set where people with blue ties are more prone to buy airplanes.

Visualization

Data can sometimes be best understood by graphing it. For example, visualization techniques can easily show *outliers*. Outliers are values that are clearly not in the range of what is expected: consider a data set where people may have incomes between $1000 and $4000 a month, but one individual earns $44,000. Having one person with such an abnormal salary can skew a model derived from such a data set.

Predictive Modeling (Forecasting)

A model can be used to successfully predict the outcomes of future events. While historical data cannot foretell the future, patterns do tend to repeat themselves, so that if a representative model of a data set can be built, predictions can be made from it.

1.6 A NOTE ON PRIVACY ISSUES

Data mining has made many people uneasy when considering its possible implications for privacy. For example, credit information for an individual allows you to learn a great deal about that individual. Medical records as well can say a lot about who you are. This information can be used for unethical purposes, like learning who to exclude for loans, credit cards, or health insurance.

The government has stepped in and provided regulations on what is allowed and what is not. The European communities do not allow banks to combine their financial data with credit information, which is something still allowed in the U.S. The U.S. government demands that banks explain why they extend or do not extend credit information. Certain variables, like gender, can get companies in a lot of hot water if they use them in their models to predict creditworthiness.

The telecommunications industry has regulations on information that cannot be used in their modeling processes. The use of Caller ID information has been heavily regulated.

Regulation in the industry of data mining has just clearly started, but it is likely to grow over time as people take advantage of the new products now available to mine data.

The most interesting thing about the tools discussed in this book when considering privacy issues is this: data mining tools widely available to business professionals provide broad access to information that was largely in the hands of the Fortune 500 only a few years ago. Is this dangerous or is it broadening the playing field?

1.7 S<small>UMMARY</small>

In this chapter, we looked at defining data mining, why it is used, and the methods and processes of data mining. We also briefly covered the models used in data mining as well as terminology. In Chapter 2, we examine the data mining process in much further detail.

Chapter
2

The Data Mining Process

This chapter explains the data mining process in much greater detail by using an example and stepping through the stages of data mining. This chapter discusses data mining using an example from the health care industry; however, the intent is to highlight the process and not discuss issues of this particular industry. The third part of this book discusses issues surrounding different industries; Chapter 8 is devoted to healthcare.

The chapter is organized as follows:

2.1 THE EXAMPLE

The example used in this chapter is one for the healthcare industry. Data from the field of healthcare make for interesting data mining studies because of the volume and variety of information available. Table 2–1 displays information on patients undergoing surgery or treatment for severe back pain. There is information about the patient, the doctor, the hospital, the insurance, and the type of medication used. From this data, a series of studies can be defined and run.

Table 2-1 *Data on patient recovery from severe back pain*

Column Name	*Values*	*Explanation*
PATIENT ID	Unique	Unique patient identifier
HOSPITAL BRANCH	Valley, Central, Western, Coast	The hospital branch patient used
RECOVERY TIME	0-2 weeks, 2-3 weeks, 3-6 weeks, 6+ weeks	How long it took for patient to be up and walking without significant pain
HOSPITAL_STAY	Outpatient, Overnight, 2-days, 3+ days	How long patient stayed in hospital
AGE	Numeric, in years	Age of patient
SMOKER	Yes, No	Whether the patient is a smoker
SMOKER_TYPE	Never,Occasional, Frequent, Daily	Smoker type, by frequency
MARITAL_STATUS	Single, Married, Divorced, Widowed	Marital status of patient
OCCUPATION	Civil servant, Manual worker, Unemployed, Retired, Professional, Business owner	Occupation of patient
INSURANCE	Self-insured, Medicare, Company policy	Type of insurance policy
PAIN RELIEVER USED	Mild, Codeine equivalent, Severe narcotic	Type of pain reliever prescribed for patient
DOCTOR_YRS	Numeric	Number of years doctor has been in practice

Column Name	Values	Explanation
DOCTOR_#_OPERATIONS_PERFORMED	High, Vhigh, Medium, Low, Vlow	Number of operations performed by a doctor
#BEDS_IN_HOSP	Numeric, Integer value	Number of beds in hospital
HIGH_BLOOD_PRESSURE	Yes, No	Whether patient has high blood pressure
ALLERGIES	Yes, No	Whether patient has allergies
ARTHRITIS	Yes, No	Whether patient has arthritis
PREVIOUS SURGERIES	Numeric, Integer	Number of surgeries patient has previously undergone
BACK_PROBLEMS	Yes, No	If patient has a history of back problems
QUARTER	Winter, Spring, Summer, Fall	The season that patient was admitted
FOLLOW_UP_EXAM	Critical, Poor, Fair, Good, Excellent	Condition of patient during follow-up exam
OBJ_PAIN	Low, Med, High	Doctors' objective findings on pain
OBJ_SWELLING	Yes, No	Doctors' objective findings on whether patient has swelling
OBJ_STIFFNESS	Yes, No	Doctors' objective findings on whether patient has stiffness
PATIENT_AREACODE	Area codes in the U.S.	Area code for patient's home phone.
HEIGHT	Numeric, in inches	Height of patient
WEIGHT	Numeric, in pounds	Weight of patient
WEIGHT_LAST_YEAR	Numeric, in pounds	Weight of patient last year

Given the data that is shown in Table 2–1, specific examples of the kinds of issues you are likely to face in preparing data mining studies appear immediately. The first issue is how to get at your data. This seems straightforward, but actually can be quite a formidable task if your data is stored in many places. This issue involves data preparation and it begins the data mining process.

2.2 DATA PREPARATION

Data preparation involves finding the answers to several
questions, including: How do you create a table like Table
2–1? How do you mine data that is not in the right form?
How do you handle data that is not entirely clean? This
section will discuss these questions and look at solutions
that are currently being used in the industry.

2.2.1 Getting at Your Data

The data for the patients suffering severe back pain looks
understandable enough when laid out in the form of a table,
but data about doctors, about insurance, about patient
information, and about hospitals may be stored in different
databases. Even if the data is in one relational database, the
data is likely to be stored in multiple tables.

Below are some alternative ways to access data for data
mining. Appendix A lists vendors who offer solutions that
make data access easier, like data warehouse vendors, data
conversion vendors, and query tool vendors.

Accessing Data Warehouses

Data mining is often discussed as an after-market for *data
warehouses* and *data marts*. This is not because data mining
requires a data warehouse or data mart. Data mining is
discussed as an after-market of data warehousing and data
marts because taking the time to build such decision
support systems forces companies to undergo the task of
bringing all their disparate data together.

An interesting trend in data mining is the integration of
data warehousing databases directly with data mining
tools. Many tools today require intermediary steps to be
performed before data in these tables can be mined.

Accessing Data through Relational Transaction-based Databases or PC-based Databases

Even if data is not in the form of a data warehouse, you can
access data from a relational, transaction-based database or
PC-based database directly by using connectivity. Many
vendors today offer integration with ODBC, a connectivity
standard to most databases of this kind. There can be a

problem of accessing multiple tables at once, but this can be solved by relational databases by creating what is known as a *view* on the database side, which is a way to make multiple tables appear as one. Using relational databases versus data warehouses for data mining increases the chances of "unclean" data, which, in turn, increases the need for more data preparation.

Accessing Data through Data Conversion Utilities

If a data warehouse is not in place or if it is in a format that a data mining tool does not understand, there are other alternatives to getting data. For example, there are several *data conversion utilities* that allow you to merge data sets and/or change formats.

A common problem you may face is that your data is stored in a different format than what the tool supports. Mainframe data is often stored in a fixed format, which is not easily transformed into comma- or tab-delimited. Often tools will require tab-delimited or comma-delimited files in lieu of a database connection.

There are a few PC-based data formatting tools out on the market today that will take data of virtually any format and put it into another, like Data Junction™ or DBMS Copy™. The data warehousing vendors also have a series of vendors who will synthesize data on a much larger scale, like Prism®.

Accessing Data Using Query Tools

Another alternative to create a data source suitable for mining is using a query tool to join tables from existing databases and then to create files from them. Vendors like Business Objects®, Brio Technology®, and Cognos Corporation® even offer levels of integration with data mining tools to facilitate this issue.

Standard query tools will solve the problem of collating data from several relational tables.

Accessing Data from Flat Files

The last alternative to get a table ready for data mining is to use a text-based file, or flat file. Almost all data mining tools today mine flat files. The main advantage is that text-based files are very fast to read. The obvious drawback is that they

	1	2	3	4	5	6	7
1	PATIENTID	HOSPITAL	RECOVERY_TIME	LENGTH_HOSP_STAY	AGE	HEIGHT	DOCTOR_YRS
2	670	CENTRAL	0-2Weeks	2days	18-25	71	2TO5
3	645	CENTRAL	0-2Weeks	2days	18-25	67	2TO5
4	13	CENTRAL	0-2Weeks	2days	18-25	68	1TO2
5	18	WESTERN	0-2Weeks	2days	18-25	67	2TO5
6	1	CENTRAL	0-2Weeks	overnight	18-25	60	1TO2
7	662	WESTERN	0-2Weeks	overnight	18-25	69	2TO5
8	83	WESTERN	0-2Weeks	overnight	18-25	73	5TO10
9	97	WESTERN	0-2Weeks	overnight	18-25	70	2TO5
10	70	VALLEY	0-2Weeks	overnight	18-25	66	5TO10
11	79	CENTRAL	0-2Weeks	overnight	18-25	62	5TO10
12	72	WESTERN	0-2Weeks	overnight	18-25	60	5TO10
13	58	WESTERN	0-2Weeks	overnight	18-25	61	10+
14	8	COAST	0-2Weeks	overnight	18-25	65	2TO5
15	597	COAST	0-2Weeks	2days	18-25	66	2TO5
16	646	CENTRAL	0-2Weeks	overnight	18-25	61	10+
17	643	VALLEY	0-2Weeks	outpatient	18-25	65	2TO5
18	676	CENTRAL	0-2Weeks	outpatient	18-25	74	1st-YEAR
19	695	CENTRAL	0-2Weeks	outpatient	18-25	75	5TO10
20	4	CENTRAL	0-2Weeks	2days	18-25	63	5TO10
21	22	COAST	0-2Weeks	overnight	18-25	70	1TO2

MEDICAL

Figure 2–1 An example of a text-based file for data mining

have to be created from somewhere and once they are created, they are difficult to manipulate.

Smaller text-based files can be loaded into spreadsheets like Microsoft Excel to manipulate, but there are limitations to this, like no more than 254 columns and roughly 16,000 rows.

An example of a healthcare data set loaded from a flat file into Excel is shown in Figure 2–1.

2.2.2 Data Qualification Issues

A common issue people face when approaching data mining is that of qualification. For example, consider the following fields of data: *Customer_ID, First_Name, Last_Name, Address, Phone_No, Area_Code, City, State,* and *Zip_Code.* You would not mine a field like *Customer_ID* because it is a unique field and there are no patterns to find in unique fields. Similarly, there are no patterns to find in *First_Name, Last_Name, Address,* or *Phone_No* because they too are unique.

Area_Code, City, State, and *Zip_Code* might be interesting fields for studies, but *City, Area_Code* and *Zip_Code* have another issue: There can be thousands of city names or zip code numbers, and hundreds of area codes. Even if you mine these data fields, are the results going to be understandable to the end user? Potentially, yes, but, on the other hand, for small data sets, these type of fields may be too unique to offer any interesting trends.

For classification studies, a data set must also have data fields that can be used as the output of a study. For example, the churn rate example in Chapter 1 had a field, *Cust_Type*, that contained the values Lost or Loyal.

Fields that are inherently qualified for the output of a data mining classification study are derived from experience. For example, over time, a bank will have information on certain customers who have balanced accounts and certain customers who have overdraft accounts. From this information, you have derived fields *good customers* and *bad customers.*

In the healthcare example in Table 2–1, there are several fields that could be used as the output of a study, including *Length_of_stay, Recovery_time,* and *Allergies.*

2.2.3 Data Quality Issues

Data is rarely 100% "clean." It is remarkable to know the quality of data on which some decisions are made. In Chapter 1, Colin Powell was referenced criticizing the data mining process during the Viet Nam war. It is safe to say that the data retrieved during that war was often misrepresented and inaccurate, and yet it was the basis for decisions that affected people's lives. Data mining is at best as good as the data it is representing.

Let us look at how data cleaning issues might affect the sample data set in Chapter 1.

Redundant Data

Look at a data distribution for an example file of our healthcare example.

| Scenario Summary | | | | | | | | |

Definition of: Scenario #1

Field Name	Usage	Type	Values	Unique values	Occur.	Category	Min	Max
PATIENTID	Input	Discrete	990		1024			
				1	1			
				2	1			
				3	1			
				4	1			
				5	1			
				6	1			
				7	1			
				8	1			
				9	1			
				10	1			
				11	1			
				12	1			
				14	1			
				930	1			
				931	1			
				932	1			
				933	1			
				934	1			
				935	1			
				936	1			
				937	34			
				938	1			
				939	1			
				940	1			
				941	1			
				942	1			
				943	1			

A

Figure 2–2 An example of unclean data

In Figure 2–2, the area circled and denoted with the letter A shows that there are 34 rows of data for the patient with patient ID 937. This particular study was supposed to show only one patient record for each patient, since it was a week's worth of data and the patient would not have undergone surgery in this period more than once. The fact that 34 rows show up means that we have redundant data in this study and it must be cleaned.

Incorrect or Inconsistent Data

Look at Figure 2–3, which shows another page of the data distribution from the same study shown in Figure 2–2.

Field Name	Usage	Type	Values	Unique values	Occur.	Category	Min	Max
PATIENTID	Input	Discrete	990		1024			
HOSPITAL_BRANCH	Input	Discrete	6		1024			
				CENTRAL	347			
				WESTERN	349			
				VALLEY	214			
				COAST	112			
				Central	1	B		
				1995	1			
RECOVERY_TIME	Output	Discrete	6		1024			
				0-2Weeks	196			
				0-2WEAeks	1	C		
				0-2WEeks	1			
				2-3Weeks	298			
				3-6Weeks	286			
				6+Weeks	242			
AGE	Input	Discrete	5		1024			
				18-25	198			
				25-35	314	D		
				35-45	221			
				45-65	211			
				65-up	80			
SMOKER_TYPE	Input	Discrete	4		1024			
				DAILY	211			
				FREQUENT	334	E		
				NO	221			
				OCCASIONAL	258			

Figure 2–3 Several data quality issues

The circles marked B and C clearly show incorrect data. The year 1995 should definitely show up in a column named region and there are inconsistencies in the value that should read 0-2Weeks.

Typos

The circles marked B and C are not only inconsistent, but also show misspellings. Note that circle B also shows the central region has been represented by CENTRAL and Central, which is a capitalization problem.

Stale Data

The data denoted by circle D may be stale. If this data set was from 1994, someone who was 24 will be 26 now. In other words, the data changed from then to now. Addresses are great examples of where stale data exists. People change addresses frequently in our society, so addresses more than a year old become suspect. A customer profile is two years old and the customer has moved, but this is not reflected in the address listed.

Variance in Defining Terms

Looking at the values marked by circle E brings up an interesting question: What makes a person an occasional smoker versus a frequent smoker? If two hospitals vary in their definition, your data is skewed. For example, the central region hospital may define frequent smokers as those who smoke more than five days a week, while the valley hospital may say frequent smokers are those who smoke more than 12 times a week.

2.2.4 Binning

The field *Age*, denoted by circle D in Figure 2–3, shows that people had been grouped into categories by age: 10-25, 25-35, 35-45, 45-55, 55-up. In this example, the field was already binned before you mined it; however, the field could have been a numeric field with each number a discrete value. When you have fields that are a range of numbers, it is often best to bin them, or rather, define them in categories not unlike what was done for you with the field *Age*.

Most data mining tools will offer ways to bin data for you. There are many different approaches to binning data and the way you bin the data can affect your overall result. In Chapter 1, a data distribution chart was shown where the categories were binned in an arbitrary way. Figure 2–4 shows the distribution chart again.

Distribution of the criterion : $SOLD_95 (Continuous)

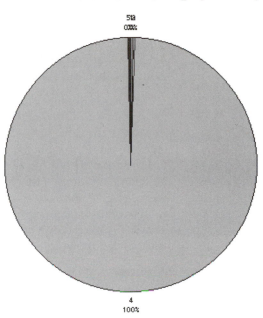

Figure 2–4 An example where most data falls into one bin

In this case, numeric values were binned into five distinct categories, but it looks like almost every data element fits into Category 4.

The question is often asked: How many bins should you have? The answer to this is not straightforward. It is necessary to look at a data distribution to figure out how many unique groupings of numbers are in your data set. Some statisticians believe data should not be binned at all; however, doing this can greatly increase the complexity and computing time of your model.

2.2.5 **Data Derivation**

There are two fields in the healthcare data set for a patient: *Weight* and *Weight_Last_Year*. The two fields are interesting for use in data mining, but what also might be interesting is to have a field that shows the difference in a patient's weight from this year to last year. A field like this can be derived by taking the difference between the two columns, *Weight* and *Weight_Last_Year*.

Data fields can be derived in several different ways. You can use SQL in a relational database to do it, query tools will allow you to do it, and this example data set is small enough that you could do it using an Excel spreadsheet and some mathematical functions.

In this study, there is another field, *Patient_AreaCode*, which for a data set of 1000 patients is not the best way to represent the data. Let us say that you want to know a patient's state, but the data set does not provide this information. This information can be derived from the area code information. In this example, the author used SQL to derive a field showing the patient's state from the area code. The patient's state may be shown by using SQL's query capability to update a field *Patient_State* with the value West for all the following area codes:

Colorado:	303,719,970
Washington:	206,360,509
Oregon:	503,541
California:	213,310,408,415,510,619,707,805,818,909,916
Idaho:	208
Utah:	801
Nevada:	702
Arizona:	520,602
Montana:	406
Wyoming:	307
New Mexico:	505

2.3 DEFINING A STUDY

Defining a study is the second step in the data mining process. You needn't have finished preparing data to perform a data mining study since data mining is a process and is likely to be honed and redone. Over time, the data you use, how you bin it, and how well it is cleaned will change and hopefully improve the overall model.

Assuming you have prepared a data set for mining, you then need to define the scope of that study. This involves several things, including understanding the limits of a study, choosing good studies to perform, determining the right elements to study, and understanding sampling.

2.3.1 Understanding Limits

In defining a study, you will be faced with many questions: Where do you start? What data should you examine? How much data should you use? Just how far will data mining go for me? Data mining has often been sold as a miracle process, and people often struggle between the reality of the benefits and the promises of the sales organizations. Here are a few of the questions concerning the limits of data mining, along with the answers.

No goal should be necessary in defining a study. Shouldn't data mining find relevant patterns for me without specifying what to look at?

While there is some truth to the statement, the choices you make in preparing data and defining how that data is presented will always reveal some goals or objectives. Even in unsupervised or clustering studies where no dependent variable is necessary, the choices in data dictate what you look at. It is not necessary to define specific goals, but, for example, if your data concerns surgeries on patients suffering from severe back pain, then your studies are likely to revolve around learning more details about these surgeries.

How will data mining work if I have bad data?

Data mining will not ignore bad data, but then, you have to start somewhere. A goal of data mining should always be to improve processes. By understanding a data set, hopefully, you will better understand how to improve its reliability.

If I have a model built, why should I continue to use a data mining tool?

Data mining is a process and it will usually raise questions when you see the results. Are there other ways to examine the data? Maybe you will perform the same study on a subset of your data. For example, you may study only surgeries performed in the central region rather than the whole.

If I perform a study and find out no new, useful information, then why should I mine data?

Data mining will not always reveal something new. If you have analyzed your data for several years and are intimately familiar with it, chances are that data mining will not provide a golden nugget.

There are two good reasons to do use data mining when data is already understood. The first is that data mining often validates what you already assume to be true. It is reassuring to have information back up your hunches. The second is that data mining can quickly spot trends. You can build the same model using new information every month and compare results. If one month's data indicates something that your previous models have not been telling you, then you may have a change in patterns and need to investigate further.

2.3.2 Choosing a Good Study

When you're not sure of the proper place to start, it is often useful to imagine presenting your overall purpose to someone else. For good studies, you should find it easy to explain how the outcome of a study will potentially provide a solution or work towards solving a need that you have.

Examples of good studies (goals):

- My purpose is to profile what type of patients have allergies or not so that we can improve the process of treating patients with or without allergies in the future.

- My purpose is to understand what type of patients undergoing surgery for severe back pain recover in 0-2 weeks, 2-3 weeks, 3-6 weeks, and 6+ weeks, so that I can potentially help reduce a lengthy recovery process, and understand areas that may hinder recovery.

- My purpose is to determine which patients are most likely to use mild pain relievers, codeine equivalent drugs, or severe narcotics in order to reduce the overall level of addiction to a certain drug.

2.3.3 Types of Studies

The following are a few suggestions of areas to consider for studies. Examples are provided for each type of study using the healthcare data set from Table 2–1.

Studies can be used both to understand why certain conditions are occurring as well as to predict sets of criteria that will cause an outcome.

Profiling Customer Habits

Example: Based on existing data of people who smoke or do not, what are the characteristics of patients who are smokers versus non-smokers?

Profiling Customer Demographics

Example: Based on information about patients' occupations, what are the differences in their patient histories?

Example: Based on information on the type of insurance people use, what are the differences in their patient histories?

Time Dependence Studies

Example: Based on the season that a surgery was performed (winter, fall, summer, spring), what are the differences in patient histories?

Retention Management

We could add a field to our data indicating whether patients, within a year's time, have continued to use this hospital system, had no further need of health services, or moved to another hospital system after this back surgery. If we added an indicator of loyal patients versus patients who have no more need of services, or those no longer using the system, we can start to understand the set of characteristics which cause a person to stay, have no need for services, or leave.

This set of data would do a retention study only for patients who had surgery for severe back pain.

Risk Forecast

Example: Based on patient recovery information, what types of patients will have the most risk of taking long to recover?

With surgeries, there is always a risk of fatalities, however small, which this data set does not cover. A more critical study is to understand what characteristics make someone likely or less likely to survive surgery.

Profitability Analysis

Example: Another column to this data set could be added to indicate the profitability of a surgery. Based on categories of net profit (e.g., high profit, low profit, low loss, high loss), what sorts of surgeries yield the highest amount of profit or loss to the organization?

Profitability studies, especially in healthcare, are the first to generate protests of the ethics of data mining. Any organization has to understand its costs to understand how to remain profitable, but there are always ethical implications of such information.

Data Trends Analysis

Example: Based on pre-built models that show trends in length of hospital stay, customer recovery rates, or any other monitoring metric, flag data that differs from what is considered normal.

Trend analysis is often performed by running a study with a data set containing past history and then running the same study using a data set with only this month's data.The differences in the results will show trends over the specified periods of time.

Employee Studies

Example: Based on the number of surgeries performed by a doctor, what set of characteristics of patients are there for doctors who perform more surgeries versus those who do not?

Regional Studies

Example: Based on where a surgery was performed (valley, central, western, or coast hospitals), what are the differences in patient histories?

Classification, Clustering, and Visualization Studies

All the examples so far have been worded so that you can perform a classification study. As an exercise, you can reread them and determine which column should be used for each type of study; however, clustering and visualization studies can be performed for each type of study.

For example, for the study profiling smokers versus non-smokers, a clustering study could be performed to potentially identify groups or segments of a patient population who are more likely to be smokers versus non-smokers.

The data on smokers and non-smokers can also be graphed against any number of other variables to visualize the importance of certain elements and characteristics of the two groups.

The number of possible studies is endless. This exercise was meant to spark thought on what you can do. In Chapters 7 through 8, specific examples will be given for several different industries.

2.3.4 What Elements to Analyze?

Whether you perform a clustering study, look at data visually, or perform a classification study, the process of choosing elements to analyze are the same. If you are data mining for the first time, then you might choose to include any number of columns and let the data mining process tell you what elements are important. The second pass may involve narrowing down the list of elements to the most important ones.

In performing a classification study, it is often important to recognize what types of data, or *dimensions*, you have and what other types you may want in the future.

There is a column, *Allergies*, in Table 2–1 from our sample healthcare data set. If we choose this as the dependent variable, then we are performing a study to classify the difference between those patients who have allergies and those who do not.

Goal: I want to understand the profile of who is likely to have allergies and who is not.

Subject of the Study: Looking at the data set in Table 2–1, there are different types of information that can be used for a study. These types of information are what the decision support industry commonly refers to as *dimensions*. It is always a good idea to identify what dimensions you may have in the data set you are studying. Here are the dimensions found in the healthcare demo:

- Patient's physical information

  Fields that tell us about a patient's physical information are: Age, Height, Weight, Weight_Last_Year

- Patient's medical information

  Fields that tell us about a patient's medical information include Recovery Time, Hospital Stay, Pain Reliever Used, High_Blood_Pressure, Allergies, Arthritis, Previous Surgeries, Back Problems, 2nd_Day_Exam, Obj_Pain, Obj_Swelling, and Obj_Stiffness

- Patient's demographic information

  Fields that tell us about a patient's demographic information include Smoker, Insurance, and Occupation

- Doctor information

  Fields that tell us about the doctor include Doctor_Yrs and Doctor_#_OP_Performed

- Hospital information

  Fields that tell us about a hospital include Hospital Branch and #Beds_in_Hosp

- Time information

  The field about time of surgery is Quarter

In all, there are six dimensions identified here: patient's physical, patient's medical, patient's demographic, doctor information, hospital information, and time information.

The first question to ask for a study on profiling people with allergies and those without is:

What dimensions are useful to profiling people with allergies and those without?

Clearly, any dimension describing the patient is useful. Is doctor information or hospital information useful? There is not as clear a link unless your purpose is to understand if certain hospitals or doctors tend to treat more people with allergies or vice versa. The time dimension is useful in determining a seasonal relation to allergies.

The second question to ask is:

How descriptive are the fields in the identified dimensions?

The patient's medical dimension has many elements, but the patient's demographic and time dimensions are sparse. If looking at what type of information to add, then the patient demographic and time dimensions would be a good place to start. Examples of patient's demographic information might include marital status, gender, income level, household type, type of exercise, or religion. The time dimension might include day of year, hour of day, or day of week.

A third question to ask is:

What types of dimension might one add to this study?

In this case, one could add a dimension about the drug a patient used, including describing side effects and efficacy rates. Another dimension might be a regional dimension describing the types of trees, animals, and environmental conditions that affect a person's allergies. If you think about it, there are several other dimensions that could be useful to a study like this.

Don't limit yourself when you are starting the data mining process. Data mining should help filter out fields that don't provide any information. More importantly, identify the dimensions of data you have and where you might add information in the future.

2.3.5 Issues of Sampling

Almost all data miners ask this question at one time or another:

How can I mine only a subset of my data and get good results if I have millions of rows of information?

Data mining does not always require your entire data set to model appropriately. The follow-up question is, how much is enough? While no exact amount can realistically be given, a fair statement would be to start out small and build up. If you are building models that accurately represent your data, increasing your data sets should not alter the results that you are finding.

Another thing to know is that a model can be created from a small sampling and then validated on the whole data set. If a sample data set is valid, then it is able to predict outcomes for other data samples and the results of known outcomes for other data sets can be compared.

2.4 READING THE DATA AND BUILDING A MODEL

For the next three sections, a classification study has been chosen to show the process of building a model. Below is the goal:

Goal: My purpose is to understand what type of patients undergoing surgery for severe back pain recover in 0-2 weeks, 2-3 weeks, 3-6 weeks, and 6+ weeks, so that I can help reduce lengthy recovery processes and understand areas that may hinder recovery.

Once this study has been defined and the input data specified to evaluate recovery time, it is left to the data mining tool to read a data set and build a model from it. Depending on the product used, the data model can look vastly different.

Chapter 1 discussed the various types of models briefly. It is not the purpose of this book to go into the details of how each type of model works. There are many works that are pointed to in Appendix A that will help with that.

For this example, a modeling tool will build a model that indicates the factors that make a person more likely to recover in 0-2 weeks, 2-3 weeks, 3-6 weeks, or 6+ weeks. The most important things with which a business professional should be comfortable are the accuracy, understandability, and performance of the model.

On Accuracy

The fact that important relationships are found that help determine why someone takes over 6 weeks to recover is one thing; proving that this relationship is a certain percentage accurate within a margin of error is another. Data mining has not completely replaced statistics toward this end; however, statistics will often miss important relationships that data mining will find.

Data mining will produce models that can be proven to have a certain degree of accuracy over time, but when accuracy is regulated by the government and must be proven, a combination of approaches is necessary. For example, HNC's Falcon is a great product for determining credit fraud, but it is not widely used to grant or deny credit because government regulations demand you know why you do what you do down to the mathematical equations.

On Understandability

Being able to understand a model can be a personal comfort issue. Some people are more comfortable with one approach over another; however, understandability is not a yes/no check-off item. There are several aspects to a model that should be understandable.

First, does the model let you understand what inputs affect an outcome?

Earlier, I mentioned that neural net approaches are often black box approaches that can be used for prediction, but it is hard to understand why predictions are made. For new generation products, this does not have to be true, but it can be an issue. Decision trees do have a good method for understanding how data segments best cluster together to affect an outcome.

Second, does a model let you understand why it fails or succeeds in predictions?

Some models will produce reports that tell you why a model succeeds in predicting (when compared against known outcomes) and where it may be falling short.

Third, does a model let you predict an outcome for complex data sets?

Decision trees have been criticized for their inability to predict outcomes of complex data sets. Again, new products may overcome past criticisms, but a model should allow you to predict outcomes on very large data sets.

Fourth, does a model validate its results?

All models should be able to tell you how accurate they are in predicting data, and where they can compare the predictions against known results.

On Performance

The performance of a model can be divided into two areas: how fast can you build a model and how fast can you predict from it. Neural nets have again historically been criticized for the time they take to build a model. HNC provides special hardware to speed the process up. Once a model has been built, prediction is very fast. The Agent Network Technology is very fast for model building and prediction. For model building, it has linear performance as a data set grows past millions of rows.

2.5 UNDERSTANDING YOUR MODEL

Understanding a model has many different dimensions to it. This section describes the types of reports and what information you might expect from a data set describing recovery time of patients.

Model Summarization

Regardless of the model you use, the reports tell you what information has a relationship to the specified outcomes. Saying the input data has an impact on a particular outcome does not necessarily mean a causal relationship. There could be a relationship between brown eyes and volleyball players, but brown eyes will not cause someone to be a volleyball player.

For our example data set, the following are some definite relationships a model should find (this is an example data set and not real data):

- Recovery: 0-2Weeks

  Roughly 7.5% of all patients who recovered in this time had the occupation of professional. If someone had the occupation professional, they always recovered in 0-2 weeks.

Roughly 73% of all patients who recovered in this time period were self-insured. If someone was self-insured, there was a very strong chance they recovered in 0-2 weeks.

- Recovery: 2-3Weeks

Roughly 34% of all patients who recovered in this time period did not smoke. If they did not smoke, there was a very strong chance that they recovered in 2-3 weeks.

- Recovery: 3-6Weeks

Roughly 41% of all patients who recovered in this time period were daily smokers. If the patient was a daily smoker, then there was a good chance they recovered in 3-6 weeks.

- Recovery: 6+Weeks

Roughly 18% of people who are retired and are over 65 years of age recovered in over 6 weeks. If someone is retired and over 65 years of age, there was a good chance that they took 6 weeks to recover.

Roughly 13% of people who recovered in 6 weeks had a history of back problems. If someone has a history of back problems, there is a strong chance they took 6 weeks to recover.

The information that was presented by the model provided several pieces of information. First, the frequencies of occurrence were calculated: How often did something happen? Second, the weight or probability that an input affected an outcome was measured in some way. Finally, something called a *conjunction* was shown. In this case the conjunction was: If someone was retired and they were over 65, then they were likely to recover in six weeks.

Specific Information

Models will also tell you what variables are specific to an outcome. For example, in the example data set, the occupation professional only occurred when patients recovered in 0-2 weeks. This is a *specific* input criterion. Also in this data set it should be known that *2nd-day-exam* never had the value "poor" for patients who recovered in 0-2 weeks. This is a *irrelevant* input criterion.

Data Distribution

One field in the example data set is *Weight*, which is a numeric value representing a patient's weight in pounds. The data for the column *weight* can be binned into five categories as follows:

Category 1	83 to 111 pounds
Category 2	111-139 pounds
Category 3	139-168 pounds
Category 4	168-196 pounds
Category 5	196-224 pounds

In order to show a data distribution, the number of values in each category is totalled. Category 1 has 75 values within its range; Category 2 has 300 values; Categories 3, 4, and 5 have 320, 211, and 115 values, repectively. The data distribution for this column looks like Figure 2–5.

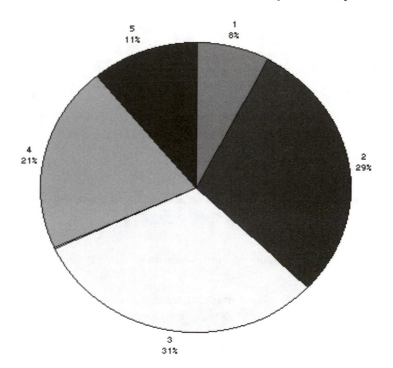

Figure 2–5 Binning data properly

The data is not evenly distributed among categories, and it creates an obvious question:

How do you bin this data to optimize your results?

There are several ways to answer this question. Decision trees, using a CHAID algorithm, are especially good at finding these types of results. Another way is to sort the values and see what the weight values look like. Figure 2–6 is an Excel chart of sorted weight values.

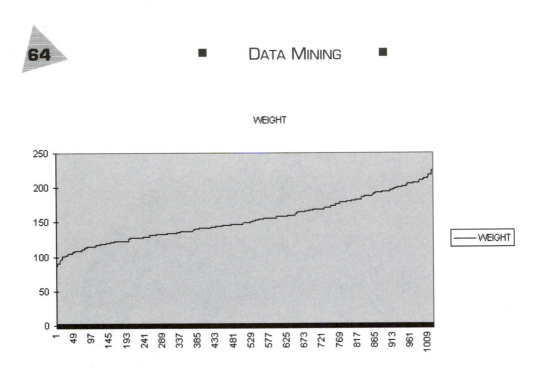

Figure 2–6 A chart showing patient weights for 1009 patients

The chart shows that the data is fairly evenly distributed among weight values and interesting groupings are not readily identifiable. Figure 2–7 shows a much more unusual distribution of patient weights.

Validation

The validation report is a way to evaluate how good your model is at predicting the data set. In one example, a model came up with these results for our sample data set:

- The model predicted patients recovering in 0-2 weeks with 84% accuracy.

- The model predicted patients recovering in 2-3 weeks with 69% accuracy.

- The model predicted patients recovering in 3-6 weeks with 62% accuracy.

- The model predicted patients recovering in over 6 weeks with 85% accuracy.

- Overall, the model predicted outcomes with a 73% accuracy.

Several things should be considered about the model that was evaluated. One, the model evaluated the same data set

WEIGHT

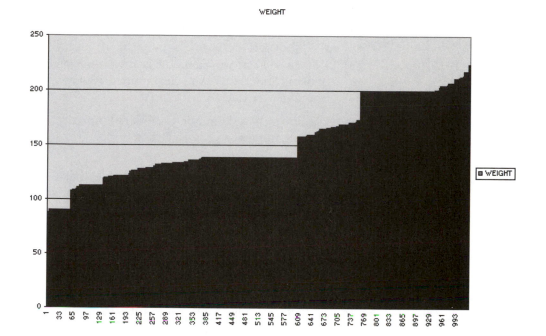

Figure 2–7 Another example of unusually distributed patients weights

that it was created with, which means it may give better results than if you evaluate it on a holdout sample. Two, the model is better at predicting certain outcomes than others. Third, the model is based on sample data, so you can always expect good results on a demo.

The results presented were from predicting an outcome for every single row. Some tools play games by only predicting on a subset of the rows and then only evaluating those rows, which skews the data and makes the prediction look better than it is.

A couple of questions that you might have about the validation process are:

How can I improve my model's predictive accuracy?

There are several ways to improve upon a model once it is created. There is, however, a danger of "over-fitting" the model, so that it is highly predictive for a training set, but is less efficient when predicting from data not used in building the model. Here are a few suggestions to improve the model.

- After identifying types of input data that have strong influence on certain outcomes, try to gather more detailed information similar to these data points.

- Data used in creating a model is always in jeopardy of being "unclean". Data cleaning will always improve a model.

- Change the way numeric values are binned. Binning ranges can have a strong impact on model efficiency

- Use evaluation information, if available, that explains when a model fails or succeeds to predict successfully. For example, the model that was evaluated reported that it failed to predict correctly for recoveries over 6 weeks when the number of operating rooms in the hospital were from 1 to 10. This condition occurred roughly 6% of the time the recovery time was 6 weeks.

- A data set can be divided into subsets and mined individually. Sometimes mining a series of subsets will yield stronger results than mining the whole.

- If you know the conditions that should always lead to a certain outcome, filter out this data and mine the rest. For example, if input A leads to output B 95% of the time, then assume all rows of data with input A are linked to output B and mine the rest.

2.6 PREDICTION

The process of prediction is straightforward. With a set of inputs, a prediction is made on a certain outcome. While the validation process uses prediction, it is really comparing known results to predictions made to calculate an accuracy level. With true prediction, the outcome to be predicted will not be known.

In our example of modeling recovery time, one row of data looks like the following:

| HOSPITAL_BRANCH | Western |
| LENGTH_HOSP_STAY | 0-2Days |

AGE	18-25
HEIGHT	Unknown
WEIGHT	Unknown
SMOKER	Yes
SMOKER_TYPE	Occasional
MARITAL_STATUS	Married
OCCUPATION	Civil Servant
INSURANCE	Self-Insured
PAIN_RELIEVER_USED	Mild-Pain-Reliever
DOCTOR_YRS	2-5
D_#_OPERS	Med
#BEDS	951-1149
#OPER_RMS	10-20
HIGH_BLOOD_PRESURE	N
ALLERGIES	N
ARTHRITIS	N
PREVIOUS_SURGERY	3
HIST_BACK_PROBS	N
BLOOD_PRESURE	High
QUARTER	Summer
2ND_DAY_EXAM	Excellent
OBJ_PAIN	LOW
OBJ_SWELLING	Y
OBJ_STIFFNESS	N
HISTORY_NEUROSIS	N

The recovery time of this particular patient will be predicted. Using one technique, the patient is predicted to recover in 0-2 weeks.

There is other information that such a prediction process may make, as discussed below.

Challenger Outcomes

Not only do you want to know what outcome will be predicted, it may be interesting to calculate challenger predictions. For example, in the case above, the patient was predicted to recover in 0-2 weeks. There are three other possible outcomes. What will be the next likely prediction to be made? In this case, 6+ weeks was predicted as the next likely outcome.

Margin of Victory

One very interesting point of data is the difference in the best prediction versus challenger outcome. If a prediction is calculated by a score or weight of some sort, then the difference in the prediction scores can also be calculated. For example, in this case, 0-2 weeks was predicted as the outcome with a score of 831 and the challenger was predicted with a score of 640, which is a margin of victory of 23%. The larger the percentage, the more likely the prediction is to be true.

You can make prediction on only the rows of data where the margin of victory is greater than some percentage. You will not make predictions for every row, but the rows you do make predictions on may have a better margin of victory.

Understanding Why a Prediction Is Made

Another item you may want to know about a prediction is why it was made. For the example above, the top three reasons this prediction was made was because the patient was self-insured, the doctor found in objective findings a low occurrence of pain, and the patient was considered in excellent shape in the 2nd day exam.

2.7 SUMMARY

This chapter has covered the data mining process in much more detail. An example data set was used to discuss issues and step through the data mining process of preparing a data set, defining a study, building a model, understanding the model, and performing prediction. The chapter explores the types of information you expect when mining. This chapter is purposely general. The subsequent chapters will explore the process in more detail. Chapter 3 discusses vendors in the data mining industry. Chapters 4 through 6 will step through the data mining process again using different tools to familiarize you with how different products approach data mining. To examine types of studies for different industries, Chapters 7 and 8 will look more at the specifics.

Chapter
3

The Data Mining Marketplace

This chapter provides insight into the data mining market today. Not only are many of the leading commercial data mining vendors discussed, this chapter also discusses useful web sites where you can learn more about them, as well as where to purchase information for data mining and, for those programmers out there, where to find public domain source code.

The chapter is organized as follows:

3.1 INTRODUCTION (TRENDS)

The preface of this book stated a few reasons why data mining is becoming more accepted by corporate America. Central to data mining's increased popularity is the advancement in computational power. Decreases in hardware costs have made data mining available to a much wider audience. Not long ago, a mainframe was required to process what PCs can do today. (The PC on which this book was written has also mined over a million rows of data.)

Beyond the rise in computational power, there also have been several trends in the industry that ensure a broader use of data mining. Below are a few of the most noticeable trends that directly affect the interest level in data mining.

Data Warehousing is Becoming Commonplace

Data warehousing has become much more widely accepted today than a few years ago. While data mining does not require the presence of a data warehouse, data mining is often viewed as an after-market product of data warehousing because people who have made the effort to create a data warehouse have the richest data available to mine. It stands to reason that the broader acceptance of data warehousing will lead to increased interest in data mining.

Data Mining Is Becoming Integrated with Relational Databases

Relational vendors are integrating data mining solutions to make the process easier than ever before. One major advantage of this is the time savings in preparing data to be mined. Other data mining solutions have traditionally required heavy workloads preparing data. Moreover, data mining directly integrated in relational engines will also prove to be easier and more accessible to end users.

Red Brick Systems, a relational database vendor specializing in data warehousing, and DataMind Corporation have just recently announced an integration with a data mining tool. Red Brick Warehouse includes Red Brick Data Mine Option™, advanced data mining functionality fully integrated into its data warehouse RDBMS. Red Brick Warehouse 5.0 is unique in providing data warehousing and data mining capabilities in a single integrated RDBMS engine.

Another announcement came from Informix Software and Neovista Solutions®, who announced they are working together to tightly couple NeoVista's Decision Series™ suite of integrated data mining tools with the INFORMIX®-Universal Server™.

EIS Tool Vendors Integrating Data Mining

EIS and query vendors are also involved in integrating data mining with traditional query and decision support tools. Query and EIS tools in the past have required end users to formulate questions in order to get interesting answers, an assumptive-based process. Integrating data mining with query and EIS tools will enable a discovery-based process, whereby an end user can be told the most interesting things to look at and then can formulate questions based on the new information.

Business Objects, in cooperation with ISoft SA®, announced a data mining integration in 1996. Business Object's data mining solution, BusinessMiner™, provides a data mining solution that's aimed at mainstream business users.

Brio Technology and DataMind Corporation announced they will leverage their technologies to provide a solution to perform predictive analysis to the desktop.

Angoss and Andyne® announced a joint relationship to provide data mining and decision support capability.

Cognos Software announced the availability of their Scenario™ data mining tool, which integrates their query and OLAP tools with data mining.

OLAP vendors have also been announcing interest in data mining. For example, Pilot Software announced an integrated data mining option with their product.

Arbor Software® and DataMind will promote the combined capabilities of the Essbase™ multidimensional OLAP server and the DataMind Professional Editions, so that customers can easily perform data mining functions on data managed by the Essbase OLAP server. This combined solution leverages the widespread popularity and power of spreadsheets as the leading desktop analysis tool.

Information More Accessible

Data mining requires information, and information is more available than ever before, as are the larger disk drives to hold the data.

Customer, household, and industry demographic information has become widely and cheaply available. Not only can one purchase a CD-ROM with millions of home and business users, but they can purchase complete geographic information from the U.S. Census Bureau. Further in this chapter, many data providers are mentioned.

While it often evokes issues of privacy, and will make many uncomfortable, it is astonishing to note how much information providers can learn about us from our credit information. For example, if you have ever purchased cat food, dog food, baby food, or squash, there are assumptions that can be made, especially if you continue a pattern.

Data Mining Vendors Focusing More on Vertical Markets

Data mining involves an implicit understanding of the data with which you are working; therefore vendors are focusing on vertical markets.

For example, HNC resells a product line named Falcon that focuses on credit fraud analysis in banking and insurance. This product has been extremely successful in this market.

DataMind Corporation has a focus on churn management in telecommunications. With deregulation and open competition in the telecommunications industry, keeping customers has become a hot area of concern.

Other data mining vendors focus on process control in manufacturing. NeuralWare worked closely with Texaco to develop a product in this market space.

3.2 DATA MINING VENDORS

Following is a list of major data mining vendors in the market today. This list is by no means complete, but is meant to represent the more dominant players. All products are trademarks or registered trademarks of their respective companies.

Angoss International Limited (KnowledgeSEEKER)
34 St. Patrick Street, Suite 200
Toronto, Ontario
Canada, M5T 1V1
(416) 593-1122
web: http://www.angoss.com

PRODUCT: KnowledgeSEEKER

PLATFORMS: Windows, Windows 95, Windows NT, UNIX

POSITION: KnowledgeSEEKER, shown in Chapter 4, performs data mining using decision tree techniques, employing two well-known algorithms: CHAID and CART. The program graphically shows decision trees, automatically forming decision trees on all significant relationships and also allowing the user to "force" a graphical tree on any relationship not already built. The program is understandable for end users and ODBC compliant to access relational back ends. Cognos, a software developer of decision support tools, has signed a relationship with Angoss to provide Angoss's technology with their product set. Angoss also has numerous other partnerships announced.

Attar Software USA (XpertRule)
Two Deerfoot Trail on Partridge Hill
Harvard, MA 01451
(508) 456-3946
web: http://www.attar.com

PRODUCTS: XpertRule, Analyzer, Profiler, Configurator

PLATFORMS: XpertRule runs on Windows, Windows 95, and Windows NT; development environment deployed on PCs, UNIX-based systems, and mainframes

POSITION: Attar is a British data mining company with a set of products for data mining. XpertRule KBS is a development package, with in-built resource optimization for building knowledge based systems. XpertRule Profiler is a client-server software package for data mining. The client-server processes are accomplished through ODBC connectivity to back end databases.

Business Objects (BusinessMiner)
20813 Stevens Creek Blvd., Suite 100
Cupertino, CA 95014
(408) 973-9300
web: http://www.businessobjects.com

PRODUCT: BusinessMiner

PLATFORMS: Windows 95, Windows NT

POSITION: BusinessMiner is an integrated client-sided data mining solution with Business Object's query, reporting, and OLAP solutions. The product is developed with the Alice technology from ISoft SA, which is a decision tree approach to data mining.

Cognos Software (Scenario)
67 S. Bedford St.
Suite 200W
Burlington, MA 01803
(800) 267-2777
web: http://www.cognos.com

PRODUCT: Scenario

PLATFORMS: Windows 95, Windows NT

POSITION: Cognos, a leader in providing query and OLAP tools, is shipping Scenario, a data mining solution for integration with their tools, Powerplay and Impromptu. This client-side data mining solution is based on decision tree CHAID (Chi-Squared Automatic Interaction Detection) technology. Cognos also announced intent to include neural network modeling based on their purchase of Right Information Systems.

DataMind Corporation (DataMind Professional Edition, DataMind DataCruncher)
2121 S. El Camino Real
Suite 1200
San Mateo, CA 94403
(415) 287-2000
web: http://www.datamindcorp.com

PRODUCTS: DataMind Professional Edition, DataMind DataCruncher

PLATFORMS: Client: Windows, Windows 95, Windows NT; Server: UNIX platforms, Windows NT

POSITION: DataMind Corporation focuses on software and solutions for business professionals. Incorporated in 1994, DataMind uses the Agent Network Technology based on research by Dr. Khai Minh Pham at the University of Paris. DataMind offers a client–server product offering DataMind Professional and DataMind DataCruncher. DataMind Professional Edition is an easy-to-use desktop front-end product with access to RDBMS systems like Informix, Oracle, Red Brick, and Sybase. DataMind DataCruncher is a server-based product for more complex modeling capabilities with direct access to several relational database systems.

In June 1996, DataMind Corporation and Red Brick Systems announced a technology partnership to jointly develop and integrate data mining functionality into the Red Brick data warehouse relational database. This is the first time where relational database technology and data mining were directly incorporated.

HNC Software Inc. (Falcon, Eagle, Colleague, AREAS, SkuPLAN, DataBase Mining Workstation)

5930 Cornerstone Court West
San Diego, California 92121-3728
619-546-8877
web: http://www.hnc.com

PRODUCTS: Falcon, Eagle, Colleague, AREAS, SkuPLAN, DataBase Mining Workstation

PLATFORMS: NetWare, Windows NT, UNIX

POSITION: HNC Software offers a suite of software applications based on neural network predictive models. Falcon is a set of software products that are used to detect credit and debit card fraud. The Eagle software offering is devoted to merchant risk. SkuPLAN is used to discover information on retail inventories. Colleague is used to help with lending decisions. AREAS is used for automatic home valuations. HNC also sells a DataBase Mining Workstation for customer information databases because of the complexities of creating neural networks. HNC manufactures their own parallel-processor boards to speed up training.

IBM Corporation (Intelligent Miner)

Old Orchard Road
Armonk, NY 10504
(914) 765-1900
web: http://www.ibm.com

PRODUCT: Intelligent Miner is a suite of software products including Explorer, Diamond, and Quest

PLATFORMS: AIX 4.1, MVS, AS/400

POSITION: IBM sells a suite of software tools under the name Intelligent Miner to provide a high-end data mining solution. IBM sells a set of different algorithms to solve separate problems. Explorer is a neural net utility for clustering. Diamond is a software product used for visualization. Quest is a tool used for what they refer to as "link analysis."

Integral Solutions LTD (Clementine)
Berk House
Basing View
Basingstoke
Hampshire RG21 4RG UK
(+44 1256 55899)
web: http://www.isl.co.uk

PRODUCT: Clementine

PLATFORMS: UNIX systems, VAX/VMS, DEC Alpha

POSITION: Clementine is based on a visual programming interface and is an application development environment as well as a data mining tool. The product uses decision tree induction and neural networks to build discovery models and perform predictions. Any neural network or decision tree model can be represented with a C source code. NCR signed a deal to represent the Clementine product in the United States.

HyperParallel, Inc. (HYPERparallel //Discovery)
282 Second Street
3rd Floor
San Francisco, CA 94105
(415) 284-7000
web: http://www.hyperparallel.com

PRODUCT: HYPERparallel //Discovery suite

PLATFORM: UNIX servers

POSITION: The HYPERparallel product is a portfolio of data mining algorithms for decision-making. HYPERparallel's //Discovery suite of products includes //Affinity //Sequence, //Induction, //Cluster, and //Neural. HyperParallel also is developing a set of solution templates, which they refer to as //Solution Framework, which can be leveraged to solve specific business problems.

Information Discovery, Inc. (IDIS)
703B Pier Avenue, Suite 169
Hermosa Beach, CA 90254
(310) 937-3600
web: http://www.datamining.com

PRODUCT: The Data Mining Suite includes Information Discovery System, PM Predictive Modeler, Map Discovery System

PLATFORMS: Windows, Windows 95, Windows NT, DOS, UNIX, SMP and MPP system

POSITION: IDIS sells a Data Mining Suite, which includes the Information Discovery System for model generation, a predictive modeler, and a mapping system. The data mining suite is sold as an automatic analysis package that discovers patterns and generates rules and performs prediction on the constructed models. The product includes spreadsheet, graphics, and mapping tools. The product supports most relational database systems. The product also has a module, referred to as the Mark Twain Edition, that automatically generates narrative to explain the relationships found with their tool.

Information Discovery has also targeted several vertical industries, including retail news, with a Customized Retail News package and INTRA/Knowledge, which works with relationship management in the financial services arena. Information Discovery also works with Oracle's Express EIS package.

ISoft (AC2, Alice)
Chemin de Moulon
F-91190 Gif sur Yvette
33-1 69 41 27 77
Fax: 33-1 69 41 25 32
email: info.isoft.fr

PRODUCTS: AC2, Alice

PLATFORMS: Alice: Windows, Windows 95, Windows NT; AC2: Windows, Windows 95, Windows NT, UNIX

POSITION: ISoft is a French company that has implemented decision tree based data mining software. Alice is a PC-based data mining solution with a graphical front end. ISoft has formed a partnership with Business Objects, where Business Objects will be adding their software as an add-in module that integrates directly with their tools.

AC2 is available as a development environment, with a C++ library and OLE support. Both products support SQL access to relational databases through ODBC.

NeoVista Solutions, Inc. (Decision Series)
10710 N. Tantau Ave.
Cupertino, CA 95014
(408) 343-4220
web: http://www.neovista.com

PRODUCTS: Decision Series: DecisionNet, DecisionCL, DecisionAR, DecisionGA, DecisionAccess

PLATFORM: UNIX servers

POSITION: NeoVista markets a suite of products, the Decision Series, that focuses on data mining. The suite of products is a server-side product offering. The products are:

DecisionNet: A neural network based solution for performing predictions.

DecisionCL: A clustering solution with advanced clustering algorithms for supervised and unsupervised learning.

DecisionAR: A solution generating association rules, used to model how likely events occur together or sequentially over time, i.e., 73% of the time events X and Y occur together, and in half of those cases, event Z occurs within a week.

DecisionGA: A solution using genetic algorithms.

DecisionAccess: A data access interface layer. This is the framework for integrating the other discovery tools with each other.

NeoVista, which has remade itself after formerly being known as Maspar, is tackling the enterprise-level data mining market. They have referenced that they aggressively market at WallMart and the Army Air Force Exchange. They were one of the first vendors to enter a relationship with Informix to construct a Data Blade for Informix's Universal Server.

Neural Applications Corporation (NetProphet, Aegis)
2600 Crosspark Rd.
Coralville, IA 52241
(319) 626-5000
web: http://www.neural.com

PRODUCTS: NetProphet, Aegis Development System

PLATFORMS: NetProphet: Windows 3.1, Windows 95; Aegis: DOS, Windows 3.1, Windows 95, Windows NT, OS/ 2, and most UNIX variants.

POSITION: Net Prophet is a stock browser for the Internet. It is a Java enabled application that monitors stock and mutual funds at home. There are intelligent stock filtering tools and neural network ratings for most stocks traded.

Aegis is a development environment for intelligent process control applications. Industrial process control applications require process optimization. Aegis makes use of neural networks, fuzzy logic, and genetic algorithms.

NeuralWare Inc. (NeuralWorks Predict, NeuralWorks Predict Professional, NeuralWorks Professional II/Plus, NeuralWorks Explorer, NeuCOP)
202 Park West Drive
Pittsburgh, PA 15275
(412) 787-8222
web: http://www.NeuralWare.com

PRODUCTS: NeuralWorks Predict, NeuralWorks Professional, NeuralWorks Explorer, Designer Pack, NeuCOP Modeler, NeuCOP Optimizer, NeuCOP Controller

PLATFORMS: With C compilation, products work on Windows 3.1, Windows 95, Windows NT, Macintosh, and most UNIX variants

POSITION: NeuralWare has several products and add-on packages to those products all centering around neural network technology. The three central products to Neural-Ware are NeuralWorks Predict, NeuralWorks Professional II/Plus, and NeuCOP.

NeuralWorks Predict is a neural network based data mining tool for business professionals, with integration into Microsoft Excel. NeuralWorks Predict utilizes genetic algorithms, fuzzy logic, statistics, Dynamic Hill Climbing techniques, along with neural networks and Kalman Filtering. For the novice user, the technology behind NeuralWorks Predict is invisible. NeuralWorks Predict SDK provides a way to directly embed Predict's technology in an application.

NeuralWorks Professional II/Plus product line focuses on the application engineer and the professional statistician. It is a general purpose environment incorporating 25 different neural network models and tools to facilitate development and implementation of the user's application. This tool includes everything needed to train and test a network, monitor training objectives, analyze performance of standard neural network models, and save and implement trained networks. An add-on pack, NeuralWorks Designer Pack, provides real-time C code generation.

NeuralWare's NeuCOP (Neural Control and Optimization Package) product line was designed and developed as a joint effort by Texaco and NeuralWare NeuCOP addresses the needs of the control engineer for an adaptive, multi-variable controller. This software utilizes neural networks, expert systems, and chaotic systems to optimize and control complex production processes inside the petrochemical, glass and metals, pharmaceutical, semiconductor fabrication, and food and beverage industries.

Pilot Software, Inc. (Pilot Discovery Server)
One Canal Park
Cambridge, MA 02141
(617) 374-9400
web: http://www.pilotsw.com

PRODUCT: Pilot Discovery Server

PLATFORMS: Windows NT, UNIX

POSITION: Pilot Software, a division of the Cognizant, markets the Pilot Discover Server data mining software as a solution that is integrated directly with Pilot's Decision Support Suite. Pilot is capitalizing on the integration of their EIS decision support software and data mining capabilities.

Pilot's Discovery Server is targeted at sales and marketing organizations. The product directly integrates with relational databases to facilitate access of information to manage customer relationships. Information is provided on a customer's lifetime value and profitability. The product also works at customer segmentation.

Red Brick Systems, Inc. (Data Mine, Data Mine Builder)
485 Alberto Way
Los Gatos, CA 95032
(408) 353-7214
web: http://www.RedBrick.com

PRODUCTS: Red Brick Data Mine, Red Brick Data Mine Builder

PLATFORMS: Client: Microsoft Windows, Windows 95, Windows NT; Server: SunOS, HP-UX, AIX, SGI UNIX, and Windows NT

POSITION: Red Brick became the first relational database company to integrate a data mining solution directly into their database, by forming a relationship with DataMind. The advantage of direct integration is the elimination of much of the data preparation time that traditional data mining solutions have offered.

The Red Brick Warehouse includes a Red Brick Data Mine Option that integrates the relational database and data mining. The Red Brick Data Mine Builder is a client-side tool for building models. Red Brick allows access to creating models from a data warehouse by extending SQL to include commands to access and create not only data tables, but data models as well.

Silicon Graphics Computer Systems (MineSet)
2011 N. Shoreline Blvd.
Mountain View, CA 94043
(415) 960-1980
web: http://www.sgi.com

PRODUCT: Silicon MineSet

PLATFORM: SGI UNIX server

POSITION: MineSet provides five visual data mining tools for visual exploration of data and data mining results. Decision tree algorithms, probabilities, and association algorithms are also incorporated. The tools utilize animated 3-D landscapes.

The MineSet version supports the following visual data mining tools:

- Map Visualizer

- Scatter Visualizer
- Tree Visualizer
- Rule Visualizer
- Evidence Visualizer

The Map Visualizer supports the analysis of spatially related data and information. By applying data onto height and color of pre-built or user-generated map elements, users have the ability to quickly identify trends, patterns, relationships, and anomalies in data.

Many times, data sets are just too complex for representation in two or even three dimensions. The MineSet Scatter Visualizer is ideal for analyzing the behavior of data in many dimensions all at once.

The Tree Visualizer provides the capability to visualize trees and hierarchical data structures. Using a three-dimensionl fly-through navigational paradigm, users can move through data to discover trends, patterns, and anomalies.

The Rule Visualizer graphically displays results from the Association Rule Generator. By analyzing rules discovered using the Association Rule Generator, users gain greater insight into the nature of a particular data set.

The Evidence Visualizer displays the structure and properties of an evidence classifier built by the Evidence Inducer. The Evidence Visualizer shows how unique values or value ranges of attributes can lead to a particular classification.

SPSS Inc. (SPSS CHAID)
444 N. Michigan Ave.
Chicago, IL 60611-3962
(800) 543-2185
web: http://www.spss.com

PRODUCT: SPSS CHAID

PLATFORMS: Windows, Windows 95, Windows NT

POSITION: SPSS is a leader in the statistical software arena, competing head-to-head with SAS Institute. SPSS has also embarked on initiatives to offer data mining solutions, and is likely to continue to add to their offerings in this area. SPSS has SPSS and SYSTAT statistical packages that perform linear regressions and achieve some of the same results with conventional statistics.

SPSS CHAID is a decision tree based data mining software tool for analysts that develops predictive models and produces easy-to-read tree diagrams. Market and customer segmentation is one key area where this product has been used. This SPSS CHAID product can also be run as an add-on module to the SPSS Base for the Windows package.

SPSS also has a neural network product, referred to as Neural Connection, which provides modeling and predictive capabilities as well as time series analysis and data segmentation.

SAS Institute Inc. (SAS, JMP)
SAS Campus Dr.
Cary, NC 27513-2414
(916) 677-8000
web: http://www.sas.com/

PRODUCTS: SAS, JMP

PLATFORMS: JMP: Macintosh, Windows, Windows 95; SAS: Most platforms available

POSITION: SAS has two commonly used statistical packages, SAS and JMP, that perform linear regressions and achieve some of the same results as comparable data mining tools using conventional statistical approaches. JMP is positioned as a stand-alone software package for end users. SAS is a widely used, scalable statistical package that runs on virtually every hardware platform and is considered a market leader.

Thinking Machines Corporation (Darwin)
14 Crosby Dr.
Bedford, MA 01730
(617) 276-0400
web: http://www.think.com

PRODUCT: Darwin

PLATFORMS: Windows NT, Bull, DEC VMS, DEC OSF, DG AViiON, HP-UX, IBM AIX, ICL, Motorola 88k, NCR System 3000, NEC, Novell

POSITION: Darwin is a suite of data mining products. Darwin exploits parallel computing to deliver in hours results that require days or weeks using traditional methods. Darwin offers five tools:

StarTree: A decision tree, Classification and Regression Tree (CART) algorithm, for data mining.

StarNet: A neural network solution for prediction, or artificial neural networks (ANNs)

StarMatch: A solution employing k-Nearest Neighbor (KNN) and memory-based reasoning (MBR) techniques for association.

StarGene : A solution using genetic algorithms (GAs) and optimization.

StarView: A tool that provides data visualization.

Thinking Machines and NeoVista are similar in several ways. Both were hardware companies that have remade themselves. Both sell a server-based product, and both offer a suite of software products.

Trajecta (dbProphet)
611 S. Congress, Suite 420
Austin, Texas 78704-1736
(512) 326-2411
web: http://www.trajecta.com

PRODUCT: dbProphet

PLATFORMS: Windows NT, UNIX, VMS

POSITION: dbProphet is a neural network based data mining tool. The tool incorporates advanced neural network algorithms as well as data visualization and variable manipulation tools. dbProphet also has a runtime model that can be accessed by a C programming interface.

3.3 VISUALIZATION

The essence of data mining is the process of creating a model. A model is a representation of complex data that makes complex data more understandable. Since pictures often represent data better than reports or numbers, data visualization is clearly another way to data mine.

3.3.1 Examples of Data Visualization

Figure 3–1 exemplifies how a picture can help make raw data more understandable. The figure, courtesy of MapInfo, shows product sales overlaid on top of a map. The map has an area zoomed in on southern Florida and shows pie charts of product sales in specific counties. This picture is a concise way to understand how product sales vary depending on the state, county, and city at which you are looking. Colors are also used to denote the number of

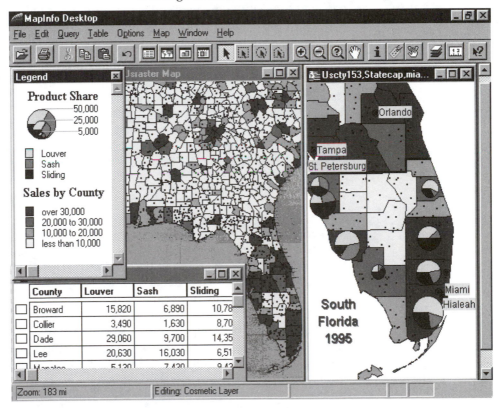

Figure 3–1 Graphically showing product share and sales by county

sales by county to help indicate where the most product sales are happening.

There are several graphical information systems, or GIS products, on the market today, and they are very useful in showing graphical representations of data. Microsoft has a mapping feature integrated directly into Microsoft Excel based on an arrangement with MapInfo.

Data visualization tools go beyond simply two-dimensional mapping data, and fortunately, with the advancements in personal computing, many of the visualization techniques that were only available on high power servers are moving into the end user market space.

Silicon Graphics is a leader in data visualization techniques. Silicon Graphic's data mining package, MineSet, has several visualization components to it. For example, they too have a map visualizer, but they allow for three dimensional visualization as well as a method to show changes over time, while mapping data like product sales over a geographic region.

Figure 3–2 shows a representation of the Map Visualizer. This tool displays quantitative and relational characteristics of your spatially oriented data. Data items are associated with graphical "bar chart" objects in the visual landscape. However, the objects have recognizable spatial shapes and positions, such as those found in geographical maps. The landscape can consist of a collection of these spatially related objects, each with individual heights and colors. You can dynamically navigate through this landscape by panning, rotating, zooming, drilling down to see increased granularity of geographic details, drilling up to aggregate data into more coarse-grained graphical objects, and using animation to see how the data changes across one or two independent dimensions.

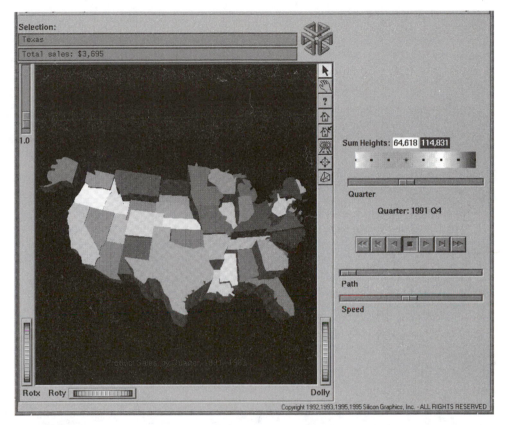

Figure 3–2 Map Visualizer

Silicon Graphics also has a tree visualizer as shown in Figure 3–3. The Tree Visualizer is a graphical interface that displays data as a three-dimensional "landscape." It presents your data as clustered, hierarchical blocks (nodes) and bars through which you can dynamically navigate, viewing part or all of the data set.

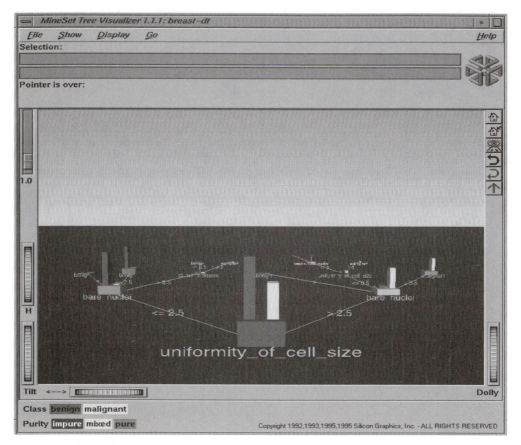

Figure 3–3 Tree Visualizer

The Tree Visualizer displays quantitative and relational characteristics of your data by showing them as hierarchically connected nodes. Each node contains bars whose height and color correspond to aggregations of data values. The lines connecting nodes show the relationship of one set of data to its subsets. Values in subgroups can be summed and displayed automatically in the next higher level. The base under the bars can provide information about the aggregate value of all the bars.

The Tree Visualizer takes data at the lowest level of the hierarchy as input. Data is then aggregated up through the visualization automatically, as defined by the user. Full support is also provided for visual filtering, querying, and marking.

The Tree Visualizer is also used for the display of the decision trees resulting from the Decision Tree Inducer. The Tree Visualizer shows decision and leaf classification nodes. Information about classification distribution and classification purity is shown at each node. The Tree Visualizer allows for further understanding and analysis of the decision trees.

3.3.2 Vendor List

Below is a list of vendors who provide data visualization tools. All products are trademarks or registered trademarks of their respective companies.

Advanced Visual Systems (AVS/Express)
300 Fifth Ave.
Waltham, MA 02115
(617) 890-4300
web: http://www.avs.com

PRODUCT: AVS/Express

PLATFORMS: Windows, Windows 95, Windows NT, UNIX

POSITION: Advanced Visual Systems provides three-dimensional visualization and imaging techniques to complex data. AVS has end user and developer versions of their products. Their graphical components include visualization blocks, image processing, and database connectivity.

Alta Analytics, Inc. (NetMap)
555 Metro Place North, Suite 175
Dublin, Ohio 43017
(614) 792-2222
web: http://www.alta-oh.com

PRODUCT: NetMap

PLATFORMS: Windows NT, UNIX workstations

POSITION: NetMap is a mapping tool designed for more sophisticated data visualization. It has features to allow for clustering, link analysis, and integration with the visualization components. This allows for graphical knowledge discovery to identify trends and patterns. The product has been used in uncovering corporate fraud as well as in analyzing corporate securities. Some customers include the Australian Securities Commission, the U.S. government, and the Special Fraud Office in London, England.

Belmont Research, Inc. (CrossGraphs)
84 Sherman St.
Cambridge, MA 02140
(617) 868-6878
web: http://www.belmont.com

PRODUCT: CrossGraphs

PLATFORMS: Window 3.X, Windows 95, Windows NT, UNIX workstations, Power Macintosh

POSITION: CrossGraphs is a unique data visualization tool that automatically divides data into subsets and displays complex data in arrays of graphs, one graph per subset, on one or many pages without programming. Graph arrays let you easily spot trends, identify anomalies, and see relationships among different variables or subsets of your data in a single display. For example, sales and marketing managers gain business knowledge by using CrossGraphs to view sales performance data in many graphs—by the competition, product, attribute, region, sales channel, market segment, time period, or a combination of these dimensions. The product can be run interactively or in batch and has links to Oracle and ODBC databases, and ASCII, dBase, and SAS data files. Belmont Research has done much work in the healthcare industry, and several of their graphs are shown in Chapter 9.

Environmental Systems Research Institute, Inc. (MapObjects, ARC/INFO, Arc GIS, Spatial Database Engine)
380 New York St.
Redlands, CA 92373
(800) GIS-XPRT (909) 793-2853
web: http://www.esri.com

PRODUCTS: MapObjects, ARC/INFO, ARC GIS, Spatial Database Engine

PLATFORMS: Windows, Windows 95, Window NT, Macintosh, UNIX

POSITION: ESRI supports a suite of GIS software products that allows for viewing maps, geocoding, and performing more sophisticated data visualization. ARC and ARC/

INFO come with a macro language to support embedding this technology into other applications. Their Spatial Database Engine allows for support of spatial information into databases like Oracle, DB2, Informix, and Sybase.

IBM Corporation (Parallel Visual Explorer)
Old Orchard Road
Armonk, NY 10504
(914) 765-1900
web: http://www.ibm.com

PRODUCT: Parallel Visual Explorer

PLATFORM: RS/6000 workstations

POSITION: IBM sells a suite of software tools under the name Intelligent Miner to provide a high-end data mining solution. IBM sells a set of different algorithms to solve separate problems. Explorer is a neural net utility for clustering. Diamond is a software package used for visualization. Quest is a tool they use for what they refer to as "link analysis."

MapInfo Corp (MapInfo, SpatialWare)
1 Global View
Troy, NY 12180
(518) 285-6000
web: http://www.mapinfo.com

PRODUCT: MapInfo Desktop, MapInfo Professional, MapMaker, SpatialWare, MapX

PLATFORMS: Windows, Windows 95, Window NT, Macintosh, UNIX

POSITION: MapInfo provides a suite of products for data visualization and mapping. They support geocoding as well as data overlay onto maps to help visualize data trends. MapInfo works with many partners and has a programming interface to its products. Its mapping technology is integrated as a module within Microsoft Excel, and it has also introduced a SpatialWare technology that allows users of relational databases like Oracle and Informix to examine and store complex data for spatial analysis within their database.

Silicon Graphics Computer Systems (MineSet)
2011 N. Shoreline Blvd.
Mountain View, CA 94043
(415) 960-1980
web: http://www.sgi.com

PRODUCT: MineSet

PLATFORM: SGI UNIX

POSITION: SGI has been discussed in this section. The Map Visualizer, the Tree Visualizer, the Scatter Visualizer, and the Evidence Visualizer all provide enhanced data visualization.

3.4 USEFUL WEB SITES/COMMERCIALLY AVAILABLE CODE

The data mining community offers several web sites with a great deal of information about data mining vendors, data, and even source code. Below is a start at listing some of the more interesting sites. You will inevitably find many more sites. Using these web sites, you may find:

- More information about data mining

- Data sites with which to experiment

- Data sources and vendors who provide this data

- Code for some data mining algorithms (for the programmer)

3.4.1 Data Mining Web Sites

Knowledge Discovery Mine
web: http://info.gte.com

DESCRIPTION: Gregory Piatestdky-Shapiro, from GTE, has put together an impressive, comprehensive data mining web site. The home page of this site provides many valuable pointers, including:

- Other web sites on data mining

- S*I*FTWARE (a list of many public domain tools available for data mining)

- KDD Nuggets—a newsletter

- Upcoming meetings for the data mining community

- Reference materials

- Pointers to available web sites.

The Data Mine
web: http://www.cs.bham.ac.uk

DESCRIPTION: This is a United Kingdom data mining web site containing references to companies, conferences, papers, and software.

Neural Networks at Pacific Northwest National Laboratory
web: http://www.emsl.pnl.gov

DESCRIPTION: This is a web site, like many others, which is devoted to neural networks. There are, as you will find, many sites devoted to neural networks. This one was listed due to a very interesting section on commercial products using neural networks. You should also find connections to many other sites through this one.

Technology Overwatch—Genetic Algorithms
web: http://www.pentagon-ai.army.mil/aic/overwatch/Genetic_Alorithms.html

DESCRIPTION: This site contains much information on genetic algorithms, including some source code.

George Mason University Genetic Algorithms Group
web: http://www.cs.gmu.edu/research/gag

DESCRIPTION: This site, while one of a number of university sites on genetic algorithms, has a "Hitchhiker's Guide to Evolutionary Computation". It is a good primer for those who have never broached this area.

3.4.2 Finding Data Sets

StatLib (sample data sets)
web: http://lib.stat.cmu.edu/datasets

DESCRIPTION: StatLib contains a collection of data sets that have been contributed by many statisticians, authors, and academicians for use by all, ranging from performance and salary ranges of major league baseball players to Dow-Jones industrial averages from 1900 to 1993. You are free to use any data set and to contribute your own. If you use any algorithm or data set from StatLib, they ask that you acknowledge Statlib and the original contributor.

The Machine Learning Database Repository (sample data sets)
web: http://www.ics.uci.edu

DESCRIPTION: The University of California has a number of data sets for machine learning.

U.S. Census Bureau
web: http://www.census.gov

DESCRIPTION: The census bureau is undergoing a massive effort to make census information available on the web. If you are interested in geographic information for the U.S., the U.S. Census Bureau has a TIGER/Line® product it distributes (at a cost) with extensive geographic information.

Edger
web: http://edgar.stern.nyu.edu

DESCRIPTION: Publicly held company files report to the SEC. These reports are available to you by visiting this web site.

3.4.3 Source Code

SGI Source (MLC++)
web: http://www.sgi.com/Technology/mlc/

DESCRIPTION: MLC++ (A Machine Learning Library) is C++ source code which provides general machine learning algorithms. This source code is developed by Silicon Graphics by Ronny Kohavi. Silicon Graphics is making source code available as public domain (compiled on SGI's IRIX 5.3 using their C++ compilers) in order to promote the development of new and better data mining algorithms. Many of the better known algorithms and graphing styles are available.

Getting Marketing Information
web: http://www.marketingtools.com

DESCRIPTION: This web site contains a number of vendors who sell information to the general public (some of which are listed in the next section). There is a wide variety of information tracked, and although it is not an all-inclusive list, it is a good starting place if you are looking to augment your own information.

Source Code for C4.5 Decision Tree Algorithm
web: http://ftp.cs.su.oz.au/pub/ml/ (patches)

DESCRIPTION: J.R. Quinlan makes the decision tree algorithm C4.5 available, with source, in his book, *C4.5— Programs for Machine Learning*, Morgan Kaufmann, 1993. Patches, papers, and more information are available on the web site mentioned above.

Source Code for OC1, a Decision Tree Algorithm
web: http://www.cs.jhu.edu/~salzberg/
web (code): ftp.cs.jhu.edu

DESCRIPTION: OC1 (Oblique Classifier 1) is a decision tree induction system available with C source code and a paper that Sreerama K. Murthy, Simon Kasif, Steven Salzberg, and Richard Beigel wrote on the algorithm for AAAI in 1993. OC1 is freely available via anonymous FTP from the Department of Computer Science at Johns Hopkins University at *ftp.cs.jhu.edu*. Go to the directory *pub/oc1*.

3.5 DATA SOURCES FOR MINING

The availability and detail of information about what people buy, where they live, how much they earn, and what types of hobbies they have is astonishing. You may be troubled by the privacy issues this raises, but the fact remains that this type of information not only exists, it is easy to get.

Adding purchased information to augment customer lists is one of the most effective ways for corporations to understand their customers. It also makes data mining an interesting endeavor. Many, if not all, data providers are involved in data mining activities of their own.

Below is a list of vendors who sell information. This is certainly not a complete list, but it is representative of the larger data providers in consumer and business-related information. All products are trademarks or registered trademarks of their respective companies. For each of them, a very brief description of their services is provided.

Acxiom Corporation
301 Industrial Blvd
Conway, AR 72032
(800) 922-9466
web: http://www.acxiom.com

DESCRIPTION: Acxiom is a leading provider of comprehensive information on consumers and businesses, for decision support activities in marketing, merchandising, and risk management. Founded in 1969 as Demographics, Axciom, by one account, has over four terabytes of data and 500,000 magnetic tapes.

CACI Marketing Systems
1100 Glebe Road
Arlington, Virginia 22201
(703) 841-7800
web: http://www.caci.com

DESCRIPTION: They provide demographic and consumer spending data, focusing on customer relationship management. Several government agencies work directly with CACI.

CorpTech
12 Alfred Street, Suite 200
Woburn, MA 01807
(617) 932-3939
web: http://www.corptech.com

DESCRIPTION: CorpTech is a provider of information of technology companies and industry markets, with over 45,000 company profiles and national, regional, and state level industry reports.

Claritas
1525 Wilson Blvd., Suite 1000
Arlington, VA 22209
(703) 812-2700
web: http://www.claritas.com

DESCRIPTION: Claritas offers customers demographic information, including a suite of products referred to as PRIZM®. Claritas supplies detailed lifestyle segmentation and PRIZM +4 micro-neighborhood segmentation.

Equifax, Inc.
1600 Peachtree St. N.W.
Atlanta, GA 30302
(404) 885-8000
web: http://www.equifax.com

DESCRIPTION: Equifax has been a leading provider of comprehensive customer and business demographic information since 1899. Equifax has expanded well beyond a credit bureau and provides a diverse range of information.

Harte-Hanks Data Technologies
25 Linnell Circle
Billerica, MA 01821-3961
(508) 436-2979
web: http://www.harte-hanks.com

DESCRIPTION: Harte-Hankes is a market leader in providing direct marketing, including consumer and business-to-business market research. Harte-Hanks Data Technologies is part of Harte-Hankes Communications based in San Antonio, Texas.

Healthdemographics
4901 Morena Blvd., Suite 701
San Diego, CA 92117
(800) 590-4545
web: http://www.healthdemographics.com

DESCRIPTION: Healthdemographics is a market leader in providing information on health demographic information for government agencies, providers, and payers. They specialize in helping sort through the complex data requirements of managed care organizations, hospitals, and pharmaceuticals.

A.C. Nielsen
150 North Martingale Rd.
Schaumburg, IL 60173
(847) 605-5000
web: http://www.Nielsen.com

DESCRIPTION: A.C. Nielsen is a market leader in providing information for consumer packaged goods manufacturers and retailers. Nielsen monitors 47,000 households in the United States and Canada electronically to understand consumer purchase behavior.

The Polk & Company
1621 18th St.
Denver, CO 80202
(303) 292-5000
web: http://www.polk.com

DESCRIPTION: Polk, at over 125 years in business, is a leading information provider to corporations. They have extensive data on motor vehicles, customer demographics, purchasing behavior, as well as many other areas.

TRW Information Systems & Services
1244 Pittsford-Mendon Center Road
Orange, CA 92668
(716)624-7390
web: http://www.trw.com

DESCRIPTION: A leading provider of consumer credit, business credit, direct marketing, and real estate information, TRW has expanded from being a credit bureau into offering a wide range of data services.

3.6 SUMMARY

This chapter discussed industry trends in the data mining industry. It also mentioned several of the leading data mining vendors today, as well as introduced visualization tools, web sites for data miners, and several of the sellers of customer and industry demographics. With this information, you can readily familiarize yourself with what is open to you in the data mining arena.

There are many vendors who are involved in data preparation and in the decision support arena who are invariably connected with data mining. For more information, refer to Appendix A, which lists many more vendors in this market space.

In the next several chapters, a few of the data mining tools are looked at much more in depth. You can get a better idea of how these tools solve industry problems.

Chapter 4

A Look at Angoss: KnowledgeSEEKER

In this chapter, we look at a popular application which uses a decision tree approach to data mining, KnowledgeSEEKER.

The chapter is organized as follows:

Section 4.1 Introduction
Section 4.2 Data Preparation
Section 4.3 Defining a Study
Section 4.4 Building the Model
Section 4.5 Understanding the Model
Section 4.6 Prediction
Section 4.7 Summary

4.1 INTRODUCTION

The purpose of this chapter is to familiarize you with a decision tree approach to data mining. While the process is demonstrated with KnowledgeSEEKER, you will find all decision tree approaches have similarities. The user interface for KnowledgeSEEKER is easy to understand.

4.1.1 More on Decision Trees

KnowledgeSEEKER, by Angoss, is a decision tree based analysis program. This program is a comprehensive program for classification tree analysis. KnowledgeSEEKER makes use of two well-known decision tree algorithms: CHAID and CART. CHAID, or Chi-Square Automatic Interaction Detection, is used to study categorical data, like states in a country or gender. CART (Classification and Regression Trees) works with continuous dependent variables, such as monthly expenses (0-1000 dollars, 1001-2000 dollars, and 2000 and above dollars). There are several commercially available decision tree algorithms (see Chapter 3). Angoss has put much work into making the process user friendly.

There are many decision tree approaches and algorithms. Dr. Gordon B. Kass introduced the CHAID method in 1976 in a doctoral presentation. CART was popularized in 1984. A popular decision tree algorithm, complete with source code, can be purchased from Morgan Kaufman Publishers, entitled C4.5 *Programming for Machine Learning*, by J. Ross Quinlan. Before C4.5, Quinlan introduced another decision tree algorithm referred to as ID3.

4.1.2 How Decision Trees Are Being Used

There are many vendors offering decision tree approaches. AC2, from Isoft, is a popular decision tree algorithm. Isoft has formed a relationship with Business Objects, where Business Objects sells a data mining module which makes use of Isoft's decision tree approach. SPSS markets a product based on the algorithm, called SI-CHAID. Many other vendors use combinations of algorithms to best fit approaches. A decision tree algorithm is also used in many data mining packages that combine a variety of approaches, including IBM's Intelligent Miner, Clementine, Thinking Machine's Darwin, and Silicon Graphic's Mineset.

Angoss recently announced a deal with Andyne, a maker of end user querying and decision support programs, to jointly market with KnowledgeSEEKER. Angoss has aggressively looked at many other partnerships to move this technology into the mainstream. For example, Customer Insight Company (CIC), a provider of database marketing tools, signed on to be a value-added reseller for KnowledgeSEEKER, and Angoss has signed up to develop a DataBlade module for INFORMIX-Universal Server.

Decision tree approaches are good at handling classification problems. Classification is the process of using historical data to build a model for the purpose of understanding and prediction. Chapter 2 discussed this in more detail.

Angoss widely advertises their product to solve a wide variety of problems and points to many industry examples. The IRS is using KnowledgeSEEKER to predict important factors associated with tax claims and the likelihood of fraud occurring. *Reader's Digest Canada* incorporates Angoss to use market segment analysis as well as predicting cost. The *Washington Post* uses KnowledgeSEEKER for direct marketing. Angoss is being used by the Oxford Transplant Center in London to analyze kidney transplants. KnowledgeSEEKER is used by Hewlett-Packard to analyze rules for production control systems. The Canadian Imperial Bank of Commerce uses the software to look at risk management.

4.2 DATA PREPARATION

This chapter uses a sample data set based on a study of high blood pressure from a community health survey, which is a data set Angoss includes with their demonstration. Table 4–1 shows the values in the data set.

Table 4-1 *Data on a hypertension study*

Column Name	Values	Explanation
TypeOfMilk	Integer: 1 - 5	Type of milk person drinks. Integer values labeled to denote whether milk is whole milk, 2%, skim, powder, or no milk at all.
DeepFriedLastWeek	Integer: 0 - 7	Number of times person had deep fried food last week.
BeefLastWeek	Integer: 0 - 7	Number of times person had beef last week.
PorkLastWeek	Integer: 0 - 7	Number of times person had pork last week.

Column Name	Values	Explanation
PoultryLastWeek	Integer: 0 - 7	Number of times person had poultry last week.
FishLastWeek	Integer: 0, 1, 2	Number of times person had pork last week.
LambLastWeek	Integer: 0 - 7	Number of times person had lamb last week.
OtherMeatLastWeek	Integer: 0, 1, 2, 3, 7	Number of times person had other meat last week.
CheeseLastWeek	Integer: 0 - 7	Number of times person had cheeses last week.
EggsLastWeek	Integer: 0 - 7, 9	Number of times person had egg last week.
Meat2MealsLstWk	Integer: 0 - 7, 9	Number of times person had meat in two meals last week.
SaltInFood	Integer: 1 - 5, 9	Does a person use salt? Numbers are labeled to denote a lot, moderate, very little, or none.
SaltConsumption	Integer: 1 - 5, 9	What is the person's level of salt consumption? Numbers are labeled to denote very low, low, moderate, high, or very high.
ButterFood	Integer: 1 - 3	Does a person butter their food? Numbers are labeled to denote frequently, sometimes, and never.
SportsActivity	Integer: 1 - 5, 9	Does a person exercise? Numbers are labeled to denote daily, weekly, occasionally, rarely, and never.
SleepTime	Integer: in hours: 0 - 24	The number of hours a person sleeps, on average.
Smoking	Integer: 1 - 4	Does a person smoke? Numbers are labeled to denote regular, occasional, former, never, and ??? (??? for unknown).
DrinkPattern	Integer: 1 - 5	Does a person drink? Numbers are labeled to denote regular, occasional, former, and never.

Column Name	Values	Explanation
DrinksEveryDay	Integer: 1, 2, 9	Does a person drink every day? Numbers are labeled to denote yes or no.
Age	Integer: 1 - 3	Age of person. Numbers are labeled to denote 32-50, 51-62, and 63-72.
YearsEducation	Integer: 1 - 5	How many years' education has a person had?
Income	Integer: 3 - 21	What is person's income?
Gender	Integer 1, 2	What is gender of person? Numbers are labeled to denote male and female.
Weight	Integer: in pounds	What is the weight of customer in pounds?
Height	Integer: in inches	What is the height of customer in inches?
Hypertension	Integer: 1,2,3	What is the level of hypertension of person? Numbers are labeled to denote low, normal, and high.

When the demonstration software included in the back of this book is loaded onto a PC and started, this data set automatically comes up prepared and ready to go. There are, however, steps that had to be taken to prepare this data set to be data mined. For example, several of the fields contain integer values to which labels were applied. *Hypertension* is a field that has the values 1, 2, and 3. These fields are labeled to be low, normal, and high. *TypeOfMilk* is another field that has labels added. The field has values 1-5 which are labeled to mean whole milk, 2%, skim, powder, or no milk at all.

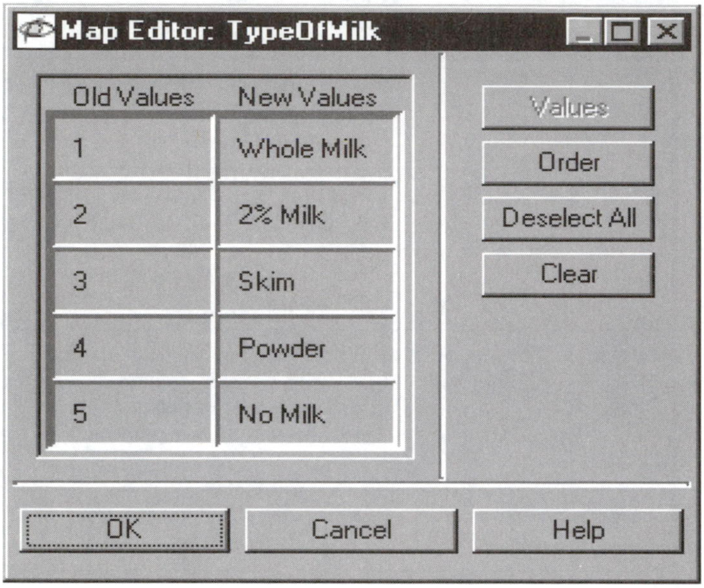

Figure 4–1 Defining data fields

In order to label these values, a user would pull down the edit menu from KnowledgeSEEKER and choose *Map Data*. You would then choose a column, like *TypeOfMilk*, and choose the *Map* push-button. The map editor for *TypeOfMilk* looks like Figure 4–1.

In Figure 4–1, integer values have been mapped to text strings with much more meaning.

Another issue to consider with this data set is that of deriving columns. For example, the column *Age* has the values 1, 2, and 3, which are labeled 32-50, 51-62, and 63-72. Normally, a column named *Age* does not come with the values 1, 2, and 3, but with the actual age of a person. In this data set, the column was derived before data mining began and the choice of the age ranges 32-50, 51-62, and 63-72 were made.

The demonstration in this chapter has already provided the data preparation for you, but it is always important to be aware of the steps that occurred to actually mine a data set. For many data sets, no mapping may be needed.

4.3 DEFINING THE STUDY

The following steps run through an example of using the KnowledgeSEEKER product. If you would like to follow along, load the demonstration by following the instructions in Appendix B.

The first step is to open the application. Open KnowledgeSEEKER. Pull down the File menu and select **Open.** You will see the screen shown in Figure 4–2.

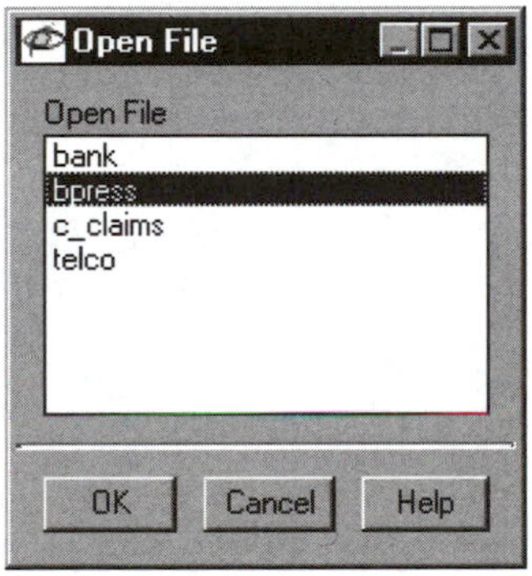

Figure 4–2 Selecting the blood pressure data set, *bpress*

By highlighting *bpress* and selecting **OK,** the data set on blood pressure, described in the last section, is automatically loaded for you.

Setting the Dependent Variable

The column *Hypertension* has been automatically set as the dependent variable. Later on, this variable will be changed.

Upon opening KnowledgeSEEKER, you will see the screen shown in Figure 4–3.

The box highlighted in black is known as the root node. Notice that the root node for the dependent variable

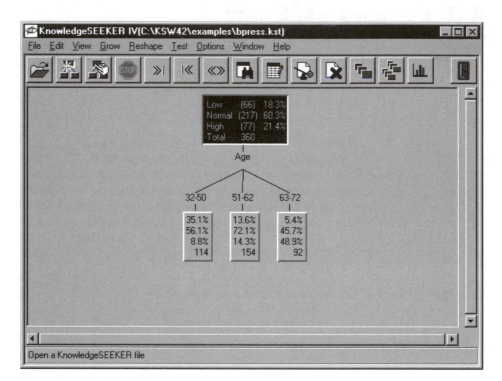

Figure 4–3 Starting Up

classifies high blood pressure into three categories: low, normal, and high. We are profiling which people are more likely to have low, normal, and high blood pressure. What you are being told here is:

- 18% of the people, or 66 people in the study, have low blood pressure

- 60% of the people, or 217 people in the study, have normal blood pressure

- 21% of the people, or 77 people in the study, have high blood pressure

4.4 BUILDING THE MODEL

KnowledgeSEEKER has built the next level of the tree model. The tree can also be generated automatically to multiple levels, as will be shown later in the chapter.

The next level of the tree in Figure 4–2 is shown dividing patients by age. Age is just one variable that affects the outcome high blood pressure, but in this case, age appears to be the most significant factor that affects whether someone has high blood pressure.

You will now see age groups as shown below:

- Age 32-50
- Age 51-62
- Age 63-72

The leaf nodes of this tree can be created using a column other than age. Specifying another column is know as a *split*. In this example, there are 12 splits automatically found. They are listed in the next section. Other splits can be created by your specification.

4.5 UNDERSTANDING THE MODEL

We can continue to grow this model, but first it is useful to explore the first leaf nodes and to clarify the concept of a split, which was just introduced. We have found age to be the most important criteria for characterizing the categories of blood pressure, but it is reasonable to assume that this is not the only factor that affects hypertension.

4.5.1 Looking at Different Splits

This application shows the importance of variables other than age on blood pressure. KnowledgeSEEKER evaluates all variables for their effectiveness in describing low, normal, and high blood pressure and constructs a ranked list of the most descriptive variables. To see another variable used to construct leaf nodes directly below the root node, you will go to another *split*. You can look at the other data elements that affect high blood pressure easily.

To see other splits, press the following button:

If you press this button, or alternatively choose **Reshape** and choose **Next Split**, you will see the next split. In this example, there are twelve different splits detected automatically. In order of importance, they are:

- Age

  Generalization: Age was divided into three groups: (32-50), (51-62), and (63-72). From this split you can make a generalization that the older you are, the higher the likelihood you will have high blood pressure. You will see that 35.1% of people age 32-50 have low blood pressure, 13.6% of people age 51-62 have low blood pressure, and only 5.4% of people age 63-72 have low blood pressure.

- Height

  Generalization: Height was divided into two groups: (565 - 654) and (654-746). It appears that taller people have lower blood pressure! Certainly something you would not expect. You can see in Figure 4–4, 32.2% of those 565 to 654 centimeters have high blood pressure while only 8.7% of people 654 to 746 have high blood pressure.

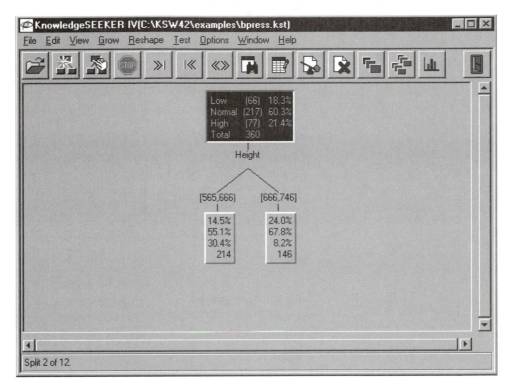

Figure 4–4 The height split

- Gender Male and Female

  Generalization: The data suggests that women are more likely to have high blood pressure. Only 14.1% of men had high blood pressure in this study versus 30% of females. Of course, follow-up studies would be valuable to determine if the study didn't just pick a lot of females with high blood pressure.

- SportsActivity

  Generalization: The tool grouped *SportsActivity* into two groups: (Daily, Weekly, Occasionally, Rarely) and Never. Those people who had some form of sports activity were much more unlikely to have high blood pressure. Only 12.8% of active people had high blood pressure versus 30.2% of inactive people.

- DrinkPattern

  Generalization: The tool grouped *DrinkPattern* into two groups: (Regular, Occasionally, Former) and (Never). Those people who had some form of drinking activity were much more unlikely to have high blood pressure. Only 16.9% of drinkers had high blood pressure versus 34.4% of non-drinkers.

- Income

  Generalization: *Income* has been grouped into five groups: (3,4,5,6,7), (8,9,10), (11), (12,13,14,15), and (16-98). The lowest blood pressure was in group 11 and 16-98 with 2.6% and 5.4% having high blood pressure, respectively. The highest blood pressure was in group 3-7 with 39.5% blood pressure.

- PorkLastWeek

  Generalization: *PorkLastWeek* has been grouped into two groups: (0-4) and (5-7). You can see 63.6% of people in group 5-7 had low blood pressure versus only 16.9% of people in group 0-4.

- SaltInFood

  Generalization: *SaltInFood* has been grouped into two groups: (A Lot, Moderate) and (Very Little, None). You can see 32.4% of people in the first group had high blood pressure versus only 16.7% of people in the second group.

- Smoking

  Generalization: *Smoking* has been grouped into two groups: (Regular) and (Occasional, Former, Never, ???). First notice that categories were grouped. We have regular smokers and all others (??? denotes unknown data). Not surprisingly, regular smokers appear to have higher blood pressure.

- TypeOfMilk

  Generalization: *TypeOfMilk* has been grouped into three groups: (Whole Milk, Powder, and No Milk), (2% Milk), and (Skim). People who regularly drink skim milk are the least likely to have high blood pressure. Only 10.5% of the people who drink skim milk have high blood pressure versus 17.7 for 2% milk and 30.9% for those who drink whole milk, powder, or no milk at all.

- YearsEducation

  Generalization: *YearsEducation* was divided into two groups, (1,2,3,4) and (5). Those whose *YearsEducation* was in Category 5 had considerably higher blood pressure, 34% versus 19.4% for the other categories.

- DeepFriedLastWeek

  Generalization: *DeepFriedLastWeek* was divided into three categories (0), (1,2,3), and (4,5,6,7). People in Category 0 were the most likely to have high blood pressure with 28.7% of them having high blood pressure, versus 15.6% for (1,2,3) and 13.8% for (4,5,6,7).

The generalizations made about each of the splits generated automatically for this data set provide food for thought about where further investigation should happen. Clearly some of the information is what you would expect. For example, the older you are, the more likely you are to have high blood pressure, or the more physically active you are, the more likely you are to have lower blood pressure. Still, this data set presented some surprises, like the relationship of a person's height to their blood pressure.

4.5.2 Going to a Specific Split

If you want to go to a specific split, you can use the following icon:

The menu in Figure 4–5 will appear. In our case, we select *smoking* from the menu and click on **OK**.

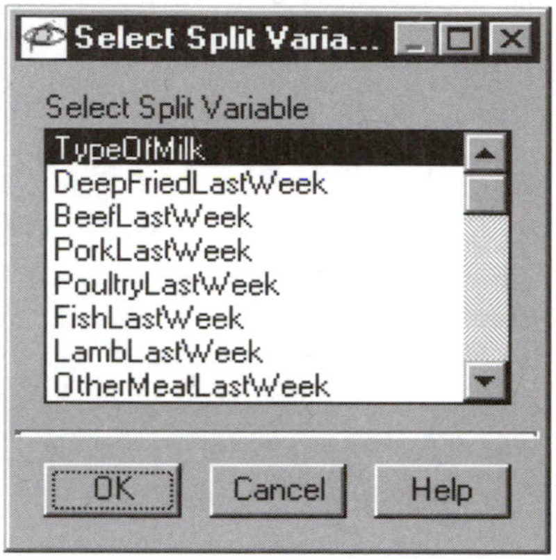

Figure 4–5 Selecting a split

4.5.3 Growing the Tree

The tree for smoking is only one level. We can grow the tree again. Choose the second level node for regular smokers shown in Figure 4–6. Pull down the *Grow* menu and choose **Find Split**. You will see the screen in Figure 4–6.

KnowledgeSEEKER found the best characterization of regular smokers is by age group. Again, for regular smokers, age is a key indicator of whether you will have high blood pressure with over 56.7% of age 63-72 having high blood pressure versus 4.8% for people age 32-50.

Regular smokers are again best characterized by age, but it found six splits in all.

Here are the six splits KnowledgeSEEKER found for regular smokers: *Age, Height, PorkLastWeek, DrinkPattern, Gender,* and *SaltConsumption.*

As an exercise, if you have loaded the CD-ROM included, take a look at these splits and try to make some generalization about them.

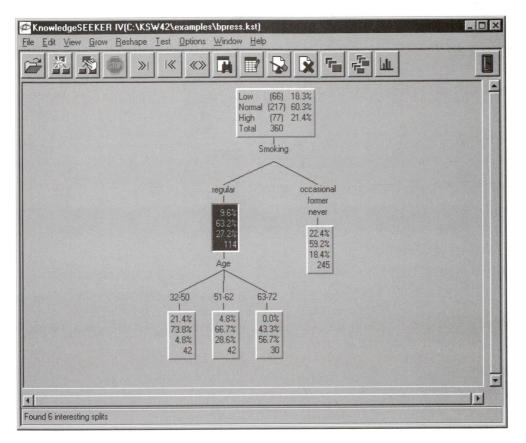

Figure 4–6 Another split

More splits can be created. The tree can be built to as many levels as the data set (or memory constraints) will allow. If there are several hundreds of variables, a tree can get quite complex.

4.5.4 Forcing a Split

Sometimes you will want to look at a variable that isn't automatically found. For example, I want to know how *PoultryLastWeek* affects high blood pressure. I can force this split, by pulling down the *Grow* menu and selecting **Force Split**.

You can see the variable list in Figure 4–7.

Figure 4–7 Forcing a split

Choose *PoultryLastWeek*, and press **OK**. For *PoultryLastWeek* there are eight values you can have: (0,1,2,3,4,5,6,7). Sometimes it is easier to get significant values by grouping these values.

You will now see the Group Categories as shown in Figure 4–8.

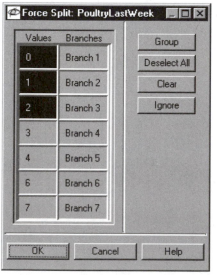

Figure 4–8 Grouping categories

Select 0, 1, and 2 and press **Group**. This will group these three categories together.

Select 3, 4, 5, 6, and 7 and press **Group**.

In effect, you have defined two groups:

- Group 1 is [0,1,2]—having had poultry unknown or two or less times last week

- Group 2 [3,4,5,6,7]—having had poultry three or more times last week

Press **OK** and you will see the results of this split with the groupings you have created in Figure 4–9.

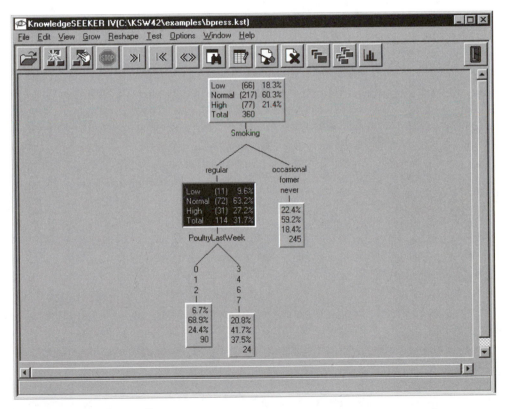

Figure 4–9 Another split

In this case, the results were not conclusive, but people who had more poultry had higher blood pressure.

4.5.5 Validation

The results from one data set are interesting, but in data mining you always want to validate your results again. Angoss refers to other data sets as *Test Partitions*.

You can use another data set, the Test Partition, to verify the findings of the discovery. You can do so by choosing the menu in Figure 4–10 (although it is not available for the demo version).

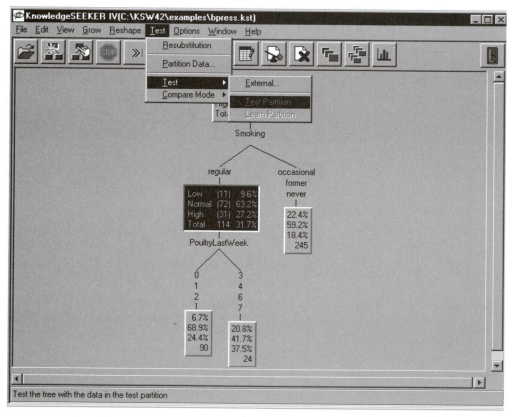

Figure 4–10 Validating a split

4.5.6 Defining a New Scenario for a Study

The demo we have done was on high blood pressure. This was our dependent variable. Suppose you want to change what you are studying. For example, you want to study the differences in people who drink different amounts.

Choose *Edit* and select the **Change Dependent Variable** option from the menu.

Figure 4–11 Changing dependent variables

You will see the variable list in Figure 4–11. Choose *DrinkPattern* and press **OK**. This effectively changes your *root node*. Your root node is now using the dependent variable, *DrinkPattern*, which has the values:

- Regular

- Occasional

- Former

- Never

Again, you can grow a new tree with *DrinkPattern* as the dependent variable. The mechanisms for using KnowledgeSEEKER remain the same, but the type of study we are doing changes dramatically. We are now studying drinking patterns and what affects this versus studying hypertension.

4.5.7 Growing a Tree Automatically

This chapter has demonstrated growing trees node by node. We can also automatically grow a tree. You can choose **Automatic** from the *Grow* menu.

To stop this process, press the *Stop* icon.

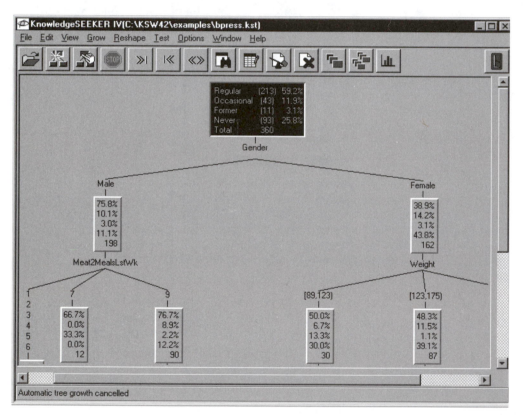

Figure 4–12 Growing a tree automatically

The process of identification of all the splits for the new root node is the same as for our previous example.

4.5.8 Data Distribution

KnowledgeSEEKER has several ways to look at the layout of the data you are studying. First, you can view the raw data that you are mining. To do this, select the **View** menu and select **Data**. You will see a window like the one in Figure 4–13.

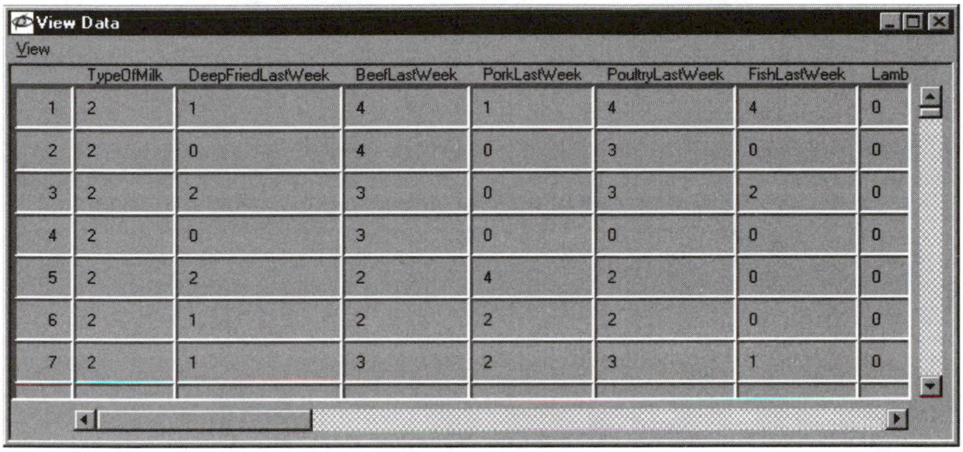

	TypeOfMilk	DeepFriedLastWeek	BeefLastWeek	PorkLastWeek	PoultryLastWeek	FishLastWeek	Lamb
1	2	1	4	1	4	4	0
2	2	0	4	0	3	0	0
3	2	2	3	0	3	2	0
4	2	0	3	0	0	0	0
5	2	2	2	4	2	0	0
6	2	1	2	2	2	0	0
7	2	1	3	2	3	1	0

Figure 4–13 A view of the hypertension data set

You can also look at the cross tabular views of different data items in your set. To do this, choose the following icon:

Selecting this icon will open up the window in Figure 4–14.

Cross Table Printing Parameters _ □ ✕

┌─Detail Level────────┐
☐ Edit View Settings
☑ Frequencies
☐ Clusters
☐ Percentages
☐ Split Statistics

Levels to Display: `100`

Column Width: `8`

☐ Use Export Format

[OK]　[Cancel]　[Help]

Figure 4–14 Printing information on input fields

If you leave the detail level selection at frequencies and select the button **OK**, you will then see the window in Figure 4–15.

Crosstable _ □ ✕
File Edit

```
********************* Split Table *********************
Root

    Cross Tabulation          Gender


DrinkPattern              Male    Female
------------------------ ------- -------
???                           0       0        0
                         ------- -------
Regular                     150      63      213
                         ------- -------
Occasional                   20      23       43
                         ------- -------
Former                        6       5       11
                         ------- -------
Never                        22      71       93
                         ======= =======
Total                       198     162      360

******************** Split Table ********************
Node:  Gender - Male
Root
```

Figure 4–15 A cross tab report for the input, Age, on hypertension

4.6 PREDICTION

You now have a model which can be used for prediction. The process of using decision trees for prediction is not automatic, but KnowledgeSEEKER allows you to save all splits of variables out to a file. The importance of each split is also calculated as a percentage. Using this information, it is possible to produce rules that will help in prediction. The *Node Detail* from the **Reshape** command gives you more information that can be used for predictions.

Decision tree approaches have historically been used more for model understanding than the automating of prediction, but they can be used for this purpose.

4.7 SUMMARY

This chapter has shown a successful decision tree based analytical product, KnowledgeSEEKER.   There are many more features of this product, but the general process of how it works has been discussed.

Such a tool can be used cross industry. One benefit of a tool like the one shown here is that data will be automatically grouped in optimal ways. For example, the variable *Income* has been grouped into five groups: (3,4,5,6,7), (8,9,10), (11), (12,13,14,15), and (16-98). This grouping characteristic is especially valuable when you are looking at market segmentation studies.

Creating decision trees for data sets helps you not only to discover brand new insight, but to confirm what you might already know, as well as look at new trends and patterns.

Chapter

5

A Look at DataMind

This chapter outlines the use of the DataMind Professional Edition product. A demonstration version of this product is included on the CD-ROM included in the back and is used for the exercises.

The chapter is organized as follows:

5.1 INTRODUCTION

DataMind Corporation develops, sells, and supports a client-server data mining software designed specifically for business professionals. While DataMind sells to a wide range of companies, DataMind specifically focuses their technology on customer retention, acquisition, and management applications used by business professionals. Customer retention, acquisition, and management applications enable marketing professionals to do such things as more efficiently target campaigns ahead of time to retain customers before they leave for a competitor.

DataMind DataCruncher is a client-server data mining engine with the capacity to analyze large volumes of data found in today's warehouses. The DataCruncher has features like the ability to connect directly with many of the leading relational database technologies today. The client-side piece to DataMind's solution is DataMind Professional, which is an easy-to-use desktop product which makes use of Microsoft Excel as the front end. DataMind Professional has ODBC access to databases like Informix, Oracle, Red Brick, and Sybase and runs on Windows NT, Windows 95, and Windows 3.1. The demonstration used in this book makes use of a demo version of DataMind Professional.

5.1.1 More on Agent Network Technology

DataMind's technology is a unique approach to data mining. Unlike regression models, neural networks, and decision tree algorithms, which are used by many vendors today, DataMind's technology is their own. This technology offers both the ability to understand a model and to use a model for prediction. While traditional approaches provide many of the same capabilities, DataMind feels that their technology is better suited to integrating model understanding and prediction using the same model. The Agent Network Technology is also extremely fast in its ability to build models, another benefit of this approach.

5.1.2 How DataMind is Being Used

DataMind's base technology was originally used in France by many large corporations. Customers mentioned in articles and literature today include Franco-Belges Malting, ADP, 360 Communications, and Land O'Lakes.

In June 1996, DataMind Corporation and Red Brick Systems announced a technology partnership to jointly develop and integrate data mining functionality into the Red Brick data warehouse relational database. This was the first time that relational database technology and data mining were directly incorporated.

Other companies that have announced integration opportunities with DataMind include Brio Corporation, Arbor Systems, and Information Advantage.

5.2 Data Preparation

The data set used in this chapter is an example of a direct mail database which keeps track of whether someone has responded or not to direct mail in the past in order to profile and predict who is most likely to respond to direct mails in the future. Data elements for direct marking models almost always include information on recency of purchases, frequency of purchases, and the monetary value of the purchases (referred to as RFM in the direct mail industry). There is also information on customer demographics, which is easily purchased from information providers like those listed in Chapter 3.

Table 5–1 shows the elements.

Table 5-1 *Data on direct mail campaign*

Column Name	Values	Explanation
CUSTID	Integer, unique	Customer identification number
CITY	City names	Cities in the state of Colorado
STATE	CO	All values for this study are from the state of Colorado
RESPONSE_95	0, 1	Did customer respond in 1995? (0) no, (1) yes
RESPONSE_96	0, 1	Did customer respond in 1996? (0) no, (1) yes
BOUGHT_SIX	0, 1	Did customer call in the last six months? (0) no, (1) yes
CALLED_MONTH	0, 1	Did customer call in the last month? (0) no, (1) yes
$SOLD_94	Real	Dollar amount customer bought in 1994
$SOLD_95	Real	Dollar amount customer bought in 1995

Column Name	Values	Explanation
$SOLD_96	Real	Dollar amount customer bought in 1996
FREQUENT_FLYER	0, 1	Is customer a frequent flyer? (0) no, (1) yes
BUS_TRAVEL	0, 1	Is customer a business traveler? (0) no, (1) yes
LEISURE_TRAVEL	0, 1	Does customer travel on leisure? (0) no, (1) yes
HOUSEHOLD	Married_Wchild, Malehead_Wchild, Malehead, Female_Head, Female_Head_Wchild, Married	Type of household
CHILDREN	Integer	Number of children
AGE	Integer	Age of customer
HOUSE_INCOME	Integer	Monthly income of household
CARTYPE	Sedan, Truck, Luxury, Compact, Wagon, Sport	Type of car a customer has
SEGMENT	Affluent, Senior, Avg_Income, Low_Income, Young_Mobile	Segment to which a customer belongs
RESPONDED	0, 1	Did customer respond? (0) no, (1) yes

The field *responded* is the dependent variable to be used in this study. It indicates whether someone has responded to a direct mailer or not.

This data set, like many data sets used in direct marketing, requires a better understanding of derived fields. For example, the field *segment* defines people by whether they are affluent, senior, avg_income, low_income, or young_mobile. The field does not, however, indicate what qualifies someone as affluent or senior or any other category. This data uses a set of standards that requires understanding.

DataMind will characterize some of the inputs in the data set as discrete, like *cartype*, which specifies the type of car a person drives. Discrete variables are variables that you treat as atomic. For example, gender has the discrete values male and female.

DataMind allows numeric variables to be either discrete or continuous. If you are treating numeric variables as continuous, then you are putting them into a series of ranges or bins. The fields *$sold_93*, *$sold_94*, and *$sold_95* are numeric values that, in this example, are classified as continuous.

5.3 DEFINING THE STUDY

In this section, we will step through a process of defining an example direct marketing study. You can follow along and do it yourself by installing DataMind's software as explained in Appendix B. Microsoft Excel is required for this product to run. DataMind uses Microsoft Excel to display reports and to examine data.

Defining the Goal

In order to start using DataMind, it is useful to define the goal or your study. The demonstration in this chapter profiles whether someone has responded to a direct mail campaign or not. This goal can be stated clearly as:

Profile and predict the set of customers who are likely to respond to a direct mail campaign and those who are not.

Choosing a Dependent Variable

Studies are defined as a set of inputs and an output. Each row of the data set corresponds to a customer who has been sent a catalog via direct mail. Each of these customers either responded or did not respond to the campaign. Based on this historical data, we can build a model that profiles these customers.

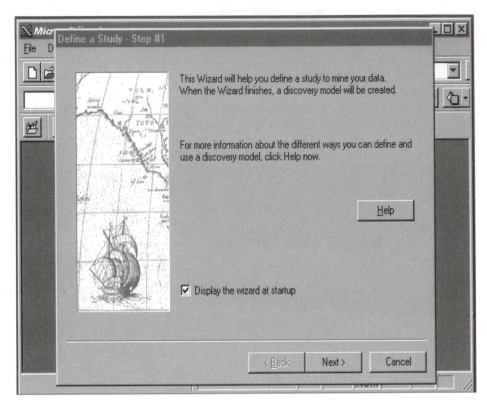

Figure 5–1 Starting up DataMind

The data set used has a column entitled *responded* which has a value of 1 or 0 depending on response or non-response. This field will be the dependent variable or output.

Starting DataMind

After installing DataMind as shown in Appendix B, you can automatically start up DataMind Professional Edition by double-clicking on the icon with that name. When you start up, you will see a wizard, as shown in Figure 5–1.

1. DataMind's Wizard steps a user through the process of defining a study. To advance, select **Next**.

2. The next window asks for the name of the study. Leave the default, Wizard #1, and select **Next** again.

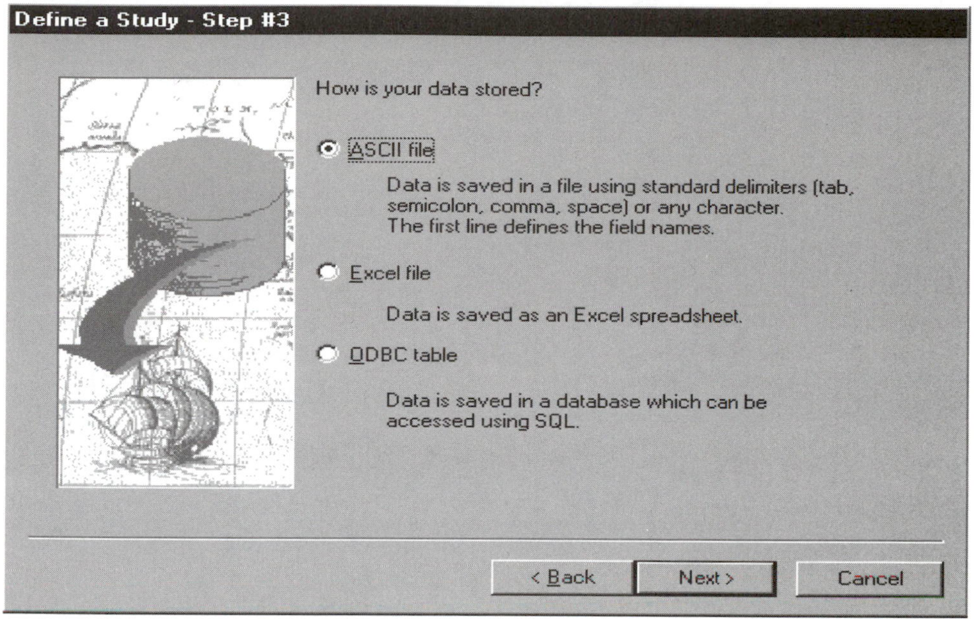

Define a Study - Step #3

How is your data stored?

○ ASCII file

   Data is saved in a file using standard delimiters (tab, semicolon, comma, space) or any character. The first line defines the field names.

○ Excel file

   Data is saved as an Excel spreadsheet.

○ ODBC table

   Data is saved in a database which can be accessed using SQL.

< Back   Next >   Cancel

Figure 5–2 Selecting a data source

Specifying Data Types

The next screen asks what type of data source is used in this study, as shown in Figure 5–2.

3. In this example, the data set is ASCII. To connect to a relational database, the ODBC connection is used. After specifying how your data is stored, select **Next**.

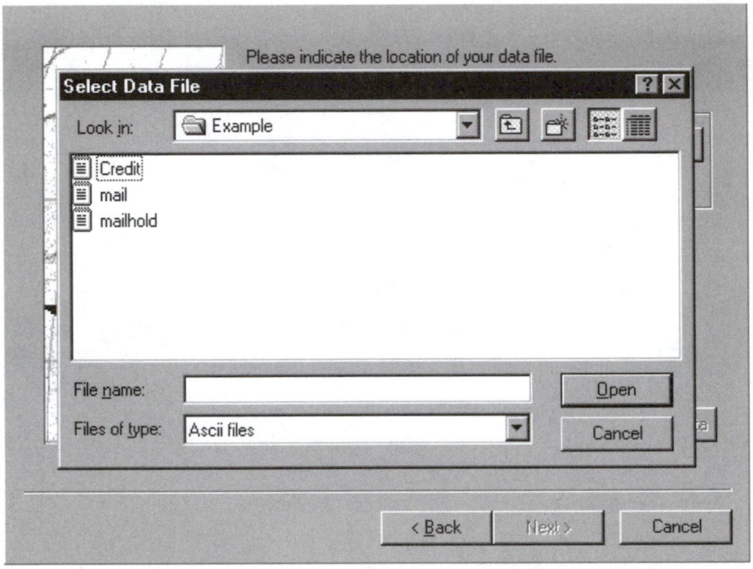

Please indicate the location of your data file.

Select Data File ? ✕

Look in: 📁 Example ▼ 🗂 🗂 ⬚⬚ ▦

📄 Credit
📄 mail
📄 mailhold

File name: [   ]   <u>O</u>pen

Files of type: Ascii files ▼   Cancel

< <u>B</u>ack   Next >   Cancel

Figure 5–3 Selecting a data file

Figure 5–3 shows the results of pushing the **Browse** button and selecting the data file *c:\datamind\example\mail.txt*.

4. Select **Open** and then **Next** to move to the next screen.

```
Define a Study - Step #5

    Mark one of the fields below as output to represent your study
    purpose. Other fields may be left as they are, or you may
    optionally tune them as indicated.

    Fields List                                        ┌─ Usage ──────┐
    ┌──────────────────────────────────────┐  ▲       │ ☐ Ignored    │
    │ CUSTID                    ▐▐▌ ▐       │  █       │ ⦿ Input      │
    │ CITY                      ▐▌▌ 100     │  ▒       │ ○ Output     │
    │ STATE                     ▐▌▌ 1       │  ▒       │ ○ Identifier │
    │ HIGHINCOME                ▐▌▌ 2       │          │              │
    │ RESPONSE_95               ▐▌▌ 2       │          │ ○ Discrete   │
    │ #MAILERS                  ▐▌▌ 10      │          │ ⦿ Continuous │
    │ BOUGHT_SIX                ▐▌▌ 2       │  ▼       └──────────────┘
    └──────────────────────────────────────┘

    Note : You may <double click> on one field to
    see the different values.                                 ┌─────────┐
                                                              │  Help   │
                                                              └─────────┘

                          ┌──────────┐  ┌──────────┐     ┌──────────┐
                          │  < Back  │  │  Next >  │     │  Cancel  │
                          └──────────┘  └──────────┘     └──────────┘
```

Figure 5–4 Defining inputs and outputs for a study

Setting Study Input/Output Specifications

The DataMind Wizard allows you to set parameters for a study as shown in Figure 5-4.

The "Usage" box shows how a field is to be designated. The choices here are:

- input

- output

- identifier (fields not used in discovery, but that appear on reports)

You can also set a field to be *ignored*. Ignoring a field means it will not be used in a data mining study.

5. The fields *city* and *state* have been selected as ignored in this figure by default. *State* is selected as ignored because there is only one state, Colorado, and since all rows have this value, it is not interesting to data mine. *City* is selected as ignored because there are nearly a thousand cities in this data set, and, although they can be mined, having nearly as many cities as rows is not

overly useful in data mining. You can select this field name and then deselect ignored and it will be used.

6. The field *custid* is a unique identifier. Because it is unique, it is not useful in model building; however, it serves to identify rows, which can be valuable in prediction. Select this row and choose the identifier button on the right to label this field accordingly.

7. Double click on the field, *bought_six*. You will see a window like the one in Figure 5–5.

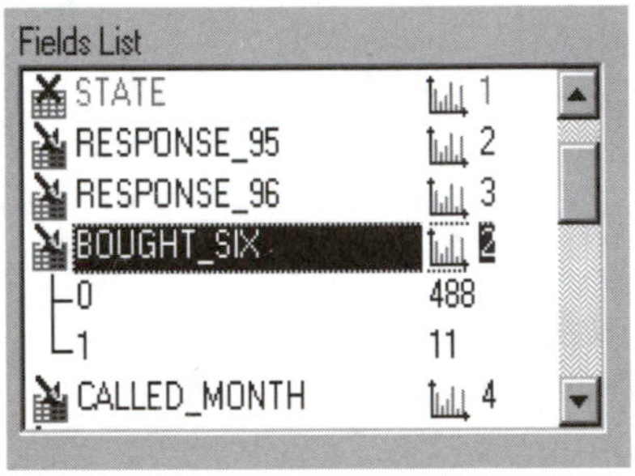

Figure 5–5 Drilling down on a field to find values in the field

The "Field List" window indicates that there are two unique values for *bought_six*, which are 0 and 1. It also shows that value 0 had 488 occurrences and the value 1 had 11 occurrences, which means 11 people in this sample set bought within the last six months.

8. Scroll down to the field *$sold_94* as shown in Figure 5–6. The "Usage" box shows that the field is continuous, meaning that is has been binned into 5 equidistant bins. Numeric amounts occurring with over 100 unique elements are automatically binned. The field can be selected as discrete by choosing that button on the "Usage" box.

The field can also be binned into different ranges, but the wizard is not the tool to do this.

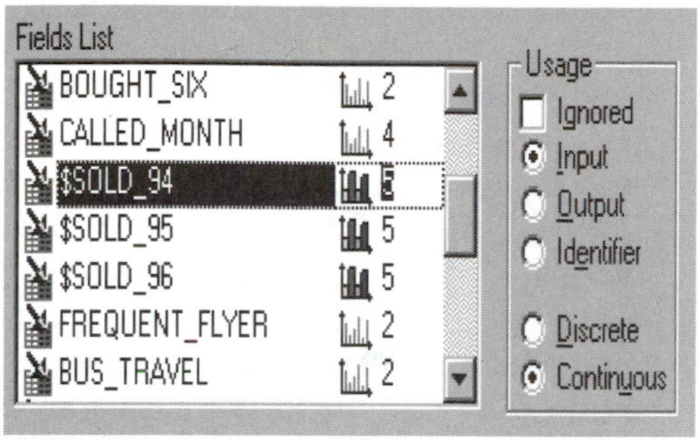

Figure 5–6 Selecting the field $sold_94

9. Scroll down to the field *responded* and select it. Click on **Output** in the "Usage" box. This selects the field to be the output, or dependent variable of the study.

10. Select **Next** at the bottom of the window, which moves you to the last screen. You can now start the model building by hitting the **Finish** button.

5.4 READ YOUR DATA/BUILD A DISCOVERY MODEL

The discovery process is put in motion by a mouse click. The Wizard does this automatically. You can also start the discovery process with the icon below.

The length of the discovery process is dependent on the number of input parameters, output categories, the number of rows of data, and the number of unique values within the data.

A spooler is started to read the data and build a model for you. This spooler runs in the background. For large volumes of data, the DataMind DataCruncher is used to build models. In the case of the DataCruncher product, it actually runs on an NT or UNIX server in the background.

DataMind's Agent Network Technology is used in the discovery process.

One advantage of the Agent Network Technology is that with the DataMind DataCruncher, you are able to build models incrementally as well as to merge models. This means that models can be created and then merged with new models as new data becomes available without having to build a model from scratch. For example, you can build a model off of 5 million rows of data from 1990-1997 and when 1998 data becomes available, you can build a new model using 1998 data and then merge that model with the model from years 1990-1997. This can save time and effort.

You will see the control panel in Figure 5–7 after the discovery process is run.

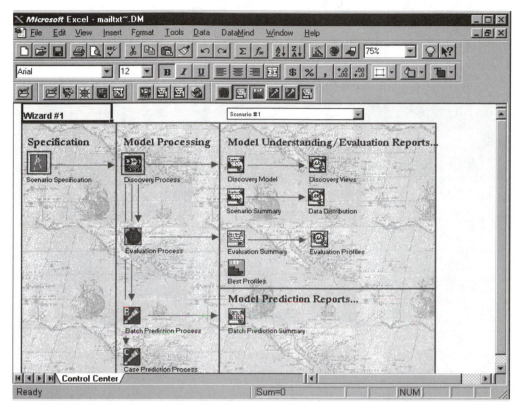

Figure 5–7 The DataMind control center

The control center screen leads you through the data mining process, from study specification to building a model to model understanding reports to prediction.

5.5 UNDERSTANDING THE MODEL

The discovery process will result in the generation of a model. Once the model is built, several reports can be generated. The Discovery Model Summary report is a good report with which to start because it provides a general overview of the model built.

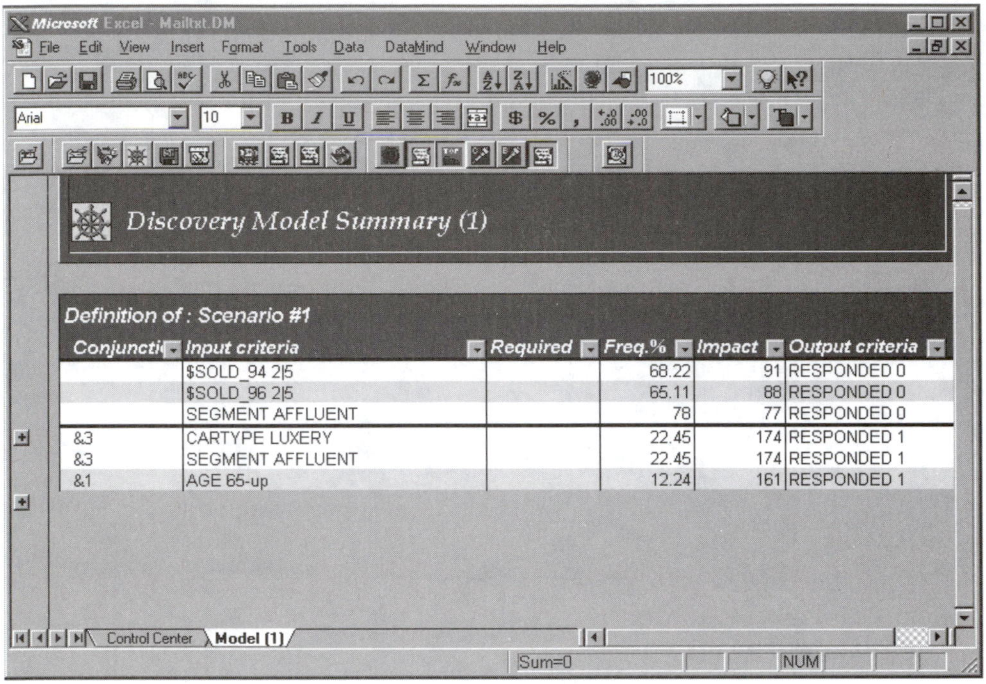

Figure 5–8 The Discovery Model Summary for the direct mail campaign

5.5.1 Model Summary Report

Figure 5–8 shows the model summary for the model built in this example.

1. To see the report in Figure 5–8, you select the icon on the control center labeled Model Summary.

This report contains much information. The first place to start is to look at the column at the far right. These are the *output criteria*. There are two sections to this report, one for the column *responded* with the value 0 (non-responders) and one for the column *responded* with the value 1 (responders).

The first section lists all the *input criteria* that describe non-responders, or rather customers who have the value 0 in the column *responded*. The input criteria are ranked in order, to indicate relative order of importance. A frequently asked question for those who look at this for the first time is:

How do you know if an input is correlated to an output?

The relative importance an input has on an output is determined by two columns, *frequency* and *impact*. High frequency and high impact together indicate a strong correlation between the output and the input criteria.

Frequency is the number of times an input criteria occurs for an output. It is a percentage. For example, Figure 5–8 shows that for non-responders, the column *segment* has the value "affluent" 78% of the time.

Impact is a relative number, based loosely on probabilities, that shows how important an input is to an output. Figure 5–8 shows that for non-responders, the column/value pair *segment* "affluent" has an impact of 77. An impact of 77 is out of a possible 100 in this case.

It is possible to make a generalization for this report that the segment of customers who have been defined as affluent in this data set are much less likely to respond to this mail campaign. The impact and frequency for this input criterion are both relatively high.

Why does the impact of the input criterion, cartype luxury, and the input criterion, segment affluent, have a value of 174? Isn't it true that the impact should never go over 100?

Impact scores for one input criteria by itself will never go over 100, but this is a *conjuction*. Conjunctions are when two or more input criteria together affect an outcome. In this case, people who drive luxury cars *and* are affluent are likely to respond to our direct mail campaign. The two input criteria together have an impact of 174 out of 200 (100 * 2 inputs), so the impact is relatively high. The frequency for these to input criteria is only 22.45%, so these two input criteria only occur for responders 22.54% of the time. In this case, there is a high impact, but a relatively low frequency. The correlation of this conjuction to the output is notable, but it would be far more predictive if the frequency was higher. (In the upcoming release of DataMind, the impact scores over 100 are always normalized to be equal to or below 100.)

It is interesting that this study points out that people characterized in the affluent segment are likely not to respond to a direct mailer unless they own a luxury car.

What does the required column mean?

```
X Microsoft Excel - Mailtxt.DM                                    _ □ X
File  Edit  View  Insert  Format  Tools  Data  DataMind  Window  Help   _ ß X
□ ☞ ⊟ ⊜ ⚲ ⚹  ⅗ ⌘ ⅔ ⚶  ⌫ ⌫  Σ ⨍  ⅔↓ ⅔↓  ⏍ ⬤ ⬤  100%    ⬤ Q ?
Arial              ▼  10  ▼  B I U  ☰ ☰ ☰ 🔲  $ % ,  +̣̣ː .ː  □ ▼  ⬤ ▼  ⓣ ▼
     I34          ▼           RESPONDED 0
```

Discovery Model Summary (1)

Definition of : Scenario #1

Conjuncti	Input criteria	Required	Freq.%	Impact	Output criteria
	$SOLD_94 2|5		68.22	91	RESPONDED 0
	$SOLD_96 2|5		65.11	88	RESPONDED 0
	SEGMENT AFFLUENT		78	77	RESPONDED 0
	CHILDREN 0		68.67	77	RESPONDED 0
	AGE 36-45		7.11	77	RESPONDED 0
	$SOLD_94 1|5		9.56	70	RESPONDED 0
	CARTYPE COMPACT		8	66	RESPONDED 0
	HOUSE_INCOME 2|5		54.67	59	RESPONDED 0
	RESPONSE_95 0		97.33	57	RESPONDED 0
	HOUSEHOLD MARRIED		8	56	RESPONDED 0
	$SOLD_95 1|5		82.67	53	RESPONDED 0
	HOUSEHOLD FEMAIL_HEAD_WCHILD		7.11	53	RESPONDED 0
	AGE 26-35		79.78	52	RESPONDED 0
	HOUSEHOLD MALEHEAD		16	52	RESPONDED 0
	LEISURE_TRAVEL 0		94.89	51	RESPONDED 0

```
◄ ◄ ► ►◄ \ Control Center \ Model [1] /         ◄ ◄                    ► ►
                                      Sum=0                    NUM
```

Figure 5–9 Expanding the Discovery Model Summary Report

Required fields are fields that occur 100% of the time of a specific outcome. Required conditions can take on special meaning in a prediction process to validated predictions.

Can I see more input criteria?

You can see more input criteria by following these directions:

2. Select one of the "+" symbols to the left of the *conjunction* column as shown in Figure 5–8 and all the input criteria for the specified output are listed as shown in Figure 5–9.

What does the $sold_94 2 | 5 mean?

This data set has a column *$sold_94* which is a numeric field. When we defined the study, the column was binned into five categories, so this input criteria reads: the column *$sold_94* has a value in the second category of five. In order to see the ranges for the five categories, the scenario summary report is now called up.

5.5.2 Scenario Summary Reports

The Scenario Summary Report is an Excel spreadsheet that shows the data distribution for all criteria.

Figure 5–10 shows a Microsoft Excel window titled "Microsoft Excel - Mailtxt.DM" displaying a Scenario Summary Report.

Definition of : Scenario #1

Field Name	Usage	Type	Values	Unique val.	Occur.	Category	Min	Max
RESPONSE_95	Input	Discrete	2		499			
RESPONSE_96	Input	Discrete	3		447			
BOUGHT_SIX	Input	Discrete	2		499			
CALLED_MONTH	Input	Discrete	4		499			
$SOLD_94	Input	Continuous	5		499	Equidistant	0	646
				1	45		0	129
				2	310		129	258
				3	110		258	387
				4	25		387	517
				5	9		517	646
$SOLD_95	Input	Continuous	5		499	Equidistant	0	723

Figure 5–10 Scenario Summary Report

3. To see the Scenario Summary Report in Figure 5–10, you return to the control center by selecting the tab marked with this name. Select the icon on the control center labeled Scenario Summary.

The question was asked, what does *$sold_94* 2 | 5 mean? By expanding this report, Figure 5–10 shows that category 2 of 5 is a range between 129 and 258. Furthermore, there are 310 occurrences of this category out of 499 rows.

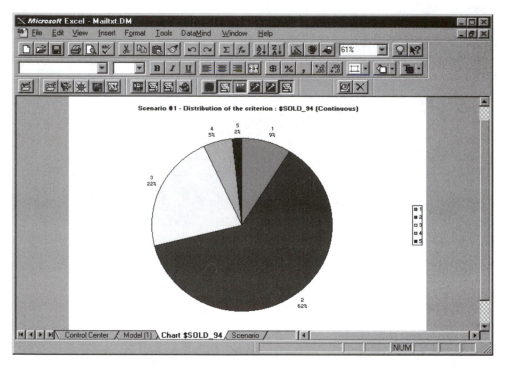

Figure 5–11 Data Distribution for the column $sold_95

4. A data distribution for one input criteria can be generated. To see the Data Distribution Report in Figure 5–11, you select the icon on the control center labeled Data Distribution.

What should be apparent by looking at this data distribution is that the five equidistant bins we used in this study are not optimal. Bin 2 has 62% of the rows; bin 3 has 22% of the rows. Bins 1, 4, and 5 have less than 10% each. It is possible in the Professional Edition to edit this study and change those ranges by selecting the Scenario Specification icon in the control center, editing the ranges of the input fields, and rebuilding the model. In more advanced usages of this product, several different scenarios can be created and compared to evaluate trends or just to improve upon the model being built by modifying inputs used and ranges specified.

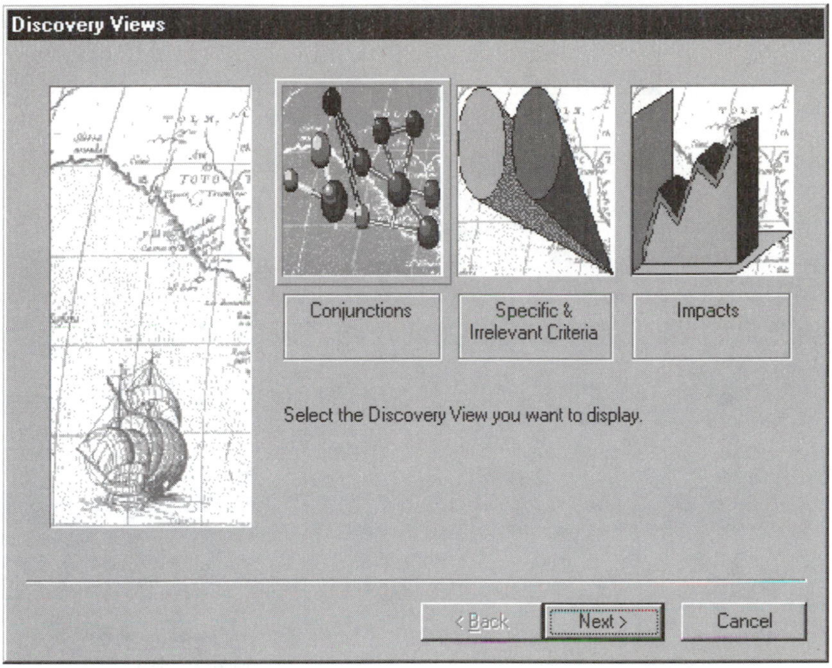

Discovery Views

Conjunctions

Specific &
Irrelevant Criteria

Impacts

Select the Discovery View you want to display.

< Back   Next >   Cancel

Figure 5–12 Discovery Views

5.5.3 Discovery Views

There are several subreports that can be generated once the model summary report is created.

5. To see the Discovery Views Report in Figure 5–12, select the icon on the control center labeled Discovery Views.

There are three different types of reports that can be generated: Conjunctions, Specific & Irrelevant Criteria, and Impacts.

Conjunctions

This report is used to just look at conjunctions. It does not provide anything extra from the model summary report, but it makes it easier to find conjunctions.

Specific & Irrelevant Criteria

The Specific & Irrelevant Criteria report shows which inputs are specific to an outcome; which are irrelevant; and when an input affects more than one outcome, the difference between the impacts of the input on the multiple outcomes. The difference between impacts on an input affecting multiple outcomes is called *differentiation*, and it is often the most useful indicator of a variable's effectiveness in predicting an outcome.

6. Select the Discovery Views Icon in the control center. Select Specific & Irrelevant Criteria and push **Next**. Select *Responded 0* as the output criteria and push **Finish**. You will see the report in Figure 5–13.

Discovery Model Views

Specific... criteria for RESPONDED 0 Scenario #1

Conjunction #	Specific criteria	Freq.%	Impact	% Differentiation
	AGE 36-45	7.11	77	MAX
	$SOLD_94 1|5	9.56	70	MAX
	CARTYPE COMPACT	8	66	MAX
Conjunction #	Differentiation criteria	Freq.%	Impact	% Differentiation
	SEGMENT AFFLUENT	78	77	100
	$SOLD_94 2|5	68.22	91	91.21
	$SOLD_96 2|5	65.11	88	87.5
	Irrelevant criteria			
	$SOLD_94 4|5			
	$SOLD_94 5|5			
	$SOLD_95 3|5			

Figure 5–13 The Specific & Irrelevant Criteria Report

This report shows three sections for criteria affecting the outcome, *responded 0*.

- **Specific criteria**—Those input criteria that only occur for this outcome. (There is a 5% noise threshold used by default, which means any input criterion that occurs less than 5% of the time for an outcome is not calculated due to possible "noise" or inaccuracy. This threshold can be changed.)

- **Differentiation criteria**—To understand differentiation, it is easiest to show an example. The input *$sold_95 2 | 5* has impact 91 for outcome *responded 0*. Also, *$sold_95 2 | 5* has impact of 8 for outcome *responded 1*. The difference between the scores of the two outcomes is (91-8)/81 which is 91.21%. This means the criteria *$sold_95 2 | 5* has 91.21% more influence on *responded 0* than on *responded 1*.

  If the differentiation was calculated for outcome *responded 1* instead of outcome *responded 0*, the differentiation in this example is (8-91)/91 which is negative at -91.21%. (You can see negative numbers by expanding the report with the "+" sign).

- **Irrelevant criteria**—In Figure 5–13, *$sold_93* has no effect on the outcome *responded 0*.

Impacts

Impacts are graphical reports that help visualize the difference of the effect of an input criterion on an outcome. There are several types of reports. For example, Figure 5–14 shows one such report.

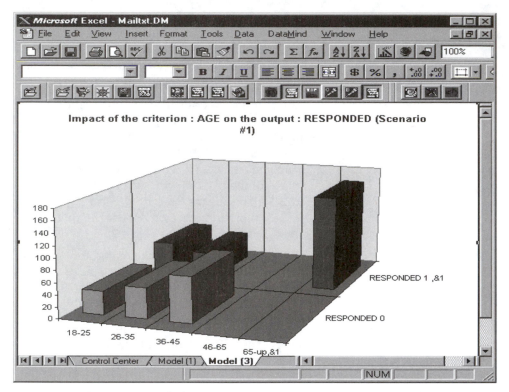

Figure 5–14 A impact graph for customer segments

This report shows how five different age groups affect response and non-response. Age group 65-up has the greatest effect on responders, but also remember that it is part of a conjunction. The "&1" you see in the graph indicates that there is a conjunction involved in this particular criterion. The "&" indicates a conjunction and "1" identifies which conjuction it is.

5.5.4 Microsoft Word Report

You can generate a report in Microsoft Word by hitting the icon on the tool bar shown in Figure 5–15 below.

Word Report Generation

Figure 5–15 Generating a Microsoft Word summary report

The report generated in Microsoft Word summarizes the results of the other generated reports for people who are not fond of Excel reports. The Microsoft Word report can also be used to generate an HTML report that can be viewed on the Internet.

5.5.5 Evaluation

The evaluation process runs a data set against your discovery model in order to see if the model created during discovery is accurate. Evaluation compares generated results against known outcomes. The evaluation process runs the data set against the discovery model in order to see if the model created during discovery is accurate.

Sometimes it is desirable to evaluate a model with a sample data set. A sample holdout data set has been provided with the direct mail set shown in this chapter.

Add the Evaluation Data Set

The following sequence cannot be done with the demonstration version of the product, but it does show how evaluation could be done against a holdout sample. Select the topic manager by clicking on the icon shown below, which is on the DataMind toolbar:

You will see the topic manager window. Go to the data sources tab as shown in Figure 5–16 and select **Browse**. Choose the file *c:\datamind\example\mailhold.txt*. Press **Close**.

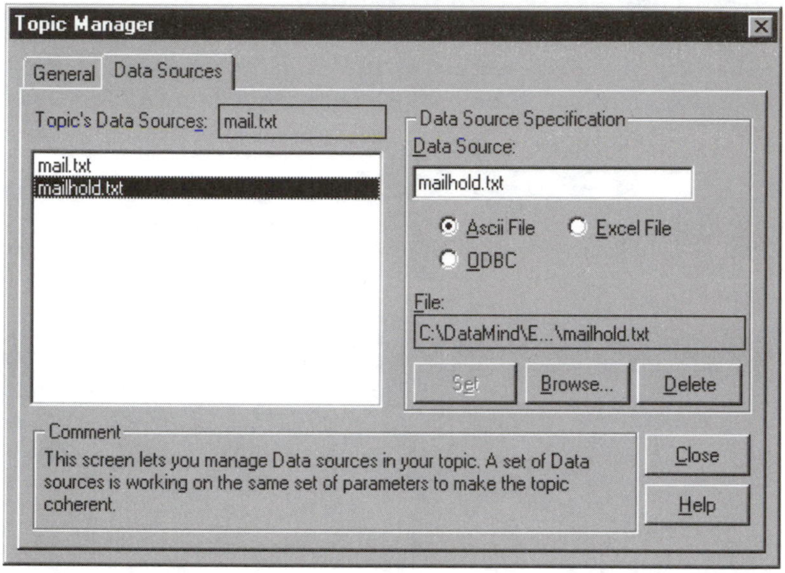

Figure 5–16 Adding a data set to the topic

Setting Up Holdout Data File for Evaluation

Select the Scenario Specification icon on the control center. The Study Setup window will come up as shown in Figure 5–17.

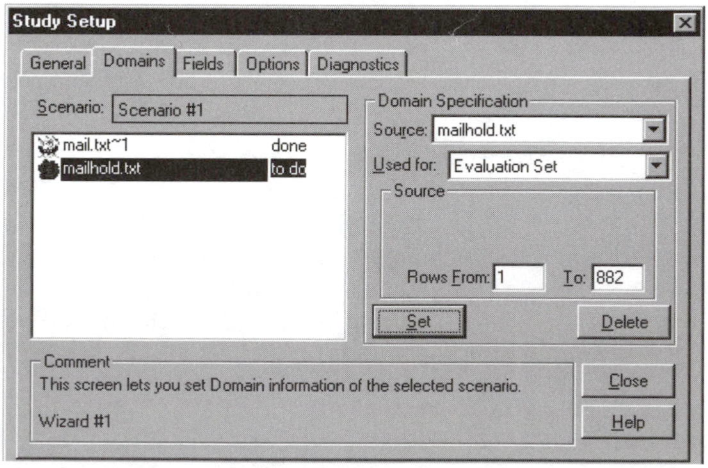

Figure 5–17 The Study Setup Window

Choose mailhold in the "Source" box. Chose Evaluation Set in the "Used for" box. Press **Set** and your screen should look like Figure 5–17. Select **Close**.

Running Evaluation

7. In the demonstration version, an evaluation can be done on the sample data file itself by hitting the **Evaluation Process** button in the Command Center.

Evaluation Summary Report

8. The Evaluation Summary Report shown in Figure 5–18 is generated by hitting the Evaluation Summary Icon in the command center.

Microsoft Excel - Mailtxt.DM
File Edit View Insert Format Tools Data DataMind Window Help
Case Prediction Process
Model Evaluation Summary (1)
Evaluation Summary
Output criteri | Prediction Success expected output found | Prediction Failure unexpected output foun | Unpredictable Too few inputs no output found | Unpredictable Missing Requi no output found | Global Number of examples
Number % | Number % | Number % | Number %
RESPONDED 0 | 377 83.78 | 73 16.22 | 0 0 | 0 0 | 450
RESPONDED 1 | 43 87.76 | 6 12.24 | 0 0 | 0 0 | 49
RESPONDED | 420 84.17 | 79 15.83 | 0 0 | 0 0 | 499
Model (1) Model (3) Evaluation (1)
Sum=0 NUM

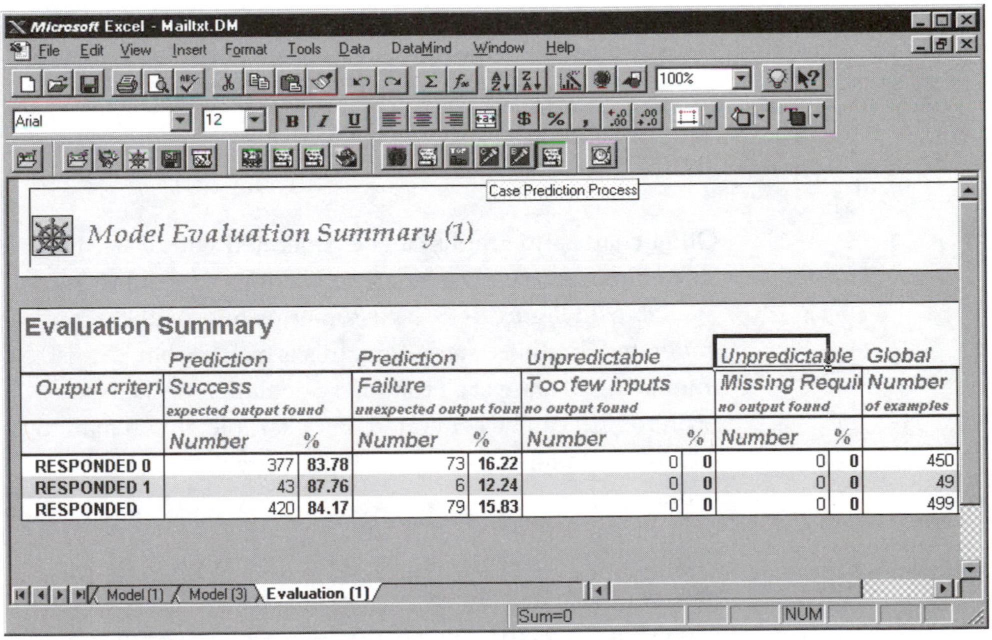

Figure 5–18 The Evaluation Report for a holdout sample

The evaluation report indications that 377, or 83.78%, of the rows are correctly predicted as non-responders and 43 rows, or 87.76%, of the rows are correctly predicted as responders. The accuracy of this model is 84.17%.

Other Reports

There are two other evaluation reports provided in the evaluation process.

- **Evaluation Profile Report**—this report shows the reasons the model predicted correctly and why it fails to predict when it does

- **Best Profile Report**—this report list rows of data that represent the best case representations of customers the model would most likely predict to be responders and non-responders.

A Customer Lift Chart

Other charts and graphs can be generated with DataMind, since direct access to resulting predictions scores are available. In Figure 5–19, a customer response lift chart was generated. In direct marketing, this is a chart that is most interesting to analysts. From it, a calculation of the best profit return can be generated. For example, if you mail to 40% of my mailing list, you will generate the maximum profit.

Figure 5–19 was generated by sorting the rows of data in order of those most likely to respond to least likely using DataMind's weights, which are discussed in Section 5.6, which discusses prediction.

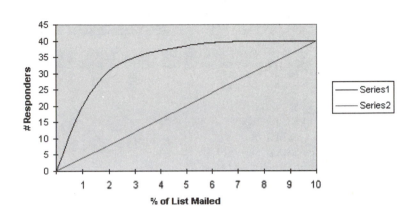

Figure 5–19 A Customer Lift Chart

In the holdout sample used for direct mailing, 42 of 846 customers receiving mailers actually responded. In Figure 5–19, it shows that using data mining, 20 of the responders were identified in the top 10% of mailers versus only 4.2 of the responders otherwise. (Ten percent of 42 responders is 4.2.) This graph might suggest that mailing to the top 30% of a mailing list could generate much more profit than mailing to the whole list, since 35 customers are identified in the top 30%.

5.6 PERFORM PREDICTION

DataMind also performs prediction. The same impact scores that were calculated for model understanding are used for prediction. There are two forms of prediction with DataMind: case and batch prediction. *Case prediction* uses your discovery model to interactively predict an outcome on a specific case. *Batch prediction* reads a series of cases and performs prediction without user interaction.

The Prediction Process is the process whereby new data sets are run against the model we have created.

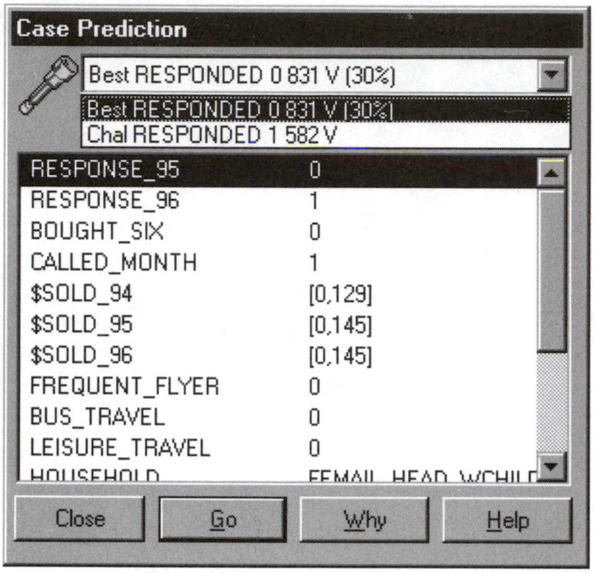

Figure 5–20 Running Case Prediction

Case Prediction

9. Prediction can be run interactively by using the "Case Prediction Process" icon on the control center. Once it opens, push **Go**.

In this case, a set of values has been set up for each input. These values can be changed by you interactively. Then, the **Go** button is pressed and a prediction is made. In the case in Figure 5–20, the prediction is made that this customer will not respond. The prediction was made with a score of 831. The challenger prediction, which is a customer response, was predicted with a score of 582. The margin of victory between these scores is 30%. The score and the margin of victory are numbers that DataMind stores. They are used to rank predictions from best prediction to worst prediction, which was used in the customer lift chart in Figure 5–19.

Prediction Influence

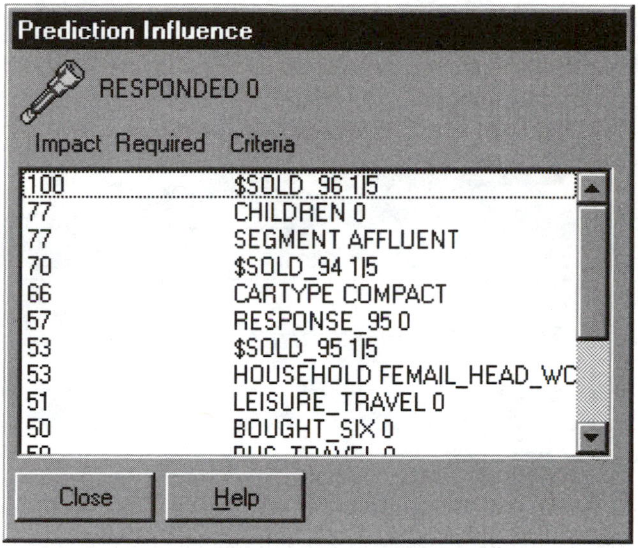

RESPONDED 0

Impact	Required	Criteria
100		$SOLD_96 1|5
77		CHILDREN 0
77		SEGMENT AFFLUENT
70		$SOLD_94 1|5
66		CARTYPE COMPACT
57		RESPONSE_95 0
53		$SOLD_95 1|5
53		HOUSEHOLD FEMAIL_HEAD_WC
51		LEISURE_TRAVEL 0
50		BOUGHT_SIX 0

Close   Help

Figure 5–21 A presentation of why this prediction is made

10. Prediction also has a *Why* button, which presents the reasons why a prediction is made. Press the **Why** button.

The Why button presents the input criteria, in order of importance, that were used to make the particular prediction. In this case, the fact that *$Sold_95 1|5*, or in English, the dollars sold in 1995 were in the lowest category, is the number one reason why the customer was predicted not to respond.

Batch Prediction Report

Batch Prediction can run in batch mode by pressing the "Batch Predition process" icon in the control center. The demonstration version does not display the results for this; however, once the process is complete, the batch prediction report can be viewed by selecting the icon with the name Batch Prediction Summary report on the control center. You will see a report like the one in Figure 5–22.

X *Microsoft* Excel - mailtxt~.DM

File   Edit   View   Insert   Format   Tools   Data   DataMind   Window   Help

Arial ▾ | 10 ▾ | **B** *I* U | ≡ ≡ ≡ 国 | $ % , | .0 .00 | □ ▾

Batch Prediction Summary

Definition of : Scenario #1

Best Prediction				Second Prediction		
RESPONDED		Level	differentiation	RESPONDED		Level
0	V	**897**	25%	1	V	675
0	V	**901**	18%	1	V	743
0	V	**903**	26%	1	V	669
0	V	**934**	21%	1	V	738
0	V	**884**	23%	1	V	688
0	V	**881**	21%	1	V	704
1	V	**826**	10%	0	V	746
1	V	**906**	5%	0	V	866
0	V	**892**	16%	1	V	752

Control Center \ **Prediction** /

Sum=25%   NUM

Figure 5–22 A batch prediction report

This report shows for each row the best case prediction, the score, the margin of victory, the challenger prediction, and the challenger prediction score. If there were more than two outcomes being predicted, a score would be calculated for each of them. The row information is also stored in the resulting prediction file and it can be used, as in the lift chart example, to rank each row by the prediction made and the confidence in each prediction.

5.7 SUMMARY

This chapter covered the basics of how to use the DataMind product. Key to the product are the concepts of *impact*, *conjunctions*, and *differentiation*, which are metrics that help a user understand the relationships between inputs used in a study and an outcome, or dependent variable.

The product provides many different views to look at the models being built; these views are Excel and Word reports that can be saved, manipulated, and printed. The look and feel of this product is very different from the approaches taken by decision trees, and demonstrated by KnowlegeSEEKER in Chapter 4, and by neural networks, which are demonstrated in the next chapter.

Chapter

6

A Look at
NeuralWorks Predict

This chapter steps through the process of data mining with a leading software product that uses a neural network approach. Many neural network based products are on the market, and, while every product differs in style and functionality, there are many similarities in all products using neural networks. NeuralWorks Predict is distinctive in its approach to making a product understandable to business professionals.

The chapter is organized as follows:

6.1 INTRODUCTION

The example discussed in this chapter uses NeuralWorks Predict, which is a product designed for business professionals. Like DataMind, discussed in Chapter 5, NeuralWorks Predict uses Microsoft Excel as an interface to make end users feel more comfortable with the product. NeuralWare sells a variety of products, including NeuralWorks Predict, NeuralWorks Predict Professional, and NeuCOP.

One advantage of a product line like NeuralWare's is its ability to be used in many ways outside of a standard interface, like Excel. For example, you can convert the trained model into code that allows you to integrate it into applications written in C, Fortran, or Visual Basic. Also NeuralWorks Predict can also be used through a command-line interface.

6.1.1 More on Neural Networks

Chapter 1 briefly discussed neural networks. Neural networks attempt to mimic the process of a neuron in a human brain, with each link described as a processing element (PE). Neural networks learn from experience and are useful in detecting unknown relationships between a set of input data and an outcome. Like other approaches, neural networks detect patterns in data, generalize about data, and predict outcomes. Neural networks have been especially noted for their ability to predict complex processes.

A processing element, or PE, processes data by summarizing and transforming it using a series of mathematical functions. One PE is limited in ability, but when connected to form a system, the neurons or PEs create an intelligent model. PEs are interconnected in any number of ways and they can be retrained over several, hundreds, or thousands of iterations to more closely fit the data they are trying to model.

If you are interested in learning more about the neural network algorithm, there are several books out and, for the developers out there, you can even get source code. One book on neural networks which provides source code is

Neural Network and Fuzzy Logic Applications in C++ by
Stephen T. Welstead.

6.1.2 How Corporate America is Using Neural Nets

Neural networks are used in many applications today. IBM,
SAS, HNC, Thinking Machines, and NeoVista are a few of
the vendors with neural network products. HNC's Falcon, a
neural network product, is used pervasively in detecting
fraud in the financial market. On searching the Web, several
hundred sites can be found discussing neural networks.
One interesting web site, already mentioned in Chapter 3,
has a section on commercial products that use neural
network technology (*www.emsl.pnl.gov*).

NeuralWorks Predict, which is discussed in this chapter, is
applied to a wide variety of applications in industry,
business, and science. For example:

- Identifying financial trends for market timing,
  stock picking, and asset allocation.

- Modeling, controlling, and optimizing production
  processes.

- Determining a customer's credit risk.

- Evaluating complex medical problems to provide
  the most effective treatment.

- Selecting geographical regions or population
  groups for target marketing or soliciting.

- Predicting your company's chance of surviving
  financial difficulties.

NeuralWare and Westinghouse Process Control division
have been working together to improve the process control
of power generation and metal and water treatment plants,
with NeuralWare's NeuCOP product line.

NeuralWare and Texaco jointly worked on a neural network
approach for the process control industry, which includes
applications in petroleum refining among other industries.
The intelligent software solution NeuCOP is involved,
which is the culmination of a four-year joint research and
development effort by NeuralWare and Texaco.

In early 1996, NeuralWare and Argonne National
Laboratory, run by University of Chicago for the
Department of Energy, entered a cooperative research and

development agreement to develop neural net signal processing identification techniques to support Argonne projects in developing, among other things, a sensor to identify gases to which it has been exposed.

6.2 DATA PREPARATION

The example used in this chapter models resolution times for problems called into support organizations.

Table 6–1 displays information on resolution time of problem tickets opened.

Table 6-1 *Data on resolution time for customer calls*

Column Name	Values	Explanation
DAY	Mon, Tue, Wed, Thu, Fri	Day of week problem call was placed
RESPONSE_TIME	Real number	The time, in minutes, it took to place the first call to the customer
REGION	Valley, Central, Western, Coast	The region in which the problem ticket was placed
PROBLEM_TYPE	Sys_Down, Question, Fix_Req, Unresolved, Unexp_Feature	The type of problem that the customer call was concerning
SEVERITY	Integer: 0, 1, 2, 3, 4, 5	The severity of the problem, with 0 being most critical
HOUROFDAY	Integer: 1 - 24	The hour of day a call was placed
TIMEONPHONE	Integer	The time a customer support representative spent on the phone with a customer
CONTACT_MADE	0, 1	Was contact made on the first call? O (no) or 1 (yes)
PREV_CALLS	Vhigh, High, Medium, Low, Vlow	Level of previous calls made by customer
SERVICE_CATEGORY	Gold, Silver, Platinum	What type of support does customer have?
CALL_SOLVED	Real	How long, in hours, did it take to resolve calls?

This example data set has been prepared from data similar to what a transaction-based system would have for a customer response center. Other types of information could be added to this data set that might be useful: for example, information about the employees receiving the calls, how long they have been doing this kind of job or how much training they have received. Similarly, we could have added information on the customer—information like their training level, their years in the industry, their age, and any descriptive information about their likelihood to understanding the product about which they are calling.

Some interesting comments can be made on this data set. The column, *prev_calls*, has the values Vhigh, High, Medium, Low, and Vlow. In transaction-based systems, the number of previous calls would have been defined as a numeric value. In this data set, we predefined values for groups of numeric values (i.e. Vhigh). It would be helpful to know what numeric ranges we have assigned to these qualitative values, since the data set, as it stands, does not tell us. Another column, *severity_level*, has been defined as a numeric value from 0 to 5. With this data set, it would be helpful to know how severity levels are defined.

6.3 Defining the Study

The goal of this study is to model how long it takes for a problem to be resolved from the time it is phoned in to when it is resolved. This is a problem that is cross-industry and frequently analyzed by corporate support organizations.

The data set has the column, *call_solved*, which is the output of our study. It tells us, in hours, how long a call has taken. Since the number is a real number, with two decimals, this output is different than what we have had previously because the number of potential outputs is much greater. In the direct mail example we had outputs (0 or 1). In this example, we have outputs from 2.45 to 29.34. The problem with having many outputs is that your predictive abilities to exactly predict a value like 2.45 versus a value like 2.46 becomes harder with the more possible outcomes you have.

There are two ways to approach a model with potentially thousands or more of numeric values as output. One way to do it is to bin the values together in ranges, so that there are only a few outputs (e.g., 2.45–5, 5.01–10, 10.01–15, 15.01–20, 20.01–25, and 25.01–29.34. It is easier to predict that a value will be in a range than it is to predict it exactly.

The other way to approach this study is to leave the values alone, and calculate a comfortable range in which our predicted value can exist. For example, if your model predicts 2.47 and your value is 2.45, then you say that the model is working within an acceptable range of accuracy.

The second approach is the one we will take for this example. Neural networks are good at predicting outputs where potentially thousands or more outputs are possible, so this is a good approach to take to highlight the technology.

6.3.1 Starting Up NeuralWorks Predict

We will step through the process that NeuralWorks Predict takes to define a study. In this study, we will use the wizard mode to build the model.

Before you can try this example out for yourself, read through Appendix B for proper installation and configurations in order to install the demonstration copy of NeuralWare Predict. The copy that has been provided is a working copy of the product except it does not allow you to save the studies you have created, like the commercial product will. There is also a professional version of NeuralWare that offers additional functionality. A few of the professional edition's features are mentioned in this chapter.

Again, we will use the wizard mode in this study. As a quick note, Predict provides different levels of interaction to fit your specific requirements and expertise in building neural network models.

- Wizard mode

  Allows you to build models without having to understand the underlying technology. You simply specify a data range and your problem type, and Predict does the rest.

- Advanced mode

  Allows you to fine-tune the network architecture, select different learning rules, and modify the training process.

- Expert mode

  Allows you to experiment with all the parameters available in Predict.

- Microsoft Excel and Command-Line Interfaces

  Predict can be used through Microsoft Excel in order to preprocess the data before supplying it to Predict, and to receive, examine, and chart the results Predict produces.

Creating a New Study and Loading the Data

1. Open Excel and Select the File menu. Click on the **Open** command.

   Scroll through the Directories list and select the directory where you installed Predict. Select Text Files (*.txt) in the List Files of Type box. Select TROUBLE.TXT, the sample data file, from the File Name list. (This file should have been copied into the directory after the installation of NeuralWorks Predict as directed in Appendix B.)

   Click **OK**.

   Excel loads the data, indicated by TROUBLE.TXT appearing in the title bar of your worksheet.

   Before you can start building a new study, you must select a setup mode and create a file in which you want the neural network to be saved.

2. Click on the Predict menu and look for the Wizards command.

   If Wizards does not have a checkmark, select it now. If Wizards has a checkmark, go to step 3. (Selecting the Wizards command when it already has a checkmark will deselect it.)

3. Click on the Predict menu and select **New**.

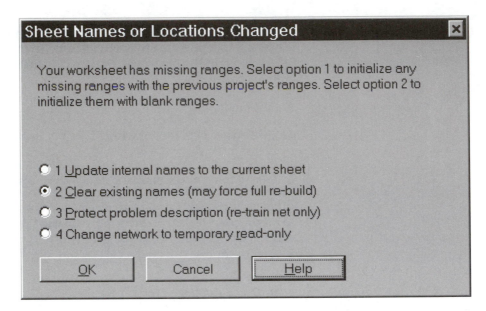

Figure 6–1 The first dialog

A dialog box appears prompting you for a name and directory for your study. Scroll through the Directories window and select the directory where you installed Predict.

Type the filename TROUBLE over or in front of .NPR (the extension for NeuralWorks Predict). Click **OK**. Predict stores the model you are about to create in this file.

4. The dialog box shown in Figure 6–1 appears.

Simply click on **Cancel**. This dialog is useful when you are updating a previously existing study.

6.3.2 Defining the New Study

A series of dialogs will now appear to specify the range of data to be studied, the type of study to be performed, and a number of other specifications the neural network needs in order to run.

5. The next step is to specify the first example input range, as shown in Figure 6–2.

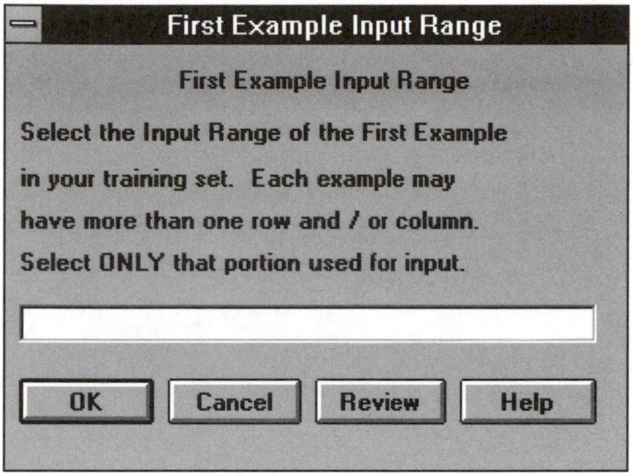

Figure 6–2 Defining inputs

You are prompted to specify the group of cells that contain the first set of your input variable values. This data will be included in the training set.

You can specify this data range by selecting it in the worksheet or by typing its first and last cell locations into the dialog box field.

In the worksheet, select cells A2 to J2, or in the dialog box enter A2:J2.Click **OK**.

6. The next step is to specify the second example input range, as shown in Figure 6–3.

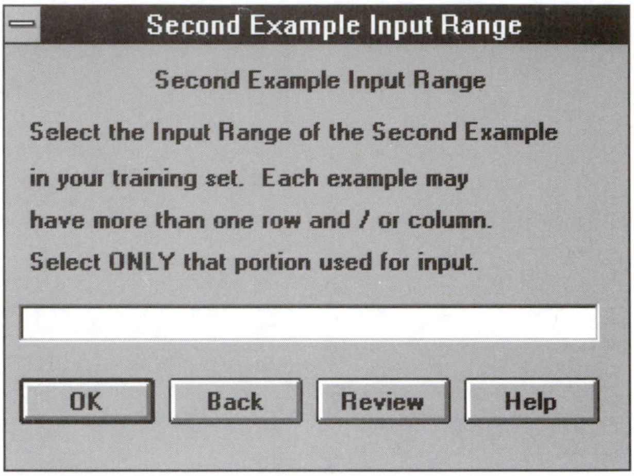

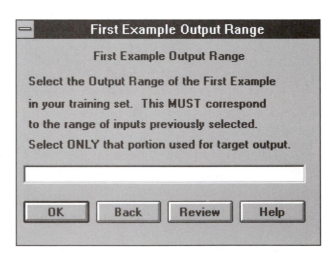

Figure 6–3 The second input field

Select cell A3 or enter A3. Click **OK**.

7. The next step is to specify the first example output range, as shown in Figure 6–4.

Figure 6–4 Specifying the output

You are prompted to specify the cell or group of cells that contain your first set of output variable values. With this information and its knowledge of the relative

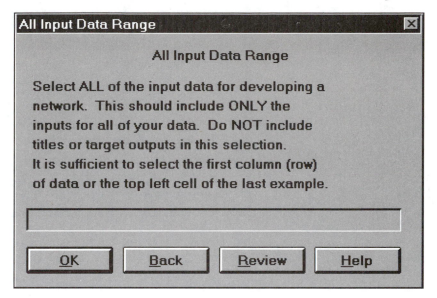

Figure 6–5 Specifying a training set

locations of the input variable sets, Predict is able to locate the remaining output variable values.

Since this project has only one output variable, select cell K2 or enter K2. Click **OK**.

8. The next step is to specify the input data range to be used for training, as shown in Figure 6–5.

You are prompted to specify the entire block of cells of input variable values that you want Predict to use for training.

You can select the entire range or enter the locations of its first (top-left) and last (bottom-right) cells. Or you can simply select the first column of this range or enter the locations of the first column's first and last cells. But be sure not to include any cells with the names (labels) of the input variables!

Select A2 to A599 or enter A2:A512. Click **OK**.

9. The next step is to specify the field names range, as shown in Figure 6–6.

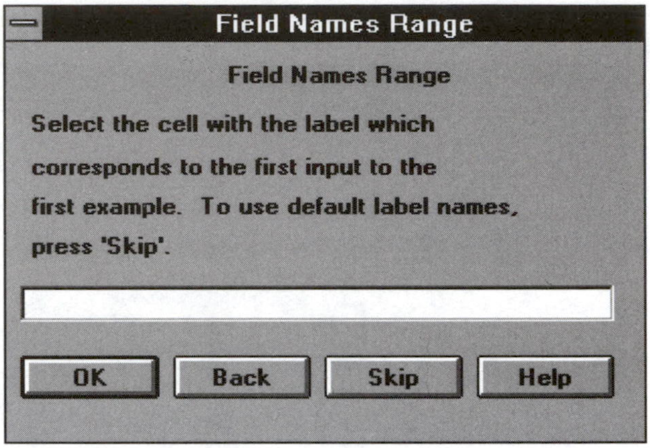

Figure 6–6 Specifying column names

You are prompted to specify the range of cells (fields) that contain the names (labels) of your input and output variables. You can specify this range by simply selecting or entering the location of its first cell.

Select cell A1 or enter A1. Click **OK**.

10. The next step is selecting the problem type, as shown in Figure 6–7.

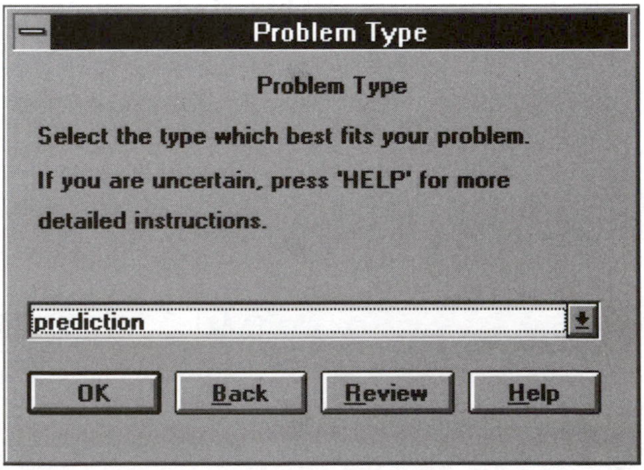

Figure 6–7 Specifying problem type

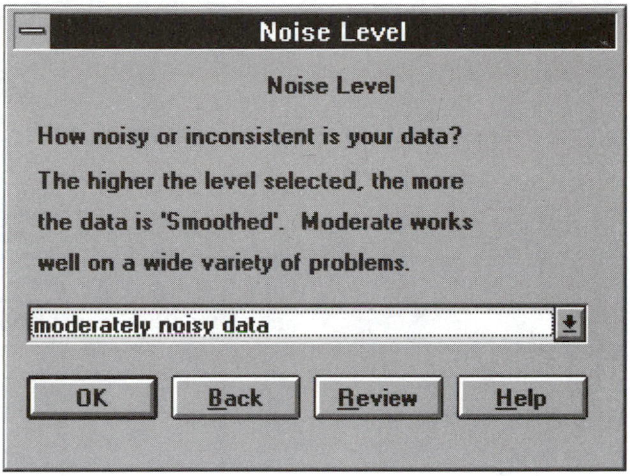

Figure 6–8 Specifying noise level of study

You are prompted to specify what type of problem you are trying to solve. The type of problem you select will determine the type of output Predict will produce. The output of a prediction problem consists of data that can have any value in a continuous or discretely ordered numeric range. If I derived a new column that ranged the output into categories titled High, Medium, and Low, I would have to change the problem type to *classification*.

Click on the arrow to see the list of options, and select *prediction*. Click **OK**.

11. The next step is to select the noise level, as shown in Figure 6–8.

    You are prompted to indicate how noisy your data is. When the data is based on physical measurements, as this sample data is, it usually contains some measurement of noise but is less noisy than the data of other applications.

    Select moderately noisy data. Click **OK**.

12. The next step is to select a data analysis and transformation level, as shown in Figure 6–9.

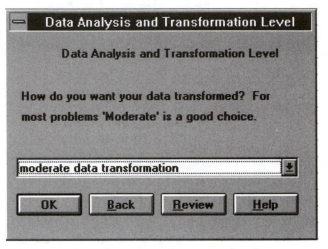

Figure 6–9 Specifying transformation level

You are prompted to decide how thoroughly you want Predict to transform your raw data. Predict analyzes the data fields and develops alternative sets of transformations for each one, according to the level specified. It then selects and combines those transformations that produce the best network output.

It would be unwise to choose a high level of data transformations when your problem has many input variables. The number of transformations would be too large, requiring a long time to build the model. A high transformation level is not even advisable for problems with small sets of input variables, since a smaller number of variables produces better generalization. A moderate level of transformations is adequate for most applications.

Select moderate data transformation. Click **OK**.

13. The next step is to set the input variable selection level, as shown in Figure 6–10.

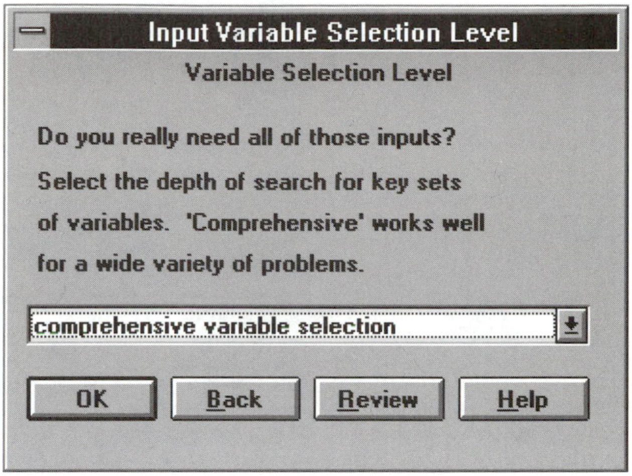

```
┌─────────────────────────────────────────────┐
│ ─    Input Variable Selection Level          │
│           Variable Selection Level            │
│                                               │
│  Do you really need all of those inputs?      │
│  Select the depth of search for key sets      │
│  of variables. 'Comprehensive' works well     │
│  for a wide variety of problems.              │
│                                               │
│  ┌─────────────────────────────────────┬───┐ │
│  │comprehensive variable selection      │ ± │ │
│  └─────────────────────────────────────┴───┘ │
│                                               │
│   ┌───────┐  ┌───────┐  ┌───────┐  ┌───────┐ │
│   │  OK   │  │ Back  │  │Review │  │ Help  │ │
│   └───────┘  └───────┘  └───────┘  └───────┘ │
└─────────────────────────────────────────────┘
```

Figure 6–10 Specifying variable selection

You are prompted to indicate how extensively you want Predict to search for combinations of input variables that produce good results. Higher settings for variable selection require more time and memory than lower settings. For a small number of input variables (as in our sample problem), the comprehensive variable selection level is effective but does not require large amounts of memory.

Select *comprehensive* variable selection. Click **OK**.

14. The next step is to set the neural network search level, as shown in Figure 6–11.

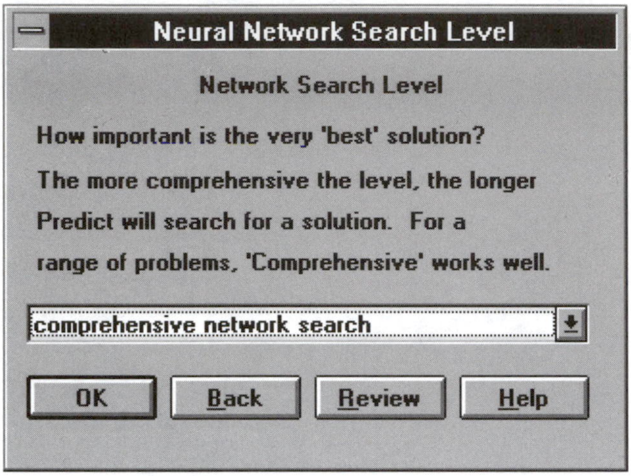

┌───┐
│ ⊟   **Neural Network Search Level**   │
│   │
│   **Network Search Level**   │
│   │
│ How important is the very 'best' solution?   │
│   │
│ The more comprehensive the level, the longer │
│   │
│ Predict will search for a solution. For a   │
│   │
│ range of problems, 'Comprehensive' works well.│
│   │
│ ┌─────────────────────────────────────┬───┐ │
│ │ comprehensive network search   │ ▼ │ │
│ └─────────────────────────────────────┴───┘ │
│   │
│ ┌────────┐ ┌────────┐ ┌────────┐ ┌────────┐ │
│ │   OK   │ │ Back │ │ Review │ │ Help │ │
│ └────────┘ └────────┘ └────────┘ └────────┘ │
└───┘

Figure 6–11 Specifying the network search level

You are prompted to specify how thoroughly you want Predict to train the network. Training thoroughly will produce a better solution but will also require more time. A comprehensive network search is recommended for most problems.

Select *comprehensive network search*. This time click on **Review**. The Edit the Network dialog box appears.

If you accidentally clicked on OK and the Build the Net dialog box appeared, simply click on Review now to bring up the Edit the Network dialog box.

Reviewing the Network Parameters

The Edit the Network dialog box allows you to review and, if necessary, edit the parameters you have entered. Your parameter settings should match the ones shown in Figure 6–12.

```
┌──────────────────────────────────────────────────────────────┐
│ ─                     Edit the Network                         │
├──────────────────────────────────────────────────────────────┤
│ ┌────────────────────────────────────┐                        │
│ │ C:\PREDICT\EVAP.NPR                 │  Project    ┌─────────┐ │
│ └────────────────────────────────────┘             │ Browse..│ │
│ ┌────────────────────────────────────┐             └─────────┘ │
│ │ EVAP.XLS!$A$2:$F$2                  │  First Example Inputs   │
│ └────────────────────────────────────┘                        │
│ ┌────────────────────────────────────┐                        │
│ │ EVAP.XLS!$A$3                       │  Second Example Inputs  │
│ └────────────────────────────────────┘                        │
│ ┌────────────────────────────────────┐                        │
│ │ EVAP.XLS!$G$2                       │  First Example Outputs  │
│ └────────────────────────────────────┘                        │
│ ┌────────────────────────────────────┐                        │
│ │ EVAP.XLS!$A$2:$A$93                 │  All Input Data         │
│ └────────────────────────────────────┘                        │
│ ┌────────────────────────────────────┐                        │
│ │ EVAP.XLS!$A$1                       │  Field Names            │
│ └────────────────────────────────────┘                        │
│ ┌────────────────────────────────┐ ┌─┐ Project                 │
│ │                                │ │↑│ Description              │
│ │                                │ └─┘ (254 characters max.)    │
│ │                                │ ┌─┐                          │
│ └────────────────────────────────┘ └↓┘                         │
│                                                                │
│ ┌──────────────────────┬─┐              ┌──────────────────┐   │
│ │ prediction           │↕│ Problem Type │    Logging...     │   │
│ └──────────────────────┴─┘              └──────────────────┘   │
│ ┌──────────────────────┬─┐              ┌──────────────────┐   │
│ │ moderately noisy data│↕│ Noise Level  │     Save         │   │
│ └──────────────────────┴─┘              └──────────────────┘   │
│ ┌──────────────────────┬─┐ Data                               │
│ │ moderate data transform│↕│ Transformation                    │
│ └──────────────────────┴─┘              ┌──────────────────┐   │
│ ┌──────────────────────┬─┐              │  Set Defaults    │   │
│ │ comprehensive variable│↕│ Variable Selection └────────────┘  │
│ └──────────────────────┴─┘              ┌──────────────────┐   │
│ ┌──────────────────────┬─┐              │   Advanced...    │   │
│ │ comprehensive network │↕│ Network Search └───────────────┘   │
│ └──────────────────────┴─┘                                     │
│ ┌──────┐ ┌────────┐ ┌──────┐            ┌──────────────────┐   │
│ │  OK  │ │ Cancel │ │ Help │            │    Expert...     │   │
│ └──────┘ └────────┘ └──────┘            └──────────────────┘   │
└──────────────────────────────────────────────────────────────┘
```

Figure 6–12 Reviewing study specifications

After you have reviewed the entries, click **OK**.

15. The (Re-)Build the Network dialog box appears, as shown in Figure 6–13. It is described in the next section. The data and network setup is now complete, and you are ready to start the building and training process.

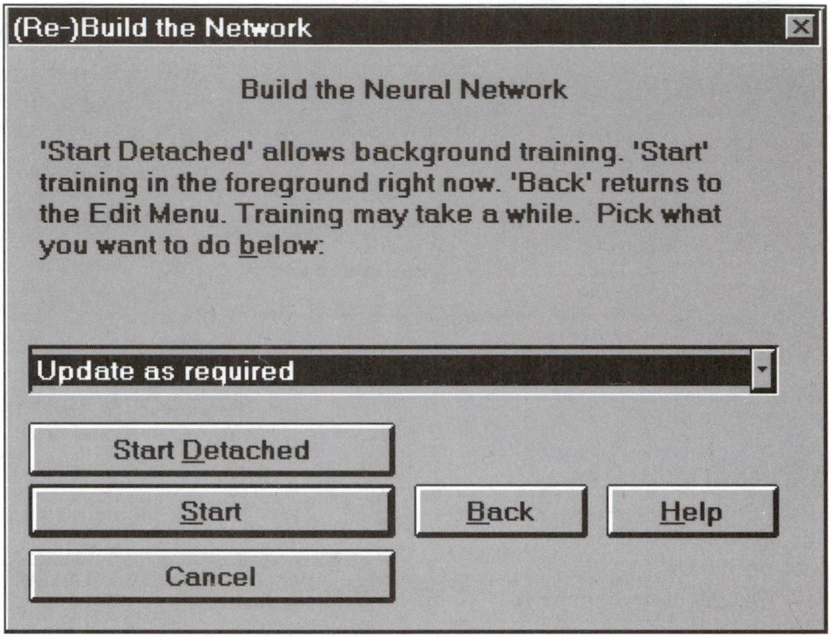

Figure box: (Re-)Build the Network

Build the Neural Network

'Start Detached' allows background training. 'Start' training in the foreground right now. 'Back' returns to the Edit Menu. Training may take a while. Pick what you want to do below:

Update as required

Start Detached

Start   Back   Help

Cancel

Figure 6–13 Starting to build the model

> In the (Re-)Build the Network dialog box (shown above), select Update as required. Click on **Start**.

6.4 BUILDING AND TRAINING THE MODEL

After the last step, the process of actually building and training the network begins. Predict automatically selects the train, test, and validation sets of data from the historical data you supply. Selection is based on mathematical procedures available in Predict that produce the best outcome values.

It is not necessary to designate specific data sets for building and training the network since Predict automatically selects these sets from the range of input data you specified above.

Training a Neural Network

Processing elements, or PEs, are linked to inputs and outputs. The process of training the network involves modifying the strength, or *weight*, of the connections from the inputs to the output. Increases or decreases in the strength of a connection is based on its importance for producing the proper outcome. A connection's strength depends on a *weight* it receives during a trial and error process. This process uses a mathematical method for adjusting the weights and is called a *learning rule*.

Training repeatedly, or iteratively, exposes a neural network to examples of historical data. PEs summarize and transform data, and the connections between PEs receive different weights. That is, a network tries various formulas for predicting the output variable for each example.

Training continues until a neural network produces outcome values that match the known outcome values within a specified accuracy level, or until it satisfies some other stopping criterion.

Predict displays brief progress messages in the status bar of your Excel window. Then it displays, in a dialog box, information about variable selection and the best test scores as training progresses. Wait for the dialog box shown in Figure 6–14 below.

Figure 6–14 Completing the study

Click **OK**.

Different Types of Models to Build—Unsupervised Learning

This example made use of what is referred to as a *feed-forward* network, which is commonly used with *supervised learning* studies. Feed-forward networks are very popular due to their relative simplicity and stability. *Back-propagation* is a feed-forward network commonly used for a variety of applications.

It is also possible to perform *unsupervised learning* with neural networks as well, although this chapter is not demonstrating this. The process is very similar, but, of course, no output is specified. In contrast to supervised learning, an unsupervised network is not given the desired response, but organizes the data in a way it sees fit. Such self-organizing networks divide input examples into clusters depending on similarity, each cluster representing an unlabeled category. *Kohonen learning* is a well-known method in self-organizing neural networks.

The Issue of Over-training

If a network is larger than need be with respect to the training data set, *over-training* can result. This was discussed briefly in Chapter 2. If a network with a large capacity for learning is trained using too few data examples to support that capacity, the network first sets about learning the general trends of the data. This is desirable, but then the network continues to learn very specific features of the training data, which is usually undesirable. Such networks are said to have memorized their training data, and lack the ability to generalize.

Over-training can be measured by periodically checking the results of your test data set. Early stages of a training session yield lower error measurements on both the training and the test data. This continues unless the network capacity is larger than need be, or unless there are too few data sets in the training file. If at some point during learning, your test data begins to produce worse results, even though the training data continues to produce improved results, over-training is occurring.

NeuralWare has an interesting feature. It has a *Savebest* function, which automates the process of watching for over-training. If these results have improved, your network is saved to disk. Should over-training occur, yielding poorer results, the network is not saved but learning continues in hopes of eventually finding improved results.

A common question asked by anyone data mining is:

How much data do I need to train the network successfully?

Generally, NeuralWare recommends having at least 10 to 40 examples per input variable. Some neural networks may require more or fewer data points depending on the complexity of the problem.

6.5   UNDERSTANDING THE MODEL

Neural networks have been criticized as being useful for prediction, but not always in understanding a model. The major challenge in many applications is to identify which input variables are the key parameters of the problem. There has been much recent work in this area, and this is not necessarily true.

While not part of the demonstration version included in the book, Predict employs a Genetic Algorithm for this phase of model development. This allows you to record groups of input variables that impact an outcome directly into your spreadsheet, providing more detailed documentation of each model. After experimenting with various models, a final model can be built by reading one of the earlier model's variable sets.

How do I tell which input has the most effect on the output?

NeuralWare's Professional Edition has an Explain command which provides a quick and easy mechanism for discerning this. Explain allows you to first dither or "jog" the input values by plus or minus a percentage and then view how much the outputs changed as a percentage of the input change. This information can be written to a result file or viewed through a dialog box. This is essentially a sensitivity analysis.

Predict's add-on module "Explain" can also be used to analyze the impact of a particular record's missing values. Explain provides insights into how a record's predicted output might change if an actual field value were present, instead of the missing value.

6.5.1   Validating the Model

Just as you might test a person's skill in a controlled environment, you test a neural network using historical data it has not seen. Test results are good if the outcome

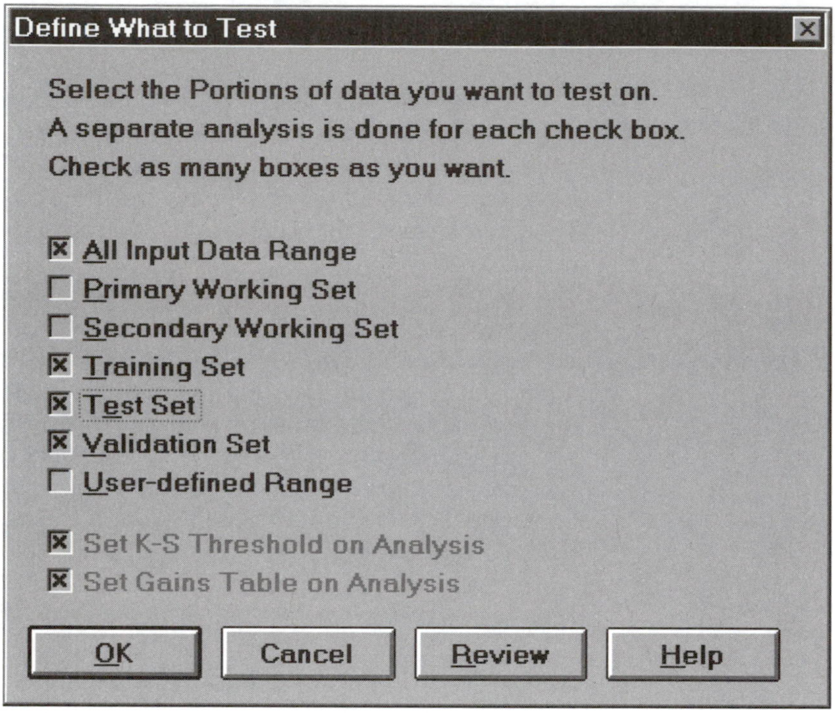

Define What to Test ☒

Select the Portions of data you want to test on.
A separate analysis is done for each check box.
Check as many boxes as you want.

☒ <u>A</u>ll Input Data Range
☐ <u>P</u>rimary Working Set
☐ <u>S</u>econdary Working Set
☒ <u>T</u>raining Set
☒ T<u>e</u>st Set
☒ <u>V</u>alidation Set
☐ <u>U</u>ser-defined Range

☒ Set K-S Threshold on Analysis
☒ Set Gains Table on Analysis

[<u>O</u>K]   [Cancel]   [<u>R</u>eview]   [<u>H</u>elp]

Figure 6–15 Defining a test

values are close enough to the actual or desired outcome
values. Then, the neural network is ready to use with a
validation set of historical data that is independent of the
train and test set data.

To test how well your model learned the problem and how
well it performs on the train, test, and validation sets,
follow these steps:

1. From the Predict menu item on the Excel toolbar, select
    Test.

    The Define What to Test dialog box appears.

2. Select the following data sets:

    • All Input Data Range

    • Training Set

    • Test Set

    • Validation Set

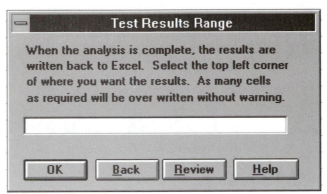

Figure 6–16 The test set range

By default, the validation set consists of all the data. Predict tests the model on these sets, calculates statistical scores for each one, and writes these scores to your worksheet. Click **OK**.

3. The Test Results Range dialog box appears as shown in Figure 6–16.

    Select cell M2 or enter M2 as the location of the first cell of the test results table that will be written to your worksheet. Click **OK**.

4. The testing process begins. When testing is complete, a statistical summary appears in your worksheet, as shown in Figure 6–17. Your results may differ slightly from the ones in the pictured table. This may be due to slight variations in parameter settings between your Predict version and the version used to create this tutorial. It may also be due to the state of the random number generator that is used in the various model-building stages.

M	N	O	P	Q	R	S	T	U
CALL_SOLVED	R	Net-R	Avg. Abs.	Max. Abs.	RMS	Accuracy (20%)	Conf. Interval	Records
All	0.87924	0.876805	1.599344	14.96959	2.468013	0.9706458	4.811147	511
Train	0.876636	0.874526	1.53224	14.96959	2.496153	0.9747899	4.872049	357
Test	0.886115	0.88323	1.754905	8.351202	2.401512	0.961039	4.712872	154
Valid	0.87924	0.876805	1.599344	14.96959	2.468013	0.9706458	4.811147	511

Figure 6–17 Statistical scores

The statistical scores given in this table are:

- *R*—The linear correlation value between the output-variable values (the "target outputs") and the corresponding real-world values produced by the model (the "predicted outputs").

- *Net-R*—The linear correlation between the target outputs and the raw predicted outputs (before they are transformed into real-world values).

- *Avg.Abs.*—The average absolute error between the real-world target and predicted output values.

- *Max. Abs.*—The maximum absolute error between the real-world target and predicted output values.

- *RMS*—The root mean square error between the real-world target and predicted outputs.

- *Accuracy*—The percentage of real-world predicted outputs that are within the specified tolerance (20%) of the corresponding real-world target outputs.

- *Conf. Interval*—This interval establishes the range [target output ± confidence interval] within which the corresponding predicted output occurs 95% of the time.

Analyzing the Results

Among the statistical scores in the summary table, those for R, RMS, Accuracy, and Confidence Interval are considered to be the key indicators of a model's performance. For example, let's look at the R values for our model on the training and test sets.

These scores are close to each other (in the 0.87 and 0.88 range), which means that the model generalizes well and is likely to make accurate predictions on data it has never seen before. A correlation value close to .9 indicates a good model. Note that correlation values as low as 0.2 can indicate a good model when the input data reflects the uncertainties of human behavior.

6.6 PREDICTION

When performance with the test and validation data is good, the neural network is ready to solve your problem by using current data to predict an outcome for which the outcome is unknown.

Computing the Predicted Outputs

To obtain the predicted values, you need to run all the data through the model. This can be done with Predict's Run command.

1. Choose Predict/Run.

    The Run Formula Inputs dialog box appears. Select the range of all your input variable data in your worksheet (A2 to A512), or enter A2:A512 in the dialog-box field. Click **OK**.

2. The Run Formula Outputs dialog box appears, prompting you to specify the range of cells into which you want Predict to write the predicted values.

    Select cell L2 in your worksheet, or enter L2 in the dialog box. Click **GO**.

    Predict writes the predicted values to your worksheet.

Graphing the Target and Predicted Values

We have generated the predicted outputs for our model! In true prediction, you will not have outputs with a known outcome; however, since we are predicting values for the data set we used to generate the model, we can also graph the target and predicted outputs.

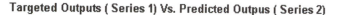

Targeted Outputs (Series 1) Vs. Predicted Outpus (Series 2)

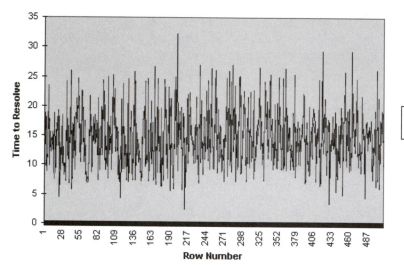

Figure 6–18 Closeness curve of actual and predicted values

You can effectively compare the predicted and target values, or a selection of them, by creating a line graph in Excel. Click on Excel's Chart Wizard button, or select the Insert/Chart command, and follow the instructions for creating a line graph.

The resulting graph looks like Figure 6–18 above.

The closeness of the curves for the target and predicted values provides another indication that the model performs well.

6.7 SUMMARY

This chapter hopefully provided insight into neural network approaches to data mining. At the very least, you should have a basic understanding of the NeuralWorks Predict product.

This is the last of three chapters discussing different data mining approaches by three software vendors. Each of these vendors is focused on allowing business professionals to gain access to data mining, but, as you should see, there are no ready-made standards in the area of data mining.

The next two chapters are devoted to providing some industry-specific examples of how products such as Angoss Knowledge SEEKER, DataMind, and NeuralWare's NeuralWorks Predict are used.

Chapter 7

Industry Applications of Data Mining

This chapter shows examples of how data mining is used in banking and finance, retail, healthcare, and telecommunications. The purpose of this chapter is to give the user some ideas of the types of activities in which data mining is already being used and what companies are using them.

The chapter is organized as follows:

Section 7.1 Data Mining Applications in Banking and Finance
Section 7.2 Data Mining Applications in Retail
Section 7.3 Data Mining Applications in Healthcare
Section 7.4 Data Mining Applications in Telecommunications
Section 7.5 Summary

7.1 DATA MINING APPLICATIONS IN BANKING AND FINANCE

Data Mining has been used extensively in the banking and financial markets. In the banking industry, data mining is used heavily in the areas of modeling and predicting credit fraud, in evaluating risk, in performing trend analysis, in analyzing profitability, as well as helping with direct marketing campaigns.

In the financial markets, neural networks have been used in stock price forecasting, in option trading, in bond rating, in portfolio management, in commodity price prediction, and in mergers and acquisitions, as well as in forecasting financial disasters.

Several of the financial companies who use neural networks and have been referenced on the Internet are Daiwa Securities, NEC Corporation, Carl & Associates, LBS Capital Management, Walkrich Investment Advisors, and O'Sullivan Brothers Investments. The number of investment companies that data mine is much more extensive than this, but you will not often find them willing to be referenced.

One interesting book in the area of global finance is *Neural Networks in the Capital Markets*, edited by Apostolos-Paul Refenes. The book explores equity applications, foreign exchange applications, bond applications, and macroeconomic and corporate performance. Most of the contributed chapters are from university professors, a group whose publishing in the areas of economic and capital market forecasting is most impressive; however, there are government and industry contributions from Citibank N.A., Daimler Benz AG, County NatWest Investment Management, and NeuroDollars.

There are many software applications on the market that use data mining techniques for stock prediction. One such application that is used for stock prediction is shown in Figure 7–1.

Figure 7–1 Stock forecasting

NETPROPHET by Neural Applications Corporation is a stock prediction application, which makes use of neural networks. The two lines shown in the graph in Figure 7–1 represent the real and the predicted stock values.

In banking, the most widespread use of data mining is in the area of fraud detection. HNC's Falcon product specifically addresses this area. HNC comments that credit fraud detection is now in place to monitor more than 160 million payment card accounts this year. They also claim a healthy return on investment. While fraud is on the decrease, applications for payment card accounts are raising as much as 50% a year.

The widespread use of data mining in banking has not been unnoticed. In 1996, *Bank Systems & Technology* commented, "Data mining is the most important application in financial services in 1996."

Finding banking companies who use data mining is not easy given their proclivity for silence, unless you look at the SEC reports of some of the data mining companies who sell into this marketplace. Data mining customers listed in such reports include: Bank of America, First USA Bank, Headlands Mortgage Company, FCC National Bank, Federal Home Loan Mortgage Corporation, Wells Fargo Bank, NationsBanc Services, Mellon Bank N.A., Advanta Mortgage Corporation, Chemical Bank, Chevy Chase Bank, U.S. Bancorp, and USAA Federal Savings Bank. Again it is reasonable to assume most all large banks are performing some sort of data mining, although many have policies not to discuss it.

7.2 DATA MINING APPLICATIONS IN RETAIL

Slim margins have pushed retailers into embracing data warehousing earlier than other industries. Retailers have seen improved decision support processes leading directly to improved efficiency in inventory management and financial forecasting. The early adoption of data warehousing by retailers has allowed them a better opportunity to take advantage of data mining. Large retail chains and groceries store vast amounts of point of sale data that is information rich. In the forefront of applications that have been adopted in retail are direct marketing applications.

Chapter 5 used the example of a direct mail campaign to show the usefulness of data mining in retail marketing activities. The direct mailing industry is an area where data mining, or data modeling, is widely used. Almost every type of retailer uses direct marketing, including catalogers, consumer retail chains, grocers, publishers, business-to-business marketers, and packaged goods manufacturers. There are many vertical applications that support direct marketing campaigns, such as HNC's Marksman product. The claim could be made that every Fortune 500 company today has used data mining in a direct marketing campaign, usually through outsourcing lists to third parties like Harte-Hanks or The Polk Company.

Direct marketers are often concerned about customer segmentation, which is a clustering problem in data mining.

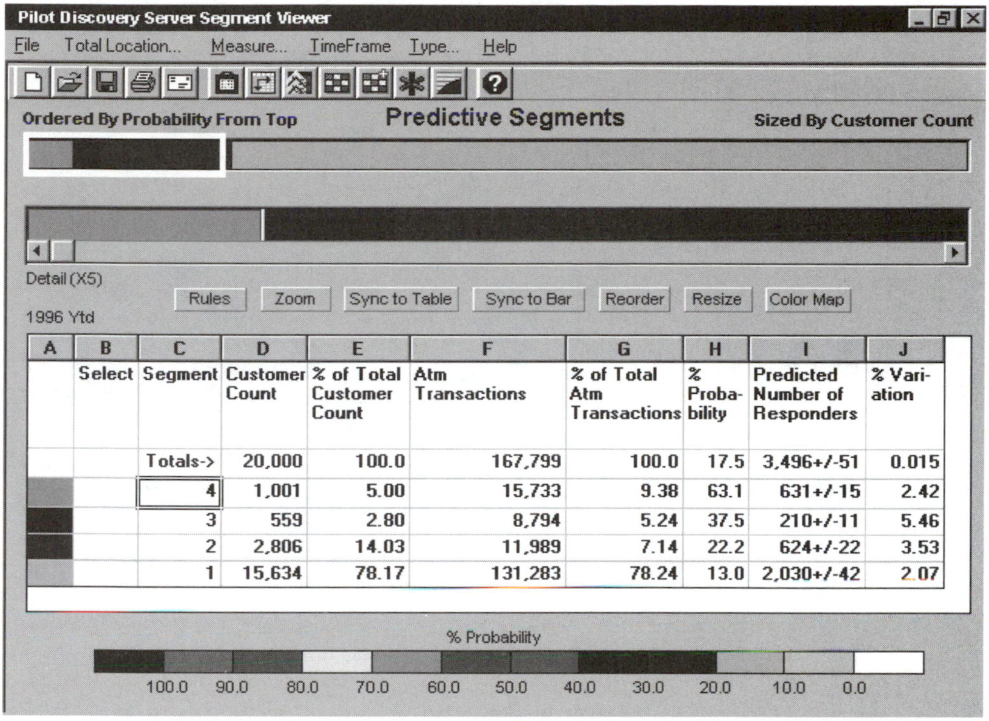

Pilot Discovery Server Segment Viewer `_ 8 ×`

File   Total Location...   Measure...   TimeFrame   Type...   Help

Ordered By Probability From Top **Predictive Segments** **Sized By Customer Count**

Detail (X5)

Rules | Zoom | Sync to Table | Sync to Bar | Reorder | Resize | Color Map

1996 Ytd

A	B	C	D	E	F	G	H	I	J
	Select	Segment	Customer Count	% of Total Customer Count	Atm Transactions	% of Total Atm Transactions	% Proba- bility	Predicted Number of Responders	% Vari- ation
		Totals->	20,000	100.0	167,799	100.0	17.5	3,496+/-51	0.015
		4	1,001	5.00	15,733	9.38	63.1	631+/-15	2.42
		3	559	2.80	8,794	5.24	37.5	210+/-11	5.46
		2	2,806	14.03	11,989	7.14	22.2	624+/-22	3.53
		1	15,634	78.17	131,283	78.24	13.0	2,030+/-42	2.07

% Probability

100.0   90.0   80.0   70.0   60.0   50.0   40.0   30.0   20.0   10.0   0.0

Figure 7–2 Customer segmentation software from Pilot Software

Many vendors offer customer segmentation packages, like the one shown in Figure 7–2.

Pilot Software also uses the customer segmentation to help in direct mailing campaigns, as shown in Figure 7–3.

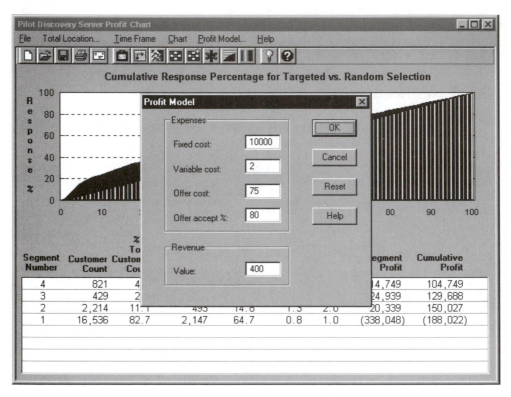

Figure 7–3 An application for a direct marketing campaign

IBM has used data mining for several retailers to analyze shopping patterns within stores based on point of sale (POS) information. For example, one retail company with $2 billion in revenue, 300,000 UPC codes, and 129 stores in 15 states found some interesting results after analyzing their sales information. A store executive comments, "... we found that people who were coming into the shop gravitated to the left-hand side of the store for promotional items and were not necessarily shopping the whole store." Such information is used to change promotional activity and provide a better understanding of how to lay out a store in order to optimize sales.

Other Types of Retail Data Mining Studies

Retailers are interested in many different types of data mining studies. In the area of marketing, retailers are interested in creating data mining models to answer questions like:

- How much are customers likely to spend over long periods of time?

- What is the frequency of customer purchasing behavior?

- What are the best types of advertisements to reach certain segments?

- What advertising mediums are most effective at reaching customers?

- What is the optimal timing at which to send mailers?

Merchandisers are beginning to profile issues such as:

- What types of customers are buying specific products?

- What determines the best product mix to sell on a regional level?

- What are the latest product trends?

- When is a merchandise department saturated?

- What are the times when a customer is most likely to buy?

- What types of products can be sold together?

In discussing customer profitability, customers may wish to build models to answer questions like:

- How does a retailer retain profitable customers?

- What are the significant customer segments that buy products?

A study by Garth Hallberg, author of *All Consumers Are Not Created Equal*, states that within a category of packaged goods, 33% of the buying households account for 67% of the sales. While this fact is not surprising to most retailers, it does clearly suggest that customer identification is critical to successful retail organizations, and is likely to become more so. Data mining helps model and identify the traits of profitable customers and to reveal the "hidden"

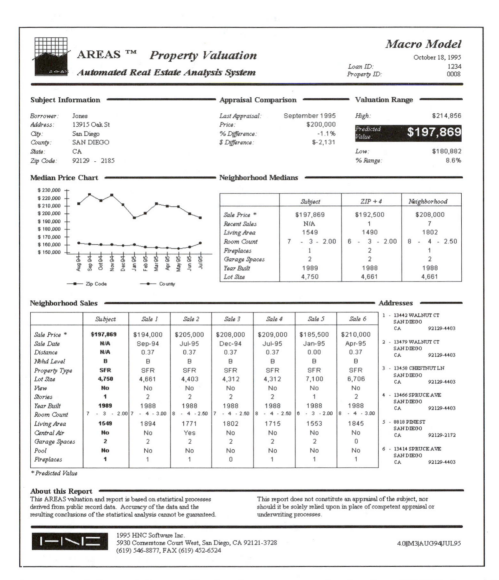

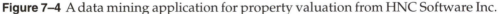

Figure 7–4 A data mining application for property valuation from HNC Software Inc.

relationship that standard query processes have not already found. For further reading on the area of customer management, one interesting work is the book *The One-to-One Future* by D. Peppers and M. Rogers.

One application of data mining in real estate is the AREAS Property Valuation product from HNC Software which performs property valuation as shown in Figure 7–4.

While some would not categorize the real estate market as a retail industry, the concept of using data mining to predict property valuations can be directly applied to any product or commodity. For example, the proper valuations of antique furniture, used cars, or clothing apparel could be predicted in the same manner.

Another application of data mining in the airline industry is a customer retention management package by SABRE Decision Technologies™. SABRE is a leader in working with the airline industry to use data warehousing to increase profitability and make better business decisions.

Some companies that use data mining in retail, and have been referenced in articles or by data mining companies, are Victoria's Secret, National Car Rental, JOCKEY International, Marriott Ownership, the Reader's Digest, and WallMart. In Chapter 1, Figure 1–2 from MapInfo Corporation shows a visualization application for locating optimal site locations for business.

7.3 DATA MINING APPLICATIONS IN HEALTHCARE

Chapter 2 discussed types of studies that can be done in the healthcare industry, as well as data preparation issues. With the amount of information and issues in the healthcare industry, not to mention the information from medical research, biotechs, and the pharmaceutical industry, the types of studies listed in Chapter 2 are only the tip of the iceberg for data mining opportunities.

Data mining has been used extensively in the medical industry already. For example, NeuroMedical Systems used neural networks to perform a pap smear diagnostic aid. Vysis uses neural networks to perform protein analysis for drug development. The University of Rochester Cancer Center and the Oxford Transplant Center use KnowledgeSEEKER, a decision tree technology to help with their research. The Southern California Spinal Disorders Hospital uses Information Discovery to data mine. Information Discovery quotes one doctor as saying, "Today alone, I came up with a diagnosis for a patient who did not even have to go through a physical exam."

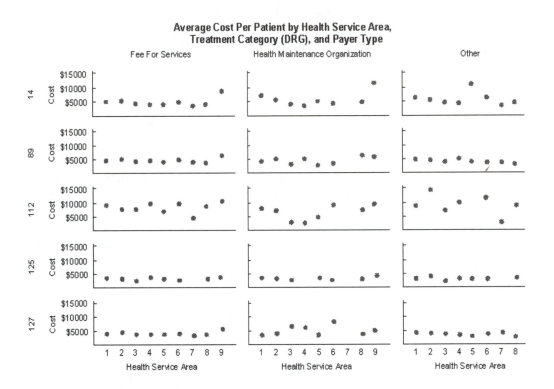

Figure 7–5 Average Cost Per Patient by Health Service Area, Treatment Category (DRG), and Payer Type (Belmont Research)

Uses of Data Visualization in the Medical Industry

Data visualization is one area that has built interest in the medical field. Belmont Research's CrossGraphs product has been used in many different applications. For example, Figure 7–5 above shows a diagram for studying healthcare costs.

The graph shows the average cost per patient for fee-for-services patients, HMO patients, and other patients. For the categories 14 and 112, costs for "other" payer types varies widely.

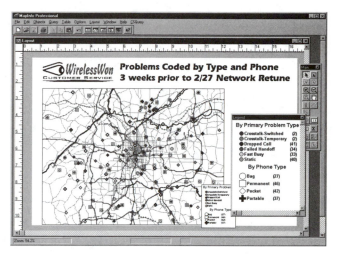

Figure 7–6 Efficacy of several antibacterial drugs over time (Belmont Research, Inc.)

Another example, Figure 7–6 above, shows an array of graphs that side-by-side show a story of antibacterial activity of Cefdinir over time.

Figure 7–6 is useful to compare the efficacy rates of different antibacterial pathogens over time. In this case, the antimicrobial agent, Cefdinir, is being studied against other agents for an eight-hour period.

Another example of a very useful application of data visualization is from MapInfo, using mapping technology to show patient location in order to deliver better service, as shown in Figure 7–7.

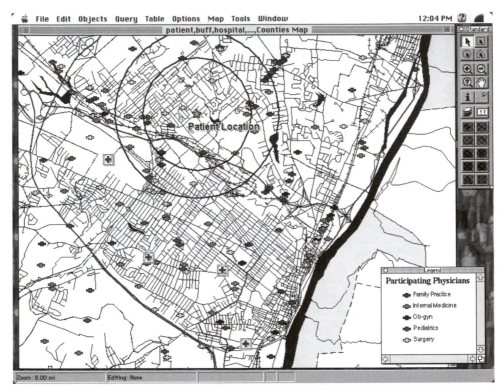

Figure 7–7 Mapping locations of physicians, patients, and patient care facilities

7.4 DATA MINING APPLICATIONS IN TELECOMMUNICATIONS

In recent years, the telecommunications industry has undergone one of the most dramatic makeovers of any industry. The U.S. Telecommunications Act of 1996 allows Regional Bell Operating Companies (RBOCS) to enter the long-distance market as well as offer "cable-like" services. The European Liberalization of Telecommunications Services, which is effective January 1, 1998, liberalizes telecommunications services in Europe and offers full competition among participating European nations. Sixty-eight nations will liberalize their telecommunications market on January 1, 1998 to coincide with the European commitment based on the World Trade Organization's Telecommunications Agreement.

Not only has there been a massive deregulation, but in the U.S., there has been a sell-off by the FCC of air waves to companies pioneering new ways to communicate. The cellular industry is rapidly taking a life of its own.

With the hyper-competitive nature of this industry, a need to understand customers, to keep them, and to model effective ways to market new products to these customers is driving a demand for data mining in telecommunications where no demand existed in distant memory.

Companies like AT&T®, GTE Telecommunications®, and AirTouch® Communications have announced use of data mining. American Management Systems® (AMS) Mobile Communications Industry Group has taken an active interest in data mining as well. AMS and AT&T offer consulting services around data mining, as do GTE and Cincinnati Bell Information Services®, among others.

Coral Systems® of Longmont, Colorado is a company which incorporates data mining techniques in their FraudBuster™ product, which tracks known types of fraud by modeling subscriber usage patterns and predicting when a carrier is suspected of fraud. There are several companies looking at cellular fraud for telecommunications, including Lightbridge® and GTE.

There are several other companies offering products to combat customer churn. For example, DataMind Corporation focuses on data mining issues in the telecommunications industry and, in particular, customer retention or churn. Industry experts have pointed out the cellular telephone market experiences a 30% churn rate in the United States. A report by Digital Equipment Corporation® by Evan Davies and Hossein Pakraven in September 1995 quantifies the cost of customer churn. In their report, they estimate that the cost of acquiring new customers is as high as $400 for each new subscriber.

Data visualization is another area with many strategic uses in telecommunications. Figure 7–8 shows a map, created by Empower Geographics® using MapInfo's technology, showing problem areas for a wireless telecommunications network.

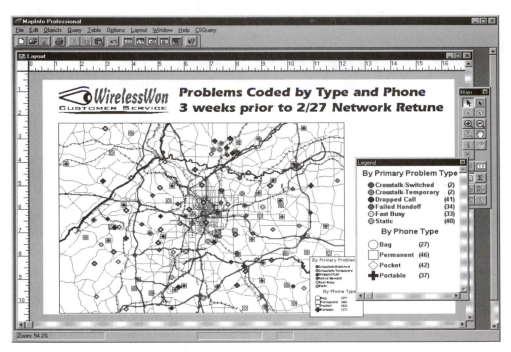

Figure 7–8 A map of a wireless telecommunications network pinpoints dropped calls

Types of Studies in Telecommunications

The telecommunications industry is interested in answering a wide variety of questions with which data mining can help. For example:

- How does one recognize and predict when cellular fraud occurs?

- How does one retain customers and keep them loyal as competitors offer special offers and reduced rates?

- Which customers are most likely to churn?

- What characteristics make a customer likely to be profitable or unprofitable?

- How does one predict whether customers will buy additional products like cellular service, call waiting, or basic services?

- What are the factors that influence customers to call more at certain times?

- What characteristics indicate high-risk investments,

such as investing in new fiber optic lines?

- What products and services yield the highest amount of profit?

- What characteristics differentiate our products from those of our customers?

- What set of characteristics indicates companies or customers who will increase their line usage?

7.5 SUMMARY

This chapter covered industry examples of data mining in banking and finance, retail, healthcare, and telecommunications. This is certainly not an inclusive list of all data mining activities, but it does provide examples of how data mining is employed today. Chapter 8 will discuss specific data mining studies for these industries and will attempt to describe many of the data preparation issues involved in performing these studies. More experienced users of data mining acknowledge that accumulation and preparation of data are the biggest hurdles to beginning the process of data mining.

Chapter 8

Enabling Data Mining Through Data Warehouses

The biggest challenge business analysts face in using data mining is how to extract, integrate, cleanse, and prepare data to solve their most pressing business problems. This issue is a formidable one and can take the bulk of the time in the data mining process. This chapter will discuss how data mining is enabled through the use of data warehousing. The purpose of this chapter is not to provide a crash course in data warehouse design, but to introduce examples of data warehouses and how they would be used for data mining. While data warehouses do not always have to be in place for data mining to occur, they do present a methodology for data integration and preparation. For a more in-depth discussion of data warehousing, I would recommend *The Data Warehouse Toolkit* by Ralph Kimball.

The chapter is organized as follows:

8.1 INTRODUCTION

Before discussing examples of data warehouses for use in
data mining, it is important to be aware of the process of
preparing data for decision support systems. Ultimately, it is
the process of data integration, cleansing, and preparation
used in deploying data warehouses that makes data
warehouses so invaluable to data mining. The most common
issue companies face when looking at data mining is that
information is not all in one place. Consider Figure 8–1. Data
resides at many different levels and in many different
organizations within a company.

Figure 8–1 A view of decentralized data

Decision Support

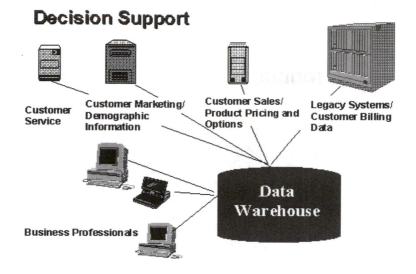

Figure 8–2 Creating a centralized data warehouse

The first step to creating an environment for data mining is to integrate all data sources as shown in Figure 8–2. Comprehensive business decisions require an integrated data repository.

The steps involved in preparing data actually extend beyond the data warehouse itself. Below is a brief sketch of this data preparation process for decision support, as well as a brief mention of some of the companies who offer solutions to make the process easier. A brief mention is also made of *data marts*, which are now a popular concept of offering smaller, targeted data warehouses, usually at a lower overhead cost.

Data Acquisition

The first step to any decision support system is acquiring data to put into a decision support system. Since data may be in many forms and often resides on legacy systems that do not have easy-to-understand formats, there are many companies that make a living by making it, including the following companies. All products are trademarks or registered trademarks of their respective companies.

Carleton Corporation
Electronic Data Systems Corporation
Evolutionary Technologies International, Inc.
Informatica Corporation
Platinum Technology, Inc.
Prism Solutions, Inc.

Data Refinement

Once data has been acquired for a decision support system, there are often many steps involved to clean the data. Among other things, there may be data that is typed incorrectly, data that is out of date, data that is redundant, or data that is simply incorrect. Again there are several vendors who offer data refinement tools including:

Acxiom Corporation
Electronic Data Systems Corporation
Harte-Hanks Data Technologies
Platinum Technology, Inc.
Prism Solutions, Inc.

Data Warehouse Design

During the process of acquiring and refining data, a data warehouse also needs to be designed, and again, there are many vendors who offer tools to facilitate this process. Vendors who automate the process of building entity level diagrams for databases include:

Bachman Software & Services
Evergreen Software Tools, Inc.
LBMS, Inc.
LogicWorks, Inc.
Popkin Software & Systems, Inc.
Sybase, Inc.

Data Warehouse and DataMart Implementation

Many vendors offer databases for data warehousing. There is also a newer market emerging for smaller data warehouses, or *data marts*. Vendors involved in data warehouse and data mart implementation include:

Broadbase Information Systems, Inc.
Informix Software, Inc.
IBM Corporation
Oracle Corporation
Red Brick Systems, Inc.
Sagent Technologies, Inc.
Sybase, Inc.
NCR Corporation

8.2 A DATA WAREHOUSE EXAMPLE IN BANKING AND FINANCE

The following data mining example uses a sample database that monitors households who have accounts with a bank. The data structure used, when compared to an actual bank, is quite simplistic, but it does help to present the issues surrounding preparing data mining studies. The data model stores transactional data as well as information that would be more fitting to a data warehouse. Since this is the case, it is helpful to first discuss the issues of having a transaction database system versus a data warehouse. Most banks today have just a transaction system, but the trend is to move towards integrating their data into a data warehouse for decision support.

A Transactional Database System Versus a Data Warehouse

Most DBMS systems today are transactional, which means they are optimized for inserting and updating information and not for decision support.

Relational systems in banks handle transactions like ATM deposits, inquiries, and withdrawals, which can process millions of transactions per day. They are designed to be fast and hold a minimal amount of information. If our fictitious bank had 4 years of data for 1 million customers who averaged 100 transactions a year, and each of those transactions needed 20 data fields to record necessary information, one table alone could require hundreds of gigabytes of data. There is a limit to what a transactional system can handle, although it is getting set higher every year.

When a decision support analyst wants to extract information from transactional information, that analyst may want to summarize information from the account or derive new information. For example, when looking at credit fraud, it may be valuable to look at the number of credit transactions a customer performs in an hour. This information is not directly stored in a transactional system but is attainable.

Data warehouses are designed specifically for decision support and will usually add many fields of information that transactional systems do not have. In fact, a data warehouse might integrate multiple transactional database systems.

Data mining is often viewed as a follow up to data warehousing because of the necessity to integrate and to derive new information that transactional systems do not provide.

Having said that, this example data model includes transactional data purposely to help distinguish types of information valuable for data mining studies and types of information not valuable for data mining.

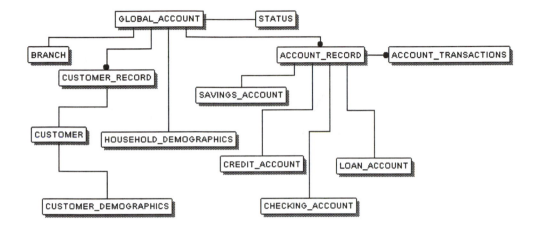

Figure 8–3 A simple data diagram for a bank

8.2.1 **The Example Data Model**

The data diagram in Figure 8–3 above represents data stored by our fictitious bank.

Below is a list of fields within the entities described in the data diagram in Figure 8–3.

Global Account Record

Figure 8–4 is the global account record for customers. A global account is an identification of a customer, or group of customers, who hold one or more different accounts with a bank. One account can have a primary and secondary account holder and one customer can have different types of accounts as well.

Figure 8–4 Global account

Customer Record/Customer

The CUSTOMER_RECORD table links one or more customers with a global account. There could be more than one person who has account privileges, but there is only one primary account holder. The *primary* field in the customer table indicates (yes or no) if the customer is the primary account holder. The CUSTOMER table in Figure 8–5 specifies the customer's name and social security number.

Figure 8–5 Customer Information

Demographic Information

Demographic information can be stored for the household as well as each customer. Information providers, like those listed in Chapter 3, can provide a great deal of demographic in information, as shown in Figure 8–6. Some data warehouses have hundreds of fields on just demographic information.

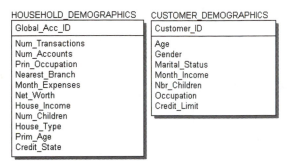

HOUSEHOLD_DEMOGRAPHICS	CUSTOMER_DEMOGRAPHICS
Global_Acc_ID	Customer_ID
Num_Transactions	Age
Num_Accounts	Gender
Prin_Occupation	Marital_Status
Nearest_Branch	Month_Income
Month_Expenses	Nbr_Children
Net_Worth	Occupation
House_Income	Credit_Limit
Num_Children	
House_Type	
Prim_Age	
Credit_State	

Figure 8–6 Demographic information at a household and customer level

Branch Information

Figure 8–7 shows the location and summary information on branches and ATM sites. Such information is useful in determining the most convenient sites for customers as well as trends in customer usage.

BRANCH
Branch_ID
Name
Address
City
State
Zip
Nbr_Customers
Avg_Nbr_Wk_Trans
Avg_Nbr_Wk_Wdwl
Avg_Nbr_Wk_Dep
Nbr_Cust_Mile_Radius
Nbr_Cust_1Mile_Radius
Total_$_Wk
Total_$_Wk_Wdwl
Total_$_Wk_Dep

Figure 8–7 Location and summary information of branches and ATMs

Account Information

Figure 8–8 shows the tables for the different accounts. In this model, the table, *ACCOUNT_RECORD*, is a master table that stores all accounts tied to a global account identifier. A global account may have several accounts. For each account, there is another view that can pull up a snapshot of account information based on the date and time requested. The information for each individual account is summary information from monthly transactions, and in this model, is created as a view that is generated from the table ACCOUNT_TRANSACTIONS to avoid the tremendous amount of space that would be needed to store this information.

ACCOUNT_RECORD	SAVINGS_ACCOUNT	CHECKING_ACCOUNT	CREDIT_ACCOUNT	LOAN_ACCOUNTS
Account_ID Global_Acc_ID	Account_ID Date	Account_ID Date	Account_ID Date	Account_ID Date
Start_Date Account_Type Card_Lost	Balance Nbr_Transactions Nbr_Deposits Nbr_Withdrawl Avg_Balance Avg_Transactions Min_Balance Fees Interest Days_Below_Min	Balance Nbr_Transaction Nbr_Deposits Nbr_Checks Nbr_Withdrawl Avg_Balance Avg_Transactions Min_Balance Fees Interest Days_Below_Min	Nbr_Transactions Avg_Nbr_Transactions Nbr_Transactions_HR Credit_Balance Fees_Paid Fraud_Before Risk_Projection New_Card Avg_Balance Yr_Charge_Avg Out_Of_State_Trans	Balance Total_Payments Nbr_Payments Interest_Paid Nbr_Late_Payments Risk_Projection Loan_Type Late_Payment Fees Mnthly_Charge

Figure 8–8 Account summary information

Account Transaction Information

The table ACCOUNT_TRANSACTIONS, shown in Figure 8–9, holds information on every deposit, withdrawal, balance inquiry, loan payment, credit charge, and any other bank transaction. This table is necessarily huge. While it is possible to data mine transactional data, summary data is very useful. The *transaction type* field, in this example specifies an ATM, mail, electronic, branch, or credit transaction. The *transaction subtype* field specifies the nature of the transaction, i.e., deposit, withdrawal, inquiry, etc.

ACCOUNT_TRANSACTIONS
Transaction_ID
Account_ID Date Transaction_Type Transaction _Subtype Fees $_Deposit $_Withdrawl Indicator Description Branch_ID Location

Figure 8–9 Transaction information

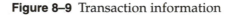

Status Information

The following table has the status information of an account. This information is used directly for decision support and includes items like an indicator of whether they have an account with another bank, an indicator of what types of services they have used with this bank in the

past, an indicator of whether they have left this bank or are still a customer, or indicators of what types of difficulties

(like foreclosure and late payments) this customer might have had.

```
STATUS
Global_Acc_ID
Account_State
Credit_Status
Savings_Status
Loan_Status
Checking_Status
Nbr_Accounts
Ever_Overdraft
Member_Other_Bank
Ever_Furclose
Ever_Payment_Late
Risk_Rating
Switched_Banks
Date_Switched
Ever_Refinanced
```

Figure 8–10 Status information

8.2.2 An Example of a Credit Fraud Study

Credit issuers are very concerned about the ability to forecast when a credit card transaction is fraudulent. There are systems in place today that check credit transactions and provide an indication of whether to allow a credit charge or not. Using the data model shown in Section 8.2.1, we can build a model that could help predict a potentially fraudulent transaction.

Preparing the Data for a Credit Fraud Model

The table ACCOUNT_TRANSACTION shown in Figure 8–9 has a field, *Transaction Type*, which indicates if the transaction was a credit card charge. It is possible to extract information on the transaction by using a query tool or formulating a SQL statement to extract the information requested. For example, a SQL statement to get transaction information on only credit charges would be:

SELECT * FROM TRANSACTION_RECORD WHERE TRANSACTION_TYPE = 'CREDIT'

In preparing data for credit fraud models, banks include more than just the transactional information itself. For example, in the table *Credit Card Account*, there are several

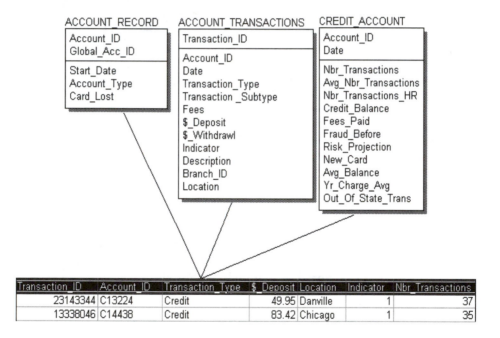

Figure 8–11 Preparing data for a study

fields that could be useful in predicting whether a credit card transaction is fraudulent, like *Nbr Transactions*, *Avg Nbr Transactions*, *Nbr Transactions Hr*, *New Card*, *Fraud Before*, or *Out of State Trans*. The field *Nbr_Transactions* shows the monthly total for transactions for a customer. The table ACCOUNT_TRANSACTIONS is also useful in determining credit fraud, since it contains a field, *Indicator*, which indicates if a card associated with this account has been reported lost.

There are three tables of information in our example that can be used to create this study. In essence, information for this study is extracted as shown in Figure 8–11.

The question with which many people struggle when trying to prepare the data to build a model is:

How do I get the information in the right form?

Three ways to approach preparing the data for this study:

- Use a query tool to extract the information from an RDBMS into the right form. Tools from vendors like Brio, Business Objects, and Cognos will create tables like the one in Figure 8–11 easily. This approach will limit the number of records extracted from the data warehouse because the data is being downloaded to a client computer.

- Create a *view* within a relational database to represent the virtual data to be mined.

- Construct a SQL statement to get data in the right form.

Ideally, data mining tools should automatically transform raw data into a form it can manage. As of this writing, that is not the case. Red Brick is the first relational vendor to integrate data mining directly with a relational database; query and OLAP vendors are integrating data mining with their tools, but data mining has, until recently, largely been done on text-based files that require a good deal of preparation.

For this model, several data fields could be derived from existing columns that might be useful. For example, it may be interesting to examine if more credit fraud occurs on Tuesdays than on Wednesdays and to do so, deriving a field to specify day-of-the-week is necessary in most data mining tools. The *Trx_Timestamp* field could be used to derive many fields, like d*ay_of_week, day_of_month, hour_of_day, month, year, week_of_year*, and so forth. Views, query tools, and SQL statements will all allow the creation of new derived fields, but this falls into the category of data preparation and is usually not automated by data mining vendors today.

Classification Versus Clustering for the Credit Fraud Model

The table ACCOUNT_TRANSACTIONS has the field *Indicator*, which indicates if a transaction is valid or not. This field is determined after a transaction is validated and is historically modified as fraud is verified. The field can be used as a dependent variable for modeling the characteristics that make some transactions more likely to be fraudulent than others. This is a traditional *classification* study.

Sometimes there may be no historical data. For example, *Indicator* may be blank because there is no historical information on which transactions are fraud or not. In this case, fraud detection may be started by *clustering* data. Since fraudulent charges will usually have unique characteristics—like with many charges made in a very short time, which is more common of new cards— clustering data should provide groupings of data that are more likely to be valid and more likely to be fraud. The discovered groups can be labeled, with some investigation as more likely to be fraudulent and more likely to not be fraudulent. Once the findings are verified, the *Indicator* field can be updated by flagging the discovered clusters and now a classification model for credit fraud can be built.

8.2.3   An Example of a Retention Management Study

Banks are always interested in understanding how to keep their customers loyal. It is much more costly to attract a new customer than to keep an existing one. Industry analysts are starting to define customer lifecycles and the needs a customer will have through each stage of life. Early on, a customer may be interested in college loans and home loans. Later in the cycle, a customer will be more interested in saving for retirement and investment opportunities. Surprisingly, building models to understand customer retention and customer lifecycles is new to many institutions and the banking industry is not alone.

Preparing the Data

The example database in Figure 8–3 has many data elements that could be of interest in creating a customer retention model. The HOUSEHOLD_STATUS table is important because it contains information on whether a customer is loyal or has left to a competitor. The actual fields in this example are *Switched_Banks* and *Date_Switched* field.

In this example, customer and household demographic information is clearly useful. Branch information may also be useful. One branch may be better at attracting and keeping customers than another. Account information is also of benefit. It may be that having multiple accounts indicates a customer will be more loyal. And finally, transaction information is useful in retention models. If a customer slows down substantially using a bank's services or if information on ATM transactions through this bank's teller machines show a customer using another bank's account, there are sure signs a customer is gravitating to a competitor.

The creation of a data table for building this model will involve joining information from all the tables.

Time Dependency in Customer Retention

This database model in Figure 8–3 shows account records as summaries for a specific period. For example, it will provide the number of account transactions in March. A customer retention model usually has a table that shows a progression of account activity over time. If a model is being built to study the likelihood someone will drop an account in July, then the account activity for January, February, March, April, May, and June may be fields in the data set for this model as shown in Figure 8–12 below.

Nbr Trans Jan	Nbr Trans Feb	Nbr Trans Mar	Nbr Trans Apr	Nbr Trans May	Nbr Trans Jun	Nbr Trans Jul	Left in Aug
20	19	14	14	15	8	7	Y
19	16	15	22	14	19	18	N
15	20	20	4	4	2	1	Y
9	8	11	7	9	3	7	N

Figure 8–12 A time-dependent data set for customer retention

The field *Nbr_Trans_May* in Figure 8–12 is the total number of transactions, but our data model in Figure 8–3 calculates number of transactions by account. *Nbr_Trans_May* would be the sum of the total number of transactions for checking and savings accounts. Also, the data model in Figure 8–3 does not have a table with fields for number of savings account and checking account transactions for January, February, March, and so forth. It does have an account record table with number of transactions and a period associated with it; so, in order to prepare columns like the one in Figure 8–12, multiple instances of account records have to be used. An example of the actual SQL to perform this type of data preparation is shown below. The example shows monthly transactions for checking and savings accounts as well as demographic information on customers.

The information stored in the table could be expanded greatly, but as an example, this is overkill.

```
CREATE TABLE MINE_CUST_RETENTION (
Global_Acc_ID                   INTEGER,
Nbr_S_Trans_6mnths_ago          INTEGER,
Nbr_C_Trans_6mnths_ago          INTEGER,
Nbr_S_Trans_5mnths_ago          INTEGER,
Nbr_C_Trans_5mnths_ago          INTEGER,
Nbr_S_Trans_4mnths_ago          INTEGER,
Nbr_C_Trans_4mnths_ago          INTEGER,
Nbr_S_Trans_3mnths_ago          INTEGER,
Nbr_C_Trans_3mnths_ago          INTEGER,
Nbr_S_Trans_2mnths_ago          INTEGER,
Nbr_C_Trans_2mnths_ago          INTEGER,
Nbr_S_Trans_1mnths_ago          INTEGER,
Nbr_C_Trans_1mnths_ago          INTEGER,
City                            VARCHAR (30),
State                           VARCHAR (30),
Net_Worth                       INTEGER,
House_Income                    INTEGER,
Num_Children                    INTEGER,
Prim_Age                        INTEGER,
Num_Accounts                    INTEGER,
Nearest_Branch                  INTEGER,
Left_This_Month                 INTEGER)



INSERT INTO MINE_CUST_RETENTION

(Global_Acc_ID
,Nbr_S_Trans_6months_ago
,Nbr_C_Trans_6months_ago
,Nbr_S_Trans_5months_ago
,Nbr_C_Trans_5months_ago
,Nbr_S_Trans_4months_ago
,Nbr_C_Trans_4months_ago
,Nbr_S_Trans_3months_ago
,Nbr_C_Trans_3months_ago
,Nbr_S_Trans_2months_ago
,Nbr_C_Trans_2months_ago
,Nbr_S_Trans_1months_ago
,Nbr_C_Trans_1months_ago
, City
, State
, Net_Worth
, House_Income
, Num_Children
, Prim_Age
, Num_Accounts
```

```
, Nearest_Branch
, Left_This_Month
)
SELECT Global_Account.Global_Acc_ID,
        sum(case when AccountType='Savings' and
                Transaction_Date between date '1997-01-01' and date
'1997-01-31'
                then 1
                else 0
                end),
        sum(case when AccountType='Checking' and
                Transaction_Date between date '1997-01-01' and date
'1997-01-31'
                then 1
                else 0
                end),
        sum(case when AccountType='Savings' and
                Transaction_Date between date '1997-02-01' and date
'1997-02-28'
                then 1
                else 0
                end),
        sum(case when AccountType='Checking' and
                Transaction_Date between date '1997-02-01' and date
'1997-02-28'
                then 1
                else 0
                end),
        sum(case when AccountType='Savings' and
                Transaction_Date between date '1997-03-01' and date '1997-03-31'
                then 1
                else 0
                end),
        sum(case when AccountType='Checking' and
                Transaction_Date between date '1997-03-01' and date '1997-03-31'
                then 1
                else 0
                end),
        sum(case when AccountType='Savings' and
                Transaction_Date between date '1997-04-01' and date '1997-04-30'
                then 1
                else 0
                end),
        sum(case when AccountType='Checking' and
                Transaction_Date between date '1997-04-01' and date '1997-04-30'
                then 1
                else 0
                end),
        sum(case when AccountType='Savings' and
                Transaction_Date between date '1997-05-01' and date '1997-05-31'
                then 1
                else 0
                end),
        sum(case when AccountType='Checking' and
                Transaction_Date between date '1997-05-01' and date '1997-05-31'
                then 1
                else 0
                end),
```

```
sum(case when AccountType='Savings' and
        Transaction_Date between date '1997-06-01' and date '1997-06-30'
        then 1
        else 0
        end),
sum(case when AccountType='Checking' and
        Transaction_Date between date '1997-06-01' and date '1997-06-30'
        then 1
        else 0
        end),
    Global_Account.City,
    Global_Account.State,
        Household_Demographics.Net_Worth,
        Household_Demographics.House_Income,
        Household_Demographics.Num_Children,
        Household_Demographics.Prim_Age,
        Household_Demographics.Num_Accounts,
        Household_Demographics.Nearest_Branch,
        case when Status.Switched_Banks = 1
        and Status.Date_Switched between
            date'1997-07-01' and date'1997-07-31'
        then 1 else 0 end as Left_This_Month
FROM Global_Account, Household_Demographics, Status,
    Account_Record, Account_Transaction
WHERE
Global_Acount.Global_Acc_ID=Household_Demographics.Global
_Acc_ID
    and Global_Acount.Global_Acc_ID=Staus.Global_Acc_ID
    and
Global_Acount.Global_Acc_ID=Account_Record.Global_Acc_ID
    and
Account_Record.Account_ID=Account_Transaction.Account_ID
        GROUP BY Global_Account.City, Global_Account.State,
Household_Demographics.Net_Worth,
        Household_Demographics.House_Income,
        Household_Demographics.Num_Children,
        Household_Demographics.Prim_Age,
        Household_Demographics.Num_Accounts,
        Household_Demographics.Nearest_Branch,
        Left_This_Month
```

The dependent variable for this study is the
Left_This_Month field that is created from information on
the *Switched_Banks* and *Date_Switched* fields.

Additionally, the actual number of transactions a month
may not be as interesting as the percent change in number
of transactions from month to month. Again, this would
require the derivation of another set of columns to calculate
the change in number of transactions.

Since customer retention is time dependent, the model that would be used in July would change in August: you would add July account activity to the August model that you didn't have a month earlier. The time dependency of this model clearly exemplifies that data mining is a process. Data mining models are continually being updated on an ongoing basis as trends and patterns change over time.

Clustering in Customer Retention

Using clustering techniques for customer retention is useful. By creating groupings of similar customers, it may be possible to identify certain segments that are more likely to leave a bank.

8.2.4 Data Trends Analysis

Another type of data mining activity is discovering trends. Trend analysis can be an additional activity on top of another data mining process. For example, if you are studying customer retention, you may build a model in August and a model in September. By comparing the models for each month, it is possible to note the most significant changes are from month to month. This may help discover seasonal changes or just unexpected changes as a business environment evolves.

Another way to perform trend analysis is to use a time field as the dependent variable. For example, with the data model in Figure 8–3, you could mine all existing account records by quarter. For every account, there would be four records: an account record summary for spring, summer, winter, and fall. A study like this may show changes in items like number of transactions, transaction amounts, or fees from season to season. Another example would be to change the time from a season to a day in a week. This model would discover changes in account behavior based on the day of a week.

8.3 A DATA WAREHOUSE EXAMPLE IN RETAIL

The example model used in this study is a point of sale (POS) model for a retail chain. When a customer buys a product or series of products at a register, that information is stored in a transactional system, which is likely to hold other information, like when the purchase happened, where it happened, what types of promotions were involved, as well as who bought the product. This information can be used to perform many types of studies, several of which are discussed here.

To see examples of data structures for data warehousing common in the retail market space, there is a book entitled *The Data Warehouse Toolkit* by Ralph Kimball. This provides numerous in-depth data modeling examples, including a model for a grocery store, an inventory warehouse, a shipment system, a value chain organization, and a subscription business.

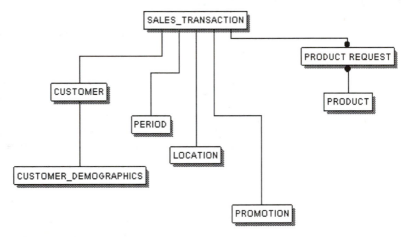

Figure 8–13 A simple retail data diagram

8.3.1 The Example Data Model

Figure 8–13 diagrams a data structure for a retail organization logging customers' transactions at their outlets in several malls across the U.S.

The descriptions of the different entities shown in Figure 8–13 are below.

Sales Transaction Information

The sales transaction is the primary table for this database. For every sale, a transaction, location, time, and customer identifier are stored as well as the total price and the number of products purchased. Transaction information excluding products purchased is stored in the SALES_TRANSACTION table.

Because any number of products can be purchased for a transaction, there is a second table, PRODUCT REQUEST, that stores a new row of data for every product purchased.

All products purchased are linked to the SALES_TRANSACTION table through the *Transaction ID* field.

Figure 8–14 Point of sale record

Customer Information

The CUSTOMER table is a list of all the customers who are know to purchase at this retail outlet.For the customers that are known, customer demographic information has been purchased through third-party sources and company demographic information has been purchased through third-party sources CUSTOMER_DEMOGRAPHIC table.

Figure 8–15 Customer information

Period

While the *Date* field in the SALES_TRANSACTION table lists the specific time a purchase has been made, it is useful

in data mining to break the time in a PERIOD table as
shown in Figure 8–16 below.

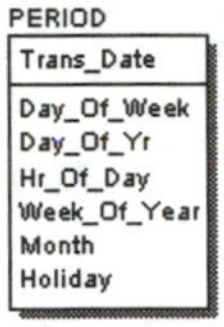

Figure 8–16 Information based on the time of purchase

Location Dimension

This LOCATION table stores information containing the
region, store, and sales representative involved in the sale
as shown in Figure 8–17 below.

Figure 8–17 Location where merchandise is purchased

Promotion Information

The PROMOTION table stores information on the type of
promotion, where the promotion was advertised, and the
type of discount offered with the promotion, if there was
any.

PROMOTION
Promotion_ID
Promotion_Type
Medium_Used
Discount_Offered

Figure 8–18 Promotion information

Product Information

The PRODUCT table stores information on a product
indicated by its *stock keeping unit* (SKU). Information
includes name, standard price, shelf placement, package
size, category, and brand. The number of descriptive
elements on a product is potentially much greater than this.
In retail chains, there can be tens of thousands of products

and they are changing all the time as products are upgraded and their SKUs change.

Figure 8–19 Product information

8.3.2 What Types of Customers are Buying Different Types of Products

In this example, assume we are looking at customer purchases of plastic containers for storage. There are several brands of plastic containers that the store carries: STOR_N'TOTE, PAK_AWAY, and DR_PACK. Each of the containers comes in 4 gallon, 7 gallon, 9 gallon, and 20 gallon sizes. So the PRODUCT table has the fields *Category, Brand, Size,* and *SKU,* which have the elements (there are 12 SKU numbers arbitrarily made up, one for each brand/size combination):

Category: Plastic Containers
Brand: STOR_N'TOTE, PAK_AWAY, and DR_PACK
Size: 4_GAL, 7_GAL, 9_GAL, and 20_GAL
SKU: 11055, 11056, 11057, 11058, 11155, 11156, 11157, 11158, 11255, 11256, 11257, 11258

The goal of this study is to determine what customers are buying the different brands and sizes of plastic containers. Retailers want to know what combinations of product (in this case containers) should be offered at different locations (in this case, at each of several outlet malls). It is not necessarily the case that 20 gallon PAK_AWAY containers will sell as well to customers from one location as those from another location.

Preparing the Data Set

This example creates a table MINE_PRODUCT, which integrates all the product and product request information for all records with a matching SKU for the products to be examined.

The SQL shown in this example can be used to profile other products by simply replacing the SKU numbers of the plastic containers with other products.

```
CREATE TABLE MINE_PRODUCT
Transaction_ID        INTEGER,
SKU                   INTEGER,
PRICE                 REAL,
Promotion_ID          INTEGER,
Trans_Date            DATE,
Total_Price           REAL,
Nbr_Products          INTEGER,
Cust_ID               INTEGER,
Location_ID           INTEGER,
State                 VARCHAR (4),
City                  VARCHAR (30),
Age                   INTEGER,
Children              INTEGER,
Type_Car              VARCHAR (30),
Income_Level          INTEGER,
Marital_Status        VARCHAR (30),
Gender                VARCHAR (4),
Lifestyle             VARCHAR (30),
Day_Of_Week           INTEGER,
Day_Of_Yr             INTEGER,
Hr_Of_Day             INTEGER,
Week_Of_Yr            INTEGER,
Month                 VARCHAR (4),
Holiday               INTEGER,
Sales_Rep             VARCHAR (30),
Store                 VARCHAR (30),
Region                VARCHAR (20),
Promotion_Type        VARCHAR (20),
Medium_Used           VARCHAR (20),
Discount_Offered      VARCHAR (20),
Product_Price         VARCHAR (20),
Shelf_Placement       VARCHAR (20),
Package_Size          VARCHAR (20),
Category              VARCHAR (30),
Brand                 VARCHAR (20))


INSERT INTO MINE_PRODUCT
SELECT (Transaction_ID, PRODUCT.Sku, Price, Comment,
Product_Type, Product_Name, Product_Description,
Product_Standard_Price, Shelf_Placement, Brand, Category,
Package_Size, Trans_Date, Total_Price, Nbr_Products, City, State,
Age, Children, Type_Car, Income_Level, Marital_Status, Gender,
Lifestyle, Sales_Rep, Store, Region, Promotion_Type,
```

Medium_Used, Discount_Offered, Day_Of_Week, Day_Of_Yr, Hr_Of_Day, Week_Of_Year, Month, Holiday)

FROM PRODUCT_REQUEST, PRODUCT, SALES_TRANSACTION, CUSTOMER, CUSTOMER_DEMOGRAPHIC, LOCATION, PROMOTION, PERIOD

WHERE PRODUCT.SKU is [11055, 11056, 11057, 11058, 11155, 11156, 11157, 11158, 11255, 11256, 11257, 11258]

AND PRODUCT.SKU=PRODUCT_REQUEST.SKU
AND PRODUCT_RREQUEST.SKU = SALES_TRANSACTION.SKU
AND PRODUCT_REQUEST.TRANSACTION_ID = SALES_TRANSACTION.TRANSACTION_ID
AND PRODUCT_REQUEST.PROMOTION_ID = PROMOTION.PROMOTION_ID
AND SALES_TRANSACTION.LOCATION_ID = LOCATION.LOCATION_ID
AND SALES_TRANSACTION.TRANS_DATE = PERIOD.TRANS_DATE
AND SALES_TRANSACTION.CUSTOMER_ID = CUSTOMER.CUSTOMER_ID
AND CUSTOMER.CUSTOMER_ID = CUSTOMER_DEMOGRAPHICS.CUSTOMER_ID

This query provides a table MINE_PRODUCT that is ready to mine! It should be noted that this is not necessarily the optimal way to perform this operation.

Choosing a Dependent Variable for the Study

To look at influencing factors on the different plastic containers' brand and size, the *SKU* field could be used as the dependent variable. To eliminate the effect of brand, the *Package_Size* field could be used and similarly to eliminate the effect of package size on the study, the *Brand* field could be used as the dependent variable.

This study will tell you the relevance of customer information on the type of brand, but since data on the promotion, location, and time have also been provided in the data set, the study will also indicate their influence on the purchase of the 12 different products.

Clustering Approach

Instead of using standard classification studies, a clustering approach can be taken to see if there are significant groupings of customers who have purchased containers in general. This type of study would help one understand profiles of individuals looking to buy containers.

8.3.3 An Example of Regional Studies and Others

The table, MINE_PRODUCT, can be used to study many other things. Simply by changing the dependent variable of the study, the emphasis of the model changes. For example, if the dependent variable was changed to the field *Region*, the study would examine the relationship of customer characteristics, time periods, product decisions, and promotions on the region where a particular container was bought.

Another approach would be to change the dependent variable of the study to be *Day_Of_Wk* and the study will focus on what factors are more common to the day of week.

As an exercise, examine the fields created in the table, MINE_PRODUCT, and see what type of model would be created if you made each specific field a dependent variable.

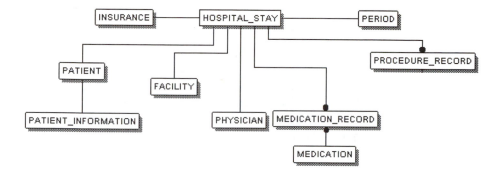

Figure 8–20 A data diagram for healthcare

8.4 A DATA WAREHOUSE EXAMPLE IN HEALTHCARE

The example healthcare data discussed in Table 2–1 in Chapter 2 had to be derived from somewhere. There is information in this table that discusses patient information, procedures performed, physician information, facility information, medications used and objective findings during examinations of a patient. The data warehouse in this section provides a starting point from which such a table of information could be created.

8.4.1 The Example Data Model

Figure 8–20 shows a data model diagram for the healthcare example.

The descriptions of the different entities in Figure 8–20 are shown below.

Hospital Stay

The HOSPITAL_STAY table is the central table of this data warehouse design. For each hospital stay, there is information on the time, the patient, the insurance, the physician, the facility, the procedures, and the medication, which are pointed to with identifiers. The cost of the stay, length of stay, and overall recovery time are also stored.

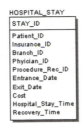

Figure 8–21 Table for hospital stay

Patient Information

The PATIENT table is a list of all the patients for this hospital with their name, phone, and address. The PATIENT_INFORMATION table includes medical history and descriptive information about a patient. The amount of information on a patient would actually be much larger than what is represented in Figure 8–22 below.

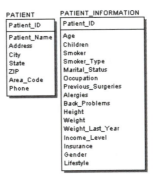

Figure 8–22 Patient information

Facility and Physician

The FACILITY and PHYSICIAN tables store information about the hospital branch at which a patient stayed as well as information on the attending physician. These tables would usually have much more data than represented in Figure 8–23 below.

Figure 8–23 Facility and physician information

Procedure Record

The PROCEDURE_RECORD table tracks all operations and procedures performed on a patient during a hospital stay, as shown in Figure 8–24 below.

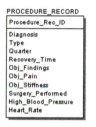

Figure 8–24 Procedure record

Medication Record/Medications

The MEDICATIONS_RECORD table tracks all medicines prescribed to a patient and the dosages used during a hospital stay. The information on medications is pointed to with the *medication_ID* field and is stored in the MEDICATION table.

MEDICATION_RECORD	MEDICATION
Medication_Rec_ID	Medication_ID
Medication_ID	Supplier
Dossage	Type
	Dossage_Rec

Figure 8–25 Medication prescribed to patient

Period

The PERIOD table stores the date of a procedure in several different time representations, as shown in Figure 8–26 below.

PERIOD
Trans_Date
Day_Of_Week
Day_Of_Yr
Hr_Of_Day
Week_Of_Year
Month
Holiday

Figure 8–26 The period table

Insurance

The INSURANCE table specifies what type of insurance a patient uses during a hospital stay, as shown in Figure 8–27 below.

INSURANCE
Insurance_ID
Insured
Insurance_Type
Co_Pay

Figure 8–27 Insurance information

8.4.2 A Look at Example Studies in Healthcare

In order to create a table like the one in Table 2–2 and discussed in Chapter 2, a view can be created in the relational database storing this example model. The code to do this would look like the code below.

The SQL is involved and a six-way join of tables is required, but it does return the desired view of information.

CREATE VIEW MINING_VIEW AS SELECT
Recovery_Time, Hospital_Stay, Age, Smoker, Smoker_Type,
Marital_Status, Occupation, Insurance,
Pain_Reliever_Used, Doctor_Yrs,
Doctor_#_Operations_Performed, Nbr_Beds_In_Hosp,
Systolic_Pressure, Diastolic_Pressure, Allergies,
Previous_Surgeries, Back_Problems, Month, Obj_Pain,
Obj_Stiffness, Area_Code, Height, Weight,
Weight_Last_Year FROM HOSPITAL_STAY a, PATIENT b,
PATIENT_INFORMATION c, FACILITY d, PHYSICIAN e,
PERIOD f, PROCEDURE_RECORD g, WHERE
a.Patient_ID = b.Patient_ID and a.Patient_ID = c.Patient_ID
and a.Facility_ID = d.Facility_ID and a.Physician_ID =
e.Physician_ID and a.Entrance_Date = f.Tran_Date and
a.Procedure_Rec_ID = g.Procedure_Rec_ID

Another reason data mining is used with data warehouses
is that data warehouses are usually optimized to handle
joins of this complexity. Transactional databases may have a
huge performance hit in trying to accomplish this join.

Choosing a Dependent Variable for the Study

Section 2.4 discussed defining a study to model recovery
times of patients. In this case, the dependent variable is the
field *Recovery_Time*. Any number of variables can be used as
the dependent variable for the data view created above.
Below are two examples of studies.

Selecting the field *Smoker*, with values "Yes" and "No," as
the dependent variable changes the focus of the study to
model the differences between smokers and non-smokers.

Selecting the field *Doctor_Yrs* as the dependent variable
shifts the focus to the differences in the surgeries performed
when a doctor is more or less experienced. In this study the
data is numeric and might possibly be binned (i.e., 0-2
years, 2-5 years, and 5 or more years).

8.4.3 A Discussion on Adding Credit Data to Our Example

One of the areas where data mining adds tremendous value
is when disparate databases are integrated and information
is then mined. It is not obvious that a person's credit
information would have any bearing on their ability to
recover from a hospital, but by adding this information to
the view MINING_VIEW (shown in Section 8.4.2), one

could easily find out if there is a connection. The reason a seemingly random data source is discussed here is that a *Wall Street Journal* article discussed a relationship that an insurance company found between someone's credit rating and their likelihood to be a good driver. Again, the connection is not always obvious, but it is interesting to try such studies if they can be managed.

8.5 A DATA WAREHOUSE EXAMPLE IN TELECOMMUNICATIONS

The following is an example data model and discussion of sample data mining models concerning promotions and competitive marketing in the cellular phone industry. Competitive information is not always easy to find. An article in *Wireless Week* entitled *Carriers Mum on Market Stats* (6/24/96) discusses the lack of competitive information. They quote several industry spokepersons about the secretiveness of information. For example, a spokeswoman for U.S. West NewVector Group commented, "We are reluctant to enable our competitors to find out market numbers." A spokeswoman for BellSouth Cellular Corporation comments, "We never give out market share information; only our subscriber numbers in aggregate." A spokeswoman for Ameritech Cellular Services commented, "What is the point of releasing [market] information"? The trend towards secrecy is widely practiced in cellular services.

The question to ask then is:

"How is data mining performed when no information is available?"

In the cellular market, only about 15% of the population used a wireless phone as of mid-1996, and none of the competitors in the market have complete, accurate information on their competition.

Hopefully, this example will argue that even with an absence of completely accurate information, *data mining is a process*, and you had to start somewhere. If models are built to describe a competitive landscape, over time, a company will be able to fill in critical information that will help create a more accurate picture. The alternative is not attractive.

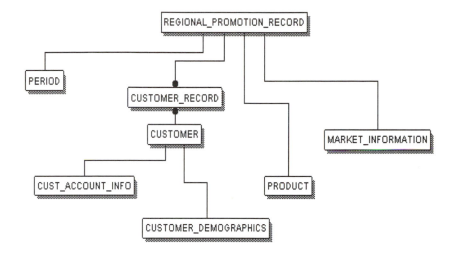

Figure 8–28 A simple diagram for the telecommunication industry

8.5.1 The Example Data Model

Figure 8–28 shows a simplified data schematic for a cellular provider tracking promotions on a rational level which has a table for competitive market share information in a given area.

Given the diagram in Figure 8–28, below is a listing of types of fields you might find for each of the tables in this schematic.

Regional Promotion Record

The table REGIONAL_PROMOTION_RECORD shows regional promotions. The promotions being tracked are ones where a customer will respond in some way if engaged.

REGIONAL_PROMOTION_RECORD

Region_Promo_ID
Period_ID
Market_ID
Product_ID
Region
Medium
Cash_Incentive
Competitive_Promo_Level
Promotion_Type

Figure 8–29 Regional promotion record

Customer Record

The CUSTOMER_RECORD table shown in Figure 8–30 is a table tracking the customers who are sent a regional promotion. If the customer responds to a marketing campaign, there is a field *Responded* to track it. The CUSTOMER table is a current list of all customers.

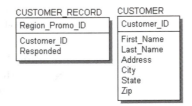

CUSTOMER_RECORD

Region_Promo_ID
Customer_ID
Responded

CUSTOMER

Customer_ID
First_Name
Last_Name
Address
City
State
Zip

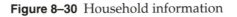

Figure 8–30 Household information

Customer Demographics/Customer_Status

Figure 8–31 stores customer demographic information as well as customer status information based on their usage patterns and information on their current activity with the company.

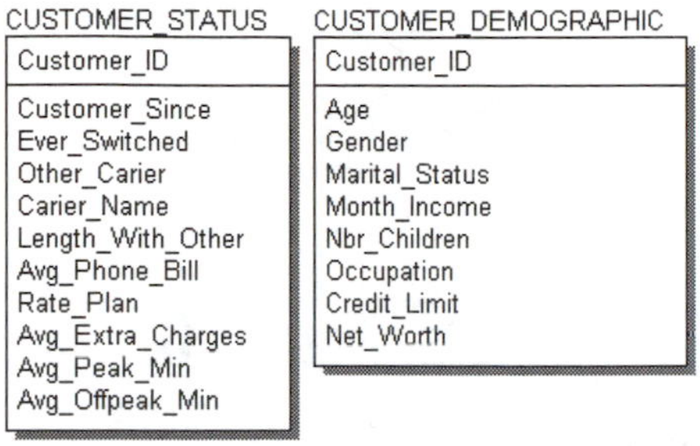

CUSTOMER_STATUS

Customer_ID
Customer_Since
Ever_Switched
Other_Carier
Carier_Name
Length_With_Other
Avg_Phone_Bill
Rate_Plan
Avg_Extra_Charges
Avg_Peak_Min
Avg_Offpeak_Min

CUSTOMER_DEMOGRAPHIC

Customer_ID
Age
Gender
Marital_Status
Month_Income
Nbr_Children
Occupation
Credit_Limit
Net_Worth

Figure 8–31 Promotional information

Market Information

Figure 8–32 lists market information that we want to collect for an account. The information provided specifies market information that can be gathered, such as the number of potential customers in a regional market, the number of actual customers in a market, this company's market share, and estimates of competitors' market shares. This model assumes two competitors, Carrier 1 and Carrier 2. The other information to be collected is market share on the regional level. Because information is not definite on market share numbers, fields for minimum and maximum market share are provided.

MARKET_INFORMATION

Market_ID
Reg_Mkt_Share
%Incr_Mkt_Share_Region
Reg_Mkt_Share_Car1_Min
Reg_Mkt_Share_Car1_Max
Reg_Mkt_Share_Car2_Min
Reg_Mkt_Share_Car2_Max
Nbr_Potential_Cust_Mkt
Nbr_Actual_Cust_Mkt

Figure 8–32 Market share information

Product Information

Figure 8–33 shows fields describing information on the product such as product name, category, and a competitive pricing metric.

PRODUCT

Product_ID
Product_Name
Product_Category
Comp_Price_Metric

Figure 8–33 Product information

Period

Figure 8–34 breaks down the data of a promotion into different time fields, such as day of the week and hour of the day.

PERIOD

Period_ID
Day_Of_Week
Day_Of_Yr
Hr_Of_Day
Week_Of_Year
Month
Holiday

Figure 8–34 Time dimension

8.5.2 Data Collection

Because market share information is not readily available, some detective work is necessary before a data set that can be mined can be created. The MARKET_INFORMATION table needs to be filled in. One suggestion is to start by collecting data on a regional level. For example, we might track competitive data in the Denver metropolitan area.

Market share information for the cellular company itself should be easy enough to create. Similarly, it is possible to purchase a listing of all the potential customers in metropolitan areas: whatever customers in the target list, who are not customers of this cellular company, could be categorized as other market share, either untapped or competitor's customers.

According to an article in *Wireless Week* entitled "Study Reveals Digital Fallacy" (11/11/96), "most cellular phone users are executives, sales staff, and administrative personnel. . . the largest percentages of users are 30- to 39- year-olds and with annual incomes of $100,000 or more." It might be necessary to start with a "customer list" that includes only the most likely people to use cellular phones (it can always be expanded as a data model gets more accurate).

The toughest part of getting market share information at a regional level is knowing the other competitor's market share. Some assumptions could be made on the minimum and maximum market share rates. This could be accomplished by survey techniques as well as by tracking in this regional area all the customers who change from another service to this company's and all those customers who move to another competitor. Over time, some general numbers can be gathered.

The same process can be used to gather information on a product level. All the data does not need to be in place before mining can take place. The process of model building needs to start at some point and, over time, the models will get better as business is better understood.

8.5.3 Creating the Data Set

The tables in this SQL example all have the *Account_ID* as an identifier. This makes the creation of a data set much easier.

CREATE VIEW MINING_VIEW AS
SELECT Promotion_ID, Month, City, State, Area_Code,
Responded, Promotion_Type, Medium, Principal_Occupation,
Region, Month_Expenses, Net_Worth, Avg_Phone_Bill,
House_Income, Num_Children, House_Type, Principal_Age,

Credit_State, Age, Gender, Marital_Status, Month_Income,
Nbr_Children, Occupation, Credit_Limit, Customer_Since,
Rate_Plan, Ever_Switched, Other_Carrier, Carrier_Name,
Length_With_Other, Reg_Mkt_Share, %Incr_Mkt_Share_Region,
Reg_Mkt_Share_Car1_Min, Reg_Mkt_Share_Car1_Max,
Reg_Mkt_Share_Car2_Min, Reg_Mkt_Share_Car2_Max,
Product_Name, Product_Category, Comp_Price_Metric

FROM REGIONAL_PROMOTION_RECORD a,
CUSTOMER_RECORD b, CUSTOMER c, CUSTOMER_STATUS d,
CUSTOMER_DEMOGRAPHIC e, MARKET_INFORMATION f,
PRODUCT g, PERIOD h

WHERE a.Region_Promo_ID IN ['101','102','103']
  and b.Responded = "Yes"

  and a.Region_Promo_ID = b.Region_Promo_ID
  and b.Customer_ID = c.Customer_ID
  and c.Customer_ID = d.Customer_ID
  and c.Customer_ID = e.Customer_ID
  and a.Market_ID = f.Market_ID
  and a.Product_ID = g.Product_ID
  and a.Period_ID = h.Period_ID

An Alternative Structure for the Example

The example above used the *Responded* field from the table
CUSTOMER_RECORD. The problem with this example is
that it tracks responders, but not the list of those to whom a
promotional was sent.

Alternatively, one could maintain two tables:
PROMO_SENT_TO and PROMO_RESPONDED_TO and
derive a view called CUSTOMER_RECORD. This is a more
flexible solution and tracks responders and non-reponders,
whereas the previous solution tracked only responders.

CREATE TABLE Promo_Sent_To
(Customer_IDdatatype NOT NULL
, Promo_IDdatatypeNOT NULL
)

CREATE TABLE Promo_Responded_To
(Customer_IDdatatype NOT NULL
, Promo _IDdatatypeNOT NULL
, RespondedCHARACTER(3) DEFAULT NULL
)
CREATE VIEW Customer_Record AS

```
SELECT Promo_Sent_To.Customer_ID,
Promo_Sent_To.Promo_ID, Promo_Responded_To.Responded
FROM Promo_Sent_To LEFT OUTER JOIN Promo_Responded_To
using Customer_ID, Promo_ID
```

8.5.4   An Example Study on Product/Market Share Analysis

We have gathered a data set of customers sent promotions in several regions taking a random sampling of cellular users of competitive basic cellular rate plans. The promotions have the identifiers 101, 102, and 103. Demographic, market share, and promotional information on each of the customers responding to one of these three promotions has been gathered. The view created in Section 8.5.3, MINING_VIEW, contains this information. The study is to look at the differences in characteristics of those that responded to one of the three promotions. The *Region_Promo_ID* field then becomes the dependent variable. The created view has been limited to only the promotions 101, 102, and 103.

8.5.5   An Example Study of a Regional Market Analysis

The same data set as described in Section 8.5.4 could be used to perform a regional/market study by setting the dependent variable to represent one of the regions where sampling took place, which is specified by the *Region* field in the REGIONAL_PROMOTION_RECORD table. In this case, the most important criteria to each region will be examined.

Some of the fields used in a study like this one might not be useful. For example, you might expect a certain promotion to figure prominently in one region because it was a regional promotion. Still, this study will show regional differences clearly.

8.6   SUMMARY

This chapter introduces the process of creating data warehouses to enable data mining studies in different industries. The chapter discussed a few studies that examine studies on customer retention, product comparisons, promotional activities, and recovery time of patients. The type of studies used in each of the four data warehouse examples purposely vary. Moreover, studies like customer retention clearly crossover between industries readily.

One fallacy of data mining is that all data must be in place before mining can take place. The process of model building needs to start at some point and, over time, the models will get better as business is better understood. Data mining used in this way is not bent on finding the million dollar piece of information, but in building the foundation to model how your business operations are doing. The central point this chapter makes is that data mining is best performed when integrated data repositories are created. The example data warehouses integrated several types of data not commonly placed together in transactional-based databases.

Data mining is a process. New models are built as data is updated and the number of studies that can be built with data mining is limitless.

Appendix A
Data Mining Vendors

Appendix A provides addresses of a number of software vendors. Not only are data mining companies listed, but useful web sites are provided, as well as information access providers, query tool, EIS and data warehousing vendors. They are listed in the following order:

Section A.1 Data Mining Players

Section A.2 Visualization Tools

Section A.3 Useful Web Sites

Section A.4 Information Access Providers

Section A.5 End User Query Vendors

Section A.6 EIS Players

Section A.7 Data Warehousing Vendors

A.1 DATA MINING PLAYERS

Angoss Software International LTC. (KnowledgeSEEKER)
34 St. Patrick Street, Suite 200
Toronto, Ontario, Canada, M5T 1V1
(416) 593-1122
web: http://www.angoss.com

Attar Software USA (XpertRule)
Two Deerfoot Trail on Partridge Hill
Harvard, MA 01451
(508) 456-3946
web: http://www.attar.com

Business Objects, Inc. (BusinessMiner)
20813 Stevens Creek Blvd., Suite 100
Cupertino, CA 95014
(408) 973-9300
web: http://www.businessobjects.com

Cognos Corporation (Scenario)
67 S. Bedford St., Suite 200 W.
Burlington, MA 01803-5164
(800) 4-COGNOS; (800) 267-2777
web: http://www.cognos.com

DataMind Corporation (DataMind Professional Edition, DataMind DataCruncher)
2121 S. El Camino Real, Suite 1200
San Mateo, CA 94403
(415) 287-2000
web: http://www.datamindcorp.com

HNC Software Inc. (Falcon, Eagle, Colleague, AREAS, SkuPLAN, DataBase Mining Workstation)
5930 Cornerstone Court West
San Diego, California 92121-3728
619-546-8877
web: http://www.hnc.com

HyperParallel (HYPERparallel//Discovery)
282 Second Street
3rd Floor
San Francisco, CA 94105
(415) 284-7000
web: http://www.hyperparallel.com

IBM Corporation (Intelligent Miner)
Old Orchard Road
Armonk, NY 10504
(914) 765-1900
web: http://www.ibm.com

Integral Solutions Ltd. (Clementine)
Berk House
Basing View
Basingstoke
Hampshire RG21 4RG UK
01256 55899 (+44 1256 55899)
web: http://www.isl.co.uk

Information Discovery, Inc. (IDIS)
703B Pier Avenue, Suite 169
Hermosa Beach, CA 90254
(310) 937-3600
web: http://www.datamining.com

ISoft (AC2, Alice)
Chemin de Moulon
F-91190 Gif sur Yvette
33-1 69 41 27 77
email: info.isoft.fr

NeoVista Solutions, Inc. (Decision Series)
10710 N. Tantau Ave
Cupertino, CA 95014
(408) 343-4220
web: http://www.neovista.com

Neural Applications Corp. (NetProphet, Aegis)
2600 Crosspark Rd.
Coralville, IA 52241
(319) 626-5000
web: http://www.Neural.com

NeuralWare Inc. (NeuralWorks Predict, NeuralWorks Professional, NeuralWorks Explorer, NeuCOP)
202 Park West Drive
Pittsburgh, PA 15275
(412) 787-8222
web: http://www.neuralWare.com

Pilot Software, Inc. (Pilot Discovery Server)
One Canal Park
Cambridge, MA 02141
(617) 374-9400
web: http://www.pilotsw.com

Red Brick Systems, Inc. (Data Mine, Data Mine Builder)
485 Alberto Way
Los Gatos, CA 95032
(408) 353-7214
web: http://www.RedBrick.com

Silicon Graphics Computer Systems (MineSet)
2011 N. Shoreline Blvd.
Mountain View, CA 94043
(415) 960-1980
web: http://www.sgi.com

SPSS, Inc. (SPSS CHAID)
444 N. Michigan Ave.
Chicago, IL 60611-3962
(800) 543-2185
web: http://www.spss.com

SAS Institute Inc. (SAS, JMP)
SAS Campus Dr.
Cary, NC 27513-2414
(916) 677-8000
web: http://www.sas.com

Thinking Machines Corporation (Darwin)
14 Crosby Dr.
Bedford, MA 01730
(617) 276-0400
web: http://www.think.com

Trajecta (dbProphet)
611 S. Congress, Suite 420
Austin, TX 78704
(512) 326-2411
web: http://www.trajecta.com

A.2 VISUALIZATION TOOLS

Advanced Visual Systems (AVS/Express)
300 Fifth Ave.
Waltham, MA 02154
(617) 890-4300
web: http://www.avs.com

Alta Analytics, Inc. (NetMap)
555 Metro Place North, Suite 175
Dublin, Ohio 43017
(614) 792-2222
web: http://www.alta-oh.com

Belmont Research, Inc. (CrossGraphs)
84 Sherman St.
Cambridge, MA 02140
(617) 868-6878
web: http://www.belmont.com

**Environmental Systems Research Institute, Inc.
(MapObjects, ARC/INFO, Arc GIS, Spatial Database
Engine)**
389 New York St.
Redlands, CA 92373
(800) GIS-XPRT; (909) 793-2853
web: http://www.esri.com

IBM (Parallel Visual Explorer)
Old Orchard Road
Armonk, NY 10504
(914) 765-1900
web: http://www.ibm.com

MapInfo Corp. (MapInfo, SpatialWare)
1 Global View
Troy, NY 12180
(518) 285-6000
web: http://www.mapinfo.com

Silicon Graphics Computer Systems (MineSet)
2011 N. Shoreline Blvd.
Mountain View, CA 94043
(415) 960-1980
web: http://www.sgi.com

A.3   USEFUL   WEB SITES

Knowledge Discovery Mine
web: http://info.gte.com

The Data Mine
web: http://www.cs.bham.ac.uk

Neural Networks at Pacific Northwest National Laboratory
web: http://www.emsl.pnl.gov

George Mason University Genetic Algorithms Group
web: http://www.cs.gmu.edu/research/gag

StatLib (Sample data sets)
web: http://lib.stat.cmu.edu/datasets

The Machine Learning Database Repository
web: http://www.ics.uci.edu

U.S. Census Bureau
web: http://www.census.gov

Edger
web: http://edgar.stern.nyu.edu

SGI Source (MLC++)
web: http://www.sgi.com/Technology/mlc/

Getting Marketing Information
web: http://www.marketingtools.com

Source Code for C4.5 Decision Tree Algorithm
web: http://ftp.cs.su.oz.au/pub/ml/ (patches)

Source Code for OC1, a Decision Tree Algorithm
web: http://www.cs.jhu.edu/

A.4 INFORMATION ACCESS PROVIDERS

Axciom Corporation
301 Industrial Blvd.
Conway, AR 72032
(800) 922-9466
web: http://www.acxiom.com

CACI Marketing Systems
1100 Glebe Road
Arlington, Virginia 22201
(703) 841-7800
web: http://www.caci.com

CorpTech
12 Alfred Street, Suite 200
Woburn, MA 01807
(617) 932-3939
web: http://www.corptech.com

Claritas
1525 Wilson Blvd., Suite 1000
Arlington, VA 22209
(703) 812-2700
web: http:/www.claritas.com

Equifax, Inc.
1600 Peachtree St. NW
Atlanta, GA 30302
(404) 885-8000
web: http://www.equifax.com

Harte-Hanks Data Technologies
25 Linnell Circle
Billerica, MA 01821
(508) 436-2979
web: http://www.harte-hanks.com

Healthdemographics
4901 Morena Blvd., Suite 701
San Diego, CA 92117
(800) 590-4545
web: http://www.healthdemographics.com

A.C. Nielsen
150 North Martingale Rd.
Schaumburg, IL 60173
(847) 605-5000
web: http://www.Nielsen.com

The Polk & Co.
1621 18th St.
Denver, CO 80202
(303) 292-5000
web: http://www.polk.com

TRW Information Systems & Services
1244 Pittsford-Mendon Center Road
Orange, CA 92668
(716) 624-7390
web: http://www.trw.com

A.5   END USER QUERY VENDORS

Andyne Computing, Ltd (GQL)
552 Princess St., 2nd
Fl. Kingston, ON, CD K7L 1C7
(800) 267-0665

Blythe Software, Inc. (True Access)
989 East Hillsdale Blvd.
Foster City, CA 94404
(415) 571-0222

Brio Technology, Inc. (BrioQuery)
444 Castro St., Suite 700
Mountain View, CA 94041
(800) 486-2746

Business Objects, Inc. (BusinessObjects)
20813 Stevens Creek Blvd., Suite 100
Cupertino, CA 95014
(408) 973-9300

Centura Software Corp. (Quest)
1060 Marsh Rd.
Menlo Park, CA 94025
(800) 584-8782; (415) 321-9500

Cognos Corp. (Impromptu)
67 S. Bedford St., Suite 200 W.
Burlington, MA 01803-5164
(800) 4-COGNOS; (800) 267-2777

Computer Associates International, Inc. (CA–Visual Express)
One Computer Associates Plaza
Islandia, NY 11788-7000
(800) CALL-CAI; (516) 342-5224

Information Builders, Inc. (Business Intelligence Suite)
1250 Broadway, 30th Fl.
New York, NY 10001-3782
(800) 969-INFO; (212) 736-4433

IntelligenceWare, Inc. (Iconic Query)
55933 W. Century Blvd., Suite 900
Los Angeles, CA 90045
(800) 888-2996; (310) 216-6177

Intersolv, Inc. (Q+E)
53200 Tower Oaks Blvd.
Rockville, MD 20852
(800) 547-4000; (301) 230-3200

IQ Software Corporation (IQ, IQ Access)
3295 River Exchange Dr., Suite 550
Norcross, GA 30092-9909
(800) 458-0386; (404) 446-8880

Microsoft Corporation (Access & MSQuery)
One Microsoft Way
Redmond, WA 98052
(206) 882-8080

Oracle Corporation (Oracle Data Query, Oracle Forms, and Oracle Reports)
500 Oracle Parkway
Redwood Shores, CA 94065
(415) 506-7000

Powersoft Corporation—a Subsidiary of Sybase
(PowerViewer, PowerMaker)
561 Virginia Rd.
Concord, MA 01742
(508) 287-1500

Software AG of North America, Inc. (Esperant)
11190 Sunrise Valley Dr.
Reston, VA 20191
(703) 860-5050

Trinzic Corporatoin—a Subsidiary of Platinum Technology
(Forest & Trees)
101 University Ave.
Palo Alto, CA 94301
(800) 952-8779

A.6   EIS PLAYERS

Andyne Computing, Ltd. (Pablo)
552 Princess St., 2nd
Fl. Kingston, ON, CD K7L 1C7
(800) 267-0665

Business Objects, Inc. (BusinessObjects)
20183 Stevens Creek Blvd., Suite 100
Cupertino, CA 95014
(408) 973-9300

Cognos Corp. (PowerPlay)
67 S. Bedford St., Suite 200W
Burlington, MA 01803
(617) 229-6600

Comshare, Inc. (Commander EIS)
3001 S. State St., P.O. Box 1588
Ann Arbor, MI 48108
(800) 922-7979

Information Advantage, Inc. (IA Decision Support Suite)
12900 Whitewater Drive, Suite 100
Minnetonka, MN 55343
(612) 938-7015

IRI Software—a Subsidiary of Oracle (Express EIS)
200 5th Ave.
Waltham, MA 02154
(617) 890-1100

Pilot Software, Inc. (Lightship)
One Canal Park
Cambridge, MA 02141
(617) 374-9400

A.7 DATA WAREHOUSING VENDORS

AT&T Global Information Services (Teradata)
1700 S. Patterson Blvd.
Dayton, OH 45479
(513) 445-5000

Carleton Corp. (Passport)
8 New England Executive Park
Burlington, MA 01803
(617) 272-4310

Evolutionary Technologies, Inc. (Extract Tool Suite)
4301 Westbank Drive
Austin, TX 78746
(512) 327-6994

IBM Corp. (IBM DB2 Parallel Edition)
Old Orchard Rd.
Armonk, NY 10504
(800) 426-3333

Informix Software, Inc. (INFORMIX-OnLine Dynamic Server)
4100 Bohannon Drive
Menlo Park, CA 94025
(415) 926-6300

Oracle Corporation (Parallel Query Option)
500 Oracle Parkway
Redwood Shores, CA 94086
(800) 633-0583

Prism Solutions, Inc. (Prism Warehouse Manager)
1000 Hamlin Court
Sunnyvale, CA 94089
(408) 752-1888

Red Brick Systems, Inc. (Red Brick Warehouse)
485 Alberto Way
Los Gatos, CA 95032
(408) 353-7214

Appendix B

Installing Demo Software

This appendix steps through the installation of the exercises and the software products discussed in Chapters 4 through 6.

This appendix is organized as follows:

B.1 INSTALLING ANGOSS KNOWLEDGESEEKER DEMO

The KnowledgeSEEKER Demo runs on Windows 95, Windows 3.1, 3.11, and 16-bit Windows NT. The requirements are:

- 8 MB RAM for Windows 3.1 and 3.11

- 12 MB RAM for Windows 95

- 4MB RAM free hard disk space

For this demo release, a data set for hypertension has been automatically loaded. You will not have the ability to load any other sample data sets. A few of the advanced features have also been grayed out.

B.1.1   Installing KnowledgeSEEKER for Windows 3.1

We are now ready to install KnowledgeSEEKER, using the included CD-ROM. To do this, follow these steps:

1.   Start Microsoft Windows on your PC.

2.   Put the CD in your CD-ROM drive. Normally, this is Drive D, but may be different for you.

     NOTE: Steps 3 through 7 discuss the Installation of Win32s, which is only required for running KnowledgeSEEKER under Windows 3.1 or Windows for Workgroups 3.11. (If you are running Windows NT or Windows 95 you can skip these steps.)

3.   Choose **Run** from the **File** menu in the Program Manager.

4.   Type *D:\Win32S\disk1\setup* in the Run dialog box.

5.   Follow the instructions in the Win32s installation program.

6.   To test the Win32s, install the FreeCell Card Game included (which can be used to test whether Win32s is functioning properly).

7.   Once Win32s is installed, you can install Predict. Choose **Run** from the **File** menu in the Program Manager.

8.   Choose **Run** from the **File** menu in the Windows Program Manager.

9.   Enter *D:\KSeeker\disk1\setup.exe* in the Run dialog box and click **OK.**

10. Follow the dialog boxes as you are asked the name of the directories where you want to install the components. The default directory names appear in the dialog box as *C:\ksw42.*

B.1.2 Installing KnowledgeSEEKER for Windows 95

We are now ready to install KnowledgeSEEKER, using the included CD-ROM. To do this, follow these steps:

1. Start Microsoft Windows 95 on your PC.

2. Put the CD in your CD-ROM drive. Normally, this is Drive D, but may be different for you.

3. Choose **Run** from the **Start** menu in the Windows95 toolbar.

4. Enter *D:\KSeeker\disk1\setup.exe* in the Run dialog box and click **OK.**

    Follow the dialog boxes as you are asked the name of the directories where you want to install the components. The default directory names appear in the dialog box as *C:\ksw42.*

5. To start, you will find a program group, KnowledgeSEEKER IV, under the **Programs** section from **Start**.

B.2 INSTALLING THE DATAMIND PROFESSIONAL EDITION DEMO

DataMind Professional Edition Demo runs on Windows 95, Windows 3.1, 3.11 and Windows NT. The requirements are:

- 12 MB RAM for Windows 3.1 and 3.11

- 16 MB RAM for Windows 95 and Windows NT

- 4MB RAM free hard disk space

- This version of DataMind requires Microsoft Excel to be present on your machine. The demo version is verified with Microsoft Excel 5.0 on Windows 3.1 and Excel 7.0 on Windows 95 and Windows NT. This DataMind demo version is not compatible with Microsoft Excel 8.0. The upcoming release of DataMind will not require Excel at all.

This demonstration release is limited in the number of columns and the number of rows that you are allowed to run. You can build studies for files with fewer than 20 columns and with less than 500 rows.

B.2.1 Installing DataMind for Windows 3.1

We are now ready to install DataMind, using the included CD-ROM. To do this, follow these steps:

1. Start Microsoft Windows on your PC.

2. Put the CD in your CD-ROM drive. Normally, this is Drive D, but may be different for you.

3. Choose **Run** from the **File** menu in the Windows Program Manager.

4. Enter *D:\DataMind\disk1\Setup* in the Run dialog box and click **OK.**

    Follow the dialog boxes as you are asked the name of the directories where you want to install the components. The default directory names appear in the dialog box as *C:\DataMind.*

5. To start, you will find a program group, DataMind, under the **Programs** section from **Start**.

B.2.2 Installing DataMind for Windows 95

We are now ready to install DataMind Solo, using the included CD-ROM. To do this, follow these steps:

1. Start Microsoft Windows 95 on your PC.

2. Put the CD in your CD-ROM drive. Normally, this is Drive D, but may be different for you.

3. Choose **Run** from the **Start** menu in the Windows 95 toolbar.

4. Enter *D:\DataMind\disk1\Setup* in the Run dialog box and click **OK.**

    Follow the dialog boxes as you are asked the name of the directories where you want to install the components. The default directory names appear in the dialog box as *C:\DataMind.*

5. To start, you will find a program group, DataMind, under the **Programs** section from **Start**.

B.3 INSTALLING NEURALWORKS PREDICT DEMO

On personal computers, NeuralWorks Predict® requires the following hardware and software configurations:

- IBM PC and compatibles with an 80386 processor and a math coprocessor, but preferably an 80486 processor or above.

- One of the following operating systems:

  Microsoft Windows version 3.1 or Windows for Workgroups version 3.11 (running on DOS 5.0 or above).

  Windows NT version 3.51 (or above).

  Windows 95 version 4.00 (or above).

- Microsoft Excel version 4.0, 5.0, or 7.0.

- 4 MB of RAM (8 or more MB strongly recommended).

- Minimum 520 K free memory prior to running Windows.

- 4 MB of disk space.

- Permanent Windows swap file (uncompressed, 32-bit mode).

The limitations for this demo release are that no study can be saved and reused. You can recreate a study, but you will have to do so each time you use Predict. Also, there is a limitation of 500 rows of data.

B.3.1 Installing NeuralWorks Predict for Windows 3.1, Windows 3.11, or Windows NT 3.5.1

We are now ready to install NeuralWorks Predict, using the included CD-ROM. To do this, follow these steps:

1. Start Microsoft Windows on your PC.

2. Put the CD in your CD-ROM drive. Normally, this is Drive D, but may be different for you.

   NOTE: Steps 3 through 7 discuss the Installation of Win32s, which is only required for running NeuralWorks Predict under Windows 3.1 or Windows for Workgroups 3.11. (If you are running Windows NT or Windows 95 you can skip these steps.)

3. Choose **Run** from the **File** menu in the Program Manager.

4. Type *D:\Win32S\disk1\setup* in the Run dialog box.

5. Follow the instructions in the Win32s installation program.

6. To test the Win32s, install the FreeCell Card Game included (which can be used to test whether Win32s is functioning properly).

7. Once Win32s is installed, you can install Predict. Choose **Run** from the **File** menu in the Program Manager.

8. Type *D:\NWorks\disk1\setup* in the Run dialog box.

9. To complete the setup, follow the instructions on the screen. The demonstration software will be installed in the *C:\predict* directory.

10. To use Predict for the first time, open Microsoft Excel. If Predict was properly installed, it is automatically loaded with Excel, and the Excel menu bar includes the Predict menu. Do not double-click on the Predict icon (which brings up the command-line interface).

If Using Excel 4 or 5.0

If you are using Excel 4 or 5.0 and the Predict menu is not included in the Excel menu bar, add the following two lines to your EXCEL4.INI or EXCEL5.INI file (located in the WINDOWS directory):

open=n:\NW\pr16xl.xll

open1=n:\NW\pr16xlr.xll

where n is the drive and NW the directory where you installed Predict. If there are other open statements in the file, number the above lines accordingly.

B.3.2 Installing NeuralWorks Predict for Windows 95 and Windows NT 4.0 and Above

We are now ready to install NeuralWorks Predict, using the included CD-ROM. To do this, follow these steps:

1. Start Microsoft Windows 95 on your PC.

2. Put the CD in your CD-ROM drive. Normally, this is Drive D, but may be different for you.

3. Choose **Run** from the **Start** menu in the Windows 95 toolbar.

4. Enter *D:\NWorks\disk1\setup* in the Run dialog box and click **OK.**

   Follow the dialog boxes as you are asked the name of the directories where you want to install the components. The default directory names appear in the dialog box as *C:\predict.*

5. To use NeuralWorks Predict for the first time, open Microsoft Excel. If Predict was properly installed, it is automatically loaded with Excel, and the Excel menu bar includes the Predict menu.

B.3.3 Copying a Sample Data File to Your Local Disk Drive

The NeuralWorks Predict demonstration for this book requires a file, *trouble.txt*, which is located on the CD-ROM in the directory *Demo_Files*.

1. Use the Windows Explorer (Windows 95) or the File Manager (Windows 3.1) to find the file, *trouble.txt*, in the directory *D:\Example* (assuming D: is the CD-ROM drive).

2. Copy this file to the directory *C:\predict*.

3. The *labs.bat* file will add files to *C:\predict*, and place all the exercises for the book in this directory. If you changed the default directory, *C:\predict*, when installing, then you will have to alter the *labs.bat* file to successfully install.

B.3.4 Getting Help

Accessing On-Line Help

For more information about any of the three products, access their on-line help system. Chapters 4 through 6 step through brief tutorials of each product using different data sets. You can also access the companies' web sites for more information. Company, product, and training information can be found at:

- http://www.angoss.com
- http://www.datamindcorp.com
- http://www.NeuralWare.com.

Appendix C
References

This following is a list of references used in this book. It also provides a good list of other books to start learning more about data mining.

Breiman, L., Fredman, J., Olshen, R.A., and Stone, C.J. (1984) "Classification and Regression Trees," Monterey, CA: Wadsworth & Brooks

Chester, M. (1993) "Neural Networks: A Tutorial," Englewood Cliffs, NJ: Prentice Hall

Fayyad, U.M.; Piatestsky-Shapiro G.; Smyth D.; and Uthurusamy R. (1996) "Advances in Knowledge Discovery and Data Mining," Cambridge, MA: AAAI Press/MIT Press

Groth, R. and Gerber, D. (1997) "Hands-On SQL: The Language, Querying, Reporting, and the Marketplace," Upper Saddle River, NJ: Prentice Hall PTR

Kimball, R. (1996) "The Data Warehouse Toolkit, Practical Techniques for Building Dimensional Data Warehouses," New York, NY: John Wiley & Sons, Inc.

Michalewicz, Z. (1994) "Genetic Algorithms + Data Structures = Evolution Programs," New York: Springer-Verlag

Quinnlan, J. (1988). "C4.5: Programs for Machine Learning," Redwood City, CA: Morgan Kaufmann

Refenes, A. (1995) "Neural Networks in the Capital Markets," New York, NY: John Wiley & Sons, Inc.

Welstead, S.T. (1994) "Neural Network and Fuzzy Logic Applications in C/C++," New York, NY: John Wiley & Sons, Inc.

Index

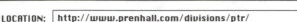

LICENSE AGREEMENT AND LIMITED WARRANTY

READ THE FOLLOWING TERMS AND CONDITIONS CAREFULLY BEFORE OPENING THIS CD PACKAGE. THIS LEGAL DOCUMENT IS AN AGREEMENT BETWEEN YOU AND PRENTICE-HALL, INC. (THE "COMPANY"). BY OPENING THIS SEALED CD PACKAGE, YOU ARE AGREEING TO BE BOUND BY THESE TERMS AND CONDITIONS. IF YOU DO NOT AGREE WITH THESE TERMS AND CONDITIONS, DO NOT OPEN THE CD PACKAGE. PROMPTLY RETURN THE UNOPENED CD PACKAGE AND ALL ACCOMPANYING ITEMS TO THE PLACE YOU OBTAINED THEM FOR A FULL REFUND OF ANY SUMS YOU HAVE PAID.

1. **GRANT OF LICENSE:** In consideration of your purchase of this book, and your agreement to abide by the terms and conditions of this Agreement, the Company grants to you a nonexclusive right to use and display the copy of the enclosed software program (hereinafter the "SOFTWARE") on a single computer (i.e., with a single CPU) at a single location so long as you comply with the terms of this Agreement. The Company reserves all rights not expressly granted to you under this Agreement.

2. **OWNERSHIP OF SOFTWARE:** You own only the magnetic or physical media (the enclosed CD) on which the SOFTWARE is recorded or fixed, but the Company and the software developers retain all the rights, title, and ownership to the SOFTWARE recorded on the original CD copy(ies) and all subsequent copies of the SOFTWARE, regardless of the form or media on which the original or other copies may exist. This license is not a sale of the original SOFTWARE or any copy to you.

3. **COPY RESTRICTIONS:** This SOFTWARE and the accompanying printed materials and user manual (the "Documentation") are the subject of copyright. The individual programs on the CD are copyrighted by the authors of each program. You may not copy the Documentation or the SOFTWARE, except that you may make a single copy of the SOFTWARE for backup or archival purposes only. You may be held legally responsible for any copying or copyright infringement which is caused or encouraged by your failure to abide by the terms of this restriction.

4. **USE RESTRICTIONS:** You may not network the SOFTWARE or otherwise use it on more than one computer or computer terminal at the same time. You may physically transfer the SOFTWARE from one computer to another provided that the SOFTWARE is used on only one computer at a time. You may not distribute copies of the SOFTWARE or Documentation to others. You may not reverse engineer, disassemble, decompile, modify, adapt, translate, or create derivative works based on the SOFTWARE or the Documentation without the prior written consent of the Company.

5. **TRANSFER RESTRICTIONS:** The enclosed SOFTWARE is licensed only to you and may not be transferred to any one else without the prior written consent of the Company. Any unauthorized transfer of the SOFTWARE shall result in the immediate termination of this Agreement.

6. **TERMINATION:** This license is effective until terminated. This license will terminate automatically without notice from the Company and become null and void if you fail to comply with any provisions or limitations of this license. Upon termination, you shall destroy the Documentation and all copies of the SOFTWARE. All provisions of this Agreement as to warranties, limitation of liability, remedies or damages, and our ownership rights shall survive termination.

7. **MISCELLANEOUS:** This Agreement shall be construed in accordance with the laws of the United States of America and the State of New York and shall benefit the Company, its affiliates, and assignees.

8. **LIMITED WARRANTY AND DISCLAIMER OF WARRANTY:** The Company warrants that the SOFTWARE, when properly used in accordance with the Documentation, will operate in substantial conformity with the description of the SOFTWARE set forth in the Documentation. The Company does not warrant that the SOFTWARE will meet your requirements or that the operation of the SOFTWARE will be uninterrupted or error-free. The Company warrants that the media on which the SOFTWARE is delivered shall be free from defects in materials and workmanship under

normal use for a period of thirty (30) days from the date of your purchase. Your only remedy and the Company's only obligation under these limited warranties is, at the Company's option, return of the warranted item for a refund of any amounts paid by you or replacement of the item. Any replacement of SOFTWARE or media under the warranties shall not extend the original warranty period. The limited warranty set forth above shall not apply to any SOFTWARE which the Company determines in good faith has been subject to misuse, neglect, improper installation, repair, alteration, or damage by you. EXCEPT FOR THE EXPRESSED WARRANTIES SET FORTH ABOVE, THE COMPANY DISCLAIMS ALL WARRANTIES, EXPRESS OR IMPLIED, INCLUDING WITHOUT LIMITATION, THE IMPLIED WARRANTIES OF MERCHANTABILITY AND FITNESS FOR A PARTICULAR PURPOSE. EXCEPT FOR THE EXPRESS WARRANTY SET FORTH ABOVE, THE COMPANY DOES NOT WARRANT, GUARANTEE, OR MAKE ANY REPRESENTATION REGARDING THE USE OR THE RESULTS OF THE USE OF THE SOFTWARE IN TERMS OF ITS CORRECTNESS, ACCURACY, RELIABILITY, CURRENTNESS, OR OTHERWISE.

IN NO EVENT, SHALL THE COMPANY OR ITS EMPLOYEES, AGENTS, SUPPLIERS, OR CONTRACTORS BE LIABLE FOR ANY INCIDENTAL, INDIRECT, SPECIAL, OR CONSEQUENTIAL DAMAGES ARISING OUT OF OR IN CONNECTION WITH THE LICENSE GRANTED UNDER THIS AGREEMENT, OR FOR LOSS OF USE, LOSS OF DATA, LOSS OF INCOME OR PROFIT, OR OTHER LOSSES, SUSTAINED AS A RESULT OF INJURY TO ANY PERSON, OR LOSS OF OR DAMAGE TO PROPERTY, OR CLAIMS OF THIRD PARTIES, EVEN IF THE COMPANY OR AN AUTHORIZED REPRESENTATIVE OF THE COMPANY HAS BEEN ADVISED OF THE POSSIBILITY OF SUCH DAMAGES. IN NO EVENT SHALL LIABILITY OF THE COMPANY FOR DAMAGES WITH RESPECT TO THE SOFTWARE EXCEED THE AMOUNTS ACTUALLY PAID BY YOU, IF ANY, FOR THE SOFTWARE.

SOME JURISDICTIONS DO NOT ALLOW THE LIMITATION OF IMPLIED WARRANTIES OR LIABILITY FOR INCIDENTAL, INDIRECT, SPECIAL, OR CONSEQUENTIAL DAMAGES, SO THE ABOVE LIMITATIONS MAY NOT ALWAYS APPLY. THE WARRANTIES IN THIS AGREEMENT GIVE YOU SPECIFIC LEGAL RIGHTS AND YOU MAY ALSO HAVE OTHER RIGHTS WHICH VARY IN ACCORDANCE WITH LOCAL LAW.

ACKNOWLEDGMENT

YOU ACKNOWLEDGE THAT YOU HAVE READ THIS AGREEMENT, UNDERSTAND IT, AND AGREE TO BE BOUND BY ITS TERMS AND CONDITIONS. YOU ALSO AGREE THAT THIS AGREEMENT IS THE COMPLETE AND EXCLUSIVE STATEMENT OF THE AGREEMENT BETWEEN YOU AND THE COMPANY AND SUPERSEDES ALL PROPOSALS OR PRIOR AGREEMENTS, ORAL, OR WRITTEN, AND ANY OTHER COMMUNICATIONS BETWEEN YOU AND THE COMPANY OR ANY REPRESENTATIVE OF THE COMPANY RELATING TO THE SUBJECT MATTER OF THIS AGREEMENT.

Should you have any questions concerning this Agreement or if you wish to contact the Company for any reason, please contact in writing at the address below.

Robin Short
Prentice Hall PTR
One Lake Street
Upper Saddle River, New Jersey 07458